THE DISCOVERY OF THE CHILD

Maria Montessori.

THE
DISCOVERY
OF THE CHILD

Revised and Enlarged Edition of *The Montessori Method*

BY
MARIA MONTESSORI

TRANSLATED BY
MARY A. JOHNSTONE

KALAKSHETRA PUBLICATIONS
ADYAR, MADRAS 20, INDIA

Sold by
The Theosophical Publishing House
Wheaton, Illinois

First Published in 1948

Reprinted   1958

,,   1962

,,   1966

PRINTED IN INDIA

At the Vasanta Press, The Theosophical Society, Adyar, Madras 20.

INTRODUCTION TO THE THIRD ITALIAN EDITION

ON the reprinting of the third Italian edition of this work, I found myself faced with the grave difficulty of having to retain a book which announces a work whilst that work has for some time been carried out and accepted in use. Another book ought to have been substituted for this, yet it is difficult to discard the first document which has laid the foundation of schools in all parts of the world. The title of the book gained for the work historical importance after Pope Benedict XV copied it in his own hand in its entirety, as a proof of his benevolent approbation of this method of education.

" May the apostolic benediction . . . bring those blessings from heaven which I pray may make fruitful of good *The Method of Scientific Pedagogy applied to Child Education in the Children's Houses.*"

BENEDICTUS S.S. XV.

21st November, 1918.

For this reason, and because this educational work has found so many admirers, I have not thought it right to let it disappear. This book, which today exists in so many languages and which in so many countries has more editions than in Italy, could not be allowed to disappear from the country of its origin owing to the action of its author.

The Method of Scientific Pedagogy Applied to Child Education in the Children's Houses exists under other and simpler titles, and where it is most widely read it is called *The Montessori Method*. It has been translated not only into English, but into German, French, Spanish (Castilian), Dutch, Swedish, Roumanian, Polish, Russian, Portuguese, Chinese, Arabian, Japanese, Gujarati, etc. In every country this has been accompanied by the founding of schools, and has excited more or less lively comments; enthusiasm has led to the creation of societies and periodicals and of centres for the training of teachers; in various places it has roused the interest of Governments, some of which, after discussions in Parliament, have officially adopted the method for public schools. In distant countries, even in those which we would least suspect of being interested in Italian matters, there sometimes exist most important and effective centres, as in the various states of Australia and New Zealand, or in the countries of Central America, like Colombia and Panama; or in the islands extending from the Philippines to Java. There is not one great continent in which schools have not been distributed—in Asia: from Syria to the Indies, China and Japan; in Africa: from Egypt and Morocco in the north to Cape Town in the extreme south; in the two Americas: the United States and Canada, and Latin America. Even in the small islands scattered throughout the great oceans, like Honolulu, half-way between California and China, there exist schools which reproduce the spirit and the essential appearance of the Italian school. A vast literature has accumulated in the course of about twenty years; it is enough to mention the numerous books which exist in the English, Spanish and Russian languages. Some are written by university professors; others by novelists who have found in the new life of the children a theme more interesting than creations of the imagination; others by Catholic priests, by teachers and by mothers, and among these last I may mention, as a mark of gratitude, Tatiana Sukotine Tolstoi, the beloved daughter of Leo Tolstoi, who was pleased to see in the Children's Houses the realization of a dream which her great father had cherished so fervently. The famous Indian poet, Rabindranath Tagore, has been kind enough to add his poetical ideas to my practical effort, and there are scattered throughout India and the island of Java Tagore-Montessori Schools.

To what has the spread of this educational method be due? It is certainly not because of the science which figures so prominently in the Italian title of the book; nor is it because an attempt is made to link up with experimental psychology many of the experiments on children which have made such extraordinary progress possible for them. Anyone who is really willing to read these efforts will find that through these new experiments an attempt is made to show (a truth which official science had already understood between the second and third editions, by its own efforts, without any help from this book) that experimental psychology has been one of the many fleeting and changeable tendencies of human thought. As it was, however, at the height of its development and success when this book was published for the first time, it is directed to opposing this erroneous idea—that it is possible to reform the school merely by studying the child in that manner. The reactions provoked instantaneously by material stimuli which are applied to the mind for a few short seconds are more illusory than can be imagined by anyone who is trying to uncover by this means some truth hidden in the human mind. It is still more illusory to suppose that not only psychology but education may be reformed by a similar theory. In fact, in the United States of America, experimental psychology applied to the study of pupils with the Binet tests and their derivatives, or with sense reactions derived from the first German experiments of Fechner and Wundt, have not led to a reform of education but to the reform of examination tests. Instead of basing the final, or State examinations, on what the child had learnt, it was proposed to base them on his human value, on his mental attitudes, as ascertained by means of mental tests. Such a substitution is the logical consequence of the application of instantaneous and stimulating reagents.

My idea of experimenting differs from this in two ways. First, because it refrains from inciting reactions depending on the will of the experimenter, and offers instead activity freely chosen by the subject; it follows that in this very choice there is manifested spontaneously the individual mental needs.   Second, because the stimuli, although they are the means analogous to those of experimental psychology, have, however, as their object the stabilization in the subject of reactions which are enduring, that is, which are capable of modifying his personality.   Education cannot exist other than in a dynamic state, in a continuous transformation of the individual who is to be raised to a higher level; and this process must develop in accordance with the inner dictates of life.   It is the creative forces which must develop, and we must not make ourselves substitutes, in an arbitrary manner, for the divine work which is accomplished in every living being.   Indeed we cannot be more than co-operators in educational work with creation; we cannot, therefore, force the child to follow our promptings, but we must provide the means best adapted to help the child in his voluntary work.

In the first edition of my book, I not only explained the dynamic idea of a " material for development," in place of that of the stimuli of experimental psychology, but I propounded a simple theory about the value of the voluntary activity of the child.   I set forth a series of facts and an experiment carried out, sufficiently extensive to deduce from it a whole practical method of education.

My experiences, however, far from being rigid, were logical conclusions corresponding to the application of an exact and positive method.   The behaviour of the children, being uncontrolled by rigid research, gave new evidence, something living, which issued from my experiments as a spring of water gushes from a rock.   In good faith, like the simple Aladdin, I thought that I held in my hand a lamp which at the most could lead me into a place hitherto unexplored, but what I discovered unexpectedly was the treasure hidden in the depths of a child's soul, and it is this new, surprising revelation, and not what might be called " the importance of my contribution to official science," which has spread my method so far over the world, so far from the land of its birth.

Professor Godefroy, lecturer in psycho-pathology in the University of Amsterdam, has expressed in the following manner his opinion of the experiment:

" In the history of culture the Montessori movement seems to me to be an almost unique example of the development and extremely rapid propagation of an attitude of life, and of a method of developing the mind and the intelligence of the young generation. This fact is explicable only when one understands that the doctrine of Madame Montessori has awakened in man a sentiment which up till now had lain unknown and still latent in hearts, and which was only waiting for the stimulant necessary to make it rapidly and powerfully conscious of itself, in order to give birth to new tendencies which seem suddenly to disclose themselves both in education and in our personal life.

" When we try to find out to what social classes the followers of Madame Montessori belong, it becomes clear that the most dissimilar currents of thought and the most diverse races have representatives among them. There are to be found Christians and Hindus, Catholics and Protestants, Radicals, Socialists, Conservatives, Javanese, Chinese, Australians, Europeans—peoples showing very different characters. When one asks any one of these what has been the attraction to the Montessori Method, it seems most frequently to be that in it they find the realization of some one or other of their own intimate, personal aspirations, of their own favourite ideas. The fact that each one finds in it what he seeks for his own soul proves that the ideas of Madame Montessori make an appeal to the universal needs of the soul.

" This, however, does not mean that the experience from which this method originates is divorced from scientific exactitude. In this respect also the Children's Houses are the results due to true work in psychology." (V. Ferriere, Geneva, *Dernieres œuvres pedagogiques*.)

The mental revelations of little children placed to live in an environment created to meet their inner needs have revealed forms of work, a capacity for perseverance, qualities of obedience and calmness, and an intellectual progress which have not been met with before. Because of this the environment of our children, which was not prepared in order to *mould* them by the suggestion of the example or the will of teachers but was meant to leave them free to express themselves, is called the *revealing environment.*

From it were removed the obstacles to profound expression, that is, the many causes of repression, which lead to permanent deformations in the child's character, were taken away. Many children's doctors who have been interested in our schools have noticed the cure of diseases of nervous character or of physiological disturbances in children, as soon as these, having come to our schools and having been removed from the causes of repression to which they had been subjected to in the family without the parents and particularly the mothers being aware of it.

To keep within the field of psychological observations, I will again quote the opinion of Professor Godefroy, expressed after he had observed for many years the Montessori Schools in Amsterdam.

" It is necessary above all to make ourselves familiar with facts, to make observations in the places where the minds of the children can actually develop without their faculties being limited, where we see displayed freely and more amply than elsewhere, not only the intellectual functions, but above all the subtle aesthetic tendencies of character, emotional and social. It will then be seen clearly that the Montessori School is the place, *par excellence,* where, more and more, there will be obtained intimate and intense contact with the depths of the child's mind, and hence, as an ultimate consequence, with the mind of every man."

Rather than to the attainment of a scientific purpose, it must be recognized that our experiments made with certain scientific

means and methods scientifically applied, have led to the discovery
of human values which up till then had remained hidden.

The child, in his elevation, has helped us to understand a
Gospel truth which was obscure: " He who would become great
in the Kingdom of Heaven must become as a little child."

Rome, 1929.   MARIA MONTESSORI

INTRODUCTION TO THE PRESENT EDITION

IF at the publication of the third Italian edition I felt compelled to justify the reprinting of a book written at the beginning of my work, I must do so even with greater reason at the publication of the present edition, 42 years later. My motives are still the same, but the development of my work and the conclusions drawn from the revelations given by the children in our schools far exceed our most legitimate expectations. It was impossible to bring this book up-to-date without re-writing it completely, not only as far as its contents, but also as far as the wording is concerned. Circumstances did not permit this and what would be needed is a complete series of specialized publications dealing with the various psychological and didactic aspects of our extensive experience all over the world. Some works have already been published (cf. *The Secret of Childhood, The Absorbent Mind, Education for a New World, Educating the Human Potential, Psycho-Arithmetic, Psycho-Geometry*, etc.), others are in preparation.

In the present edition I have tried merely to clarify certain matters and especially to stress the fact that the result of our work has been more than the creation of a new method of education. The conclusions reached are expressed in the new title: THE DISCOVERY OF THE CHILD. After some chapters I have given a short survey of more recent developments. The reader is requested, therefore, to bear in mind that the greater portion of this book was written at the very beginning of our experiments and often refers to scientific theories and experiments then prevalent or to situations of those days. The times have changed, science has made great progress and so has our work, but our principles have only been confirmed and also our conviction that humanity can hope for a solution of its problems, the most urgent of which are those of peace and unity, only by turning its attention and energies to the discovery of the child and the development of the great potentialities of the human personality in course of construction.

Poona, November, 1948.   MARIA MONTESSORI

CONTENTS

ILLUSTRATIONS

C H A P T E R I

CRITICAL CONSIDERATIONS ON SCIENCE
APPLIED TO THE SCHOOL [1]

I HAVE no intention of producing a treatise on Scientific Pedagogy; these preliminary notes have the modest aim of making known the rather interesting results of a teaching experience which would seem to open up a way for the practical application of new methods, capable of giving to teaching a wider application of scientific experiments without depriving it of its natural bases on theoritical principles. It is asserted in an exaggerated manner, and has been talked of for many years, that pedagogy, as has already been done in medicine, should tend to forsake the purely theoritical fields in order to set its bases on the positive findings of experiments. The physiological or experimental psychology which, from Weber and Fechner to Wundt and Binet, has come to be organized into a new science, would seem to be destined to furnish for it that substratum of preparation which the old psychology furnished to philosophic pedagogy. And morphological anthropology also, when applied to the physical study of the pupils, appears to furnish another link with the new pedagogy. But the truth is that the

---

[1] The reader must keep in mind that these notes form part of the text of this book when it first appeared in 1909.

so-called scientific pedagogy has never yet been either worked out or defined. It is something vague about which one talks, but which, in reality, does not exist.

Some years ago, there arose in Italy, under the directions of practical doctors, some so-called *Schools of Scientific Pedagogy* which had for their object the training of teachers in the new trend of pedagogy. These schools were a great success, and gathered together, it may be said, all Italian teachers. The teachers, before the new ideas had come to us from Germany and France, had already been interested by the Italian schools of anthropology in the methodical observation of children during the various periods of growth and in measurements made with exact instruments. Sergi, for example, for about thirty years had been spreading assiduously among the teachers the idea of seeking through scientifically directed observation a source for reforming education. "Today in social life," said Sergi, "there exists an urgent need—that of reforming methods of education and instruction, and whoever strives to reach this goal is striving for the regeneration of man."

In his pedagogical writings collected in one volume—*Educazione de Istruzione* [1] (Pensieri)—in which he gathers together his propaganda lessons and lectures, he indicates as a path leading to the desired reform the methodical study of the person being educated, conducted under the guidance of pedagogic anthropology and experimental psychology.

"For several years I have struggled with an idea which, the more I think of it, the more do I find right and useful for human instruction and education; it is that, if we are to have natural methods to attain these objects, it is necessary that we have numerous exact and reasoned observations made about man, and particularly about the stage of infancy, in which there must be laid the foundations of education and culture.

"Measuring the head, the height, etc. does not, it is true, constitute pedagogy, but it means following the way which leads

[1] Trevesini Publishers, 1892.

to it, for we cannot educate anyone unless we possess direct knowledge of them."

The authority of Sergi gave rise to the conviction that once the individual was known through the medium of experiments the art of education would come into existence almost naturally, and, as often happens, that gave rise in his followers to confusion of ideas, namely of confusing the experimental study of the pupil with his education. And since the one was made to appear as the way to reach the other, which ought to spring from it naturally, pedagogic anthropology founded by Sergi was therefore called in Italy *Scientific Pedagogy*. The converts to the new term carried as their standard the " Biographical Chart," supposing that once the flag was boldly raised on the school battlefield, the victory would be won.

Hence the school of Scientific Pedagogy taught the teachers to make anthropometric measurements, to use instruments for ascertaining tactile sensibility, to collect data for case histories. In this way the body of scientific masters was formed.

Certainly, in other countries, nothing better or more extensive was done.

In France, in England and especially in America, there were attempted studies in anthropology and pedagogic psychology in the elementary schools, inspired by the illusion of extracting from anthropometry and from psychometry the reform of the school. Following this came the study of the individual, extending from the psychology of Wundt to the tests of Binet, but all the theories were vitiated by the same mistake. Besides, scarcely ever was it the teacher who carried out such research, but doctors who were more interested in their own special science than in education, and who sought to make experimental contributions to psychology and anthropometry rather than to organize their work and their objects for the building up of scientific pedagogy. Finally, the anthropology and the psychology were never applied to educating the children in the schools; never did the teachers in their practice rise to the level of the theoritical scientist.

Instead of that, practical progress in the school required real co-ordination between the guidance of study and of thought, such as is required directly in the most important branches of science which would raise the teachers' level of culture from the state to which they are confined today. To make provision for this eminently practical idea there was founded in Rome University a Faculty for Pedagogy, with the intention of raising Pedagogy from being merely a secondary branch of the Faculty of Philosophy, as it had been hitherto in Italy, to being an independent Faculty, which like that of Medicine would include various subjects, among which would be Pedagogic Hygiene, Pedagogic Anthropology and Experimental Psychology.

Nevertheless these sciences continued to move along their own ways, and Pedagogy itself remained in the old philosophic obscurity in which it had been born, without letting itself be touched, far less be transformed.

It was a mistake to suppose that by carrying the stones of hard, dry experiments from the laboratory into the old, ruinous school one could rebuild it; this narrow way could not lead to renovation in the art of preparing new generations.

Furthermore, to train teachers in the principles of experimental science is not easy in practice. Teaching them in the most painstaking fashion anthropometry and psychometry only resulted in our producing machines, the utility of which became very problematical. By teaching them to experiment, new teachers were certainly not created. And above all the educators were left on the threshold of experimental sciences, and were not admitted to their noblest and most intimate precincts, where the scientists are created.

What in fact is a scientist?

Certainly it is not the man who is capable of manipulating all the physical apparatus in a laboratory, or who can carry out with complete confidence the reactions in a chemical laboratory, or who knows how to prepare microscopic sections in biology. It is very often persons much below the standing of scientists, such as assistants and laboratory staff, who, rather than the scientists, are the greatest experts in experimental technique.

He is a scientist who has found out a way leading to an understanding of the profound truths of life and has learnt how to raise the veil covering its fascinating secrets. He is one who through such research has felt coming to life within him so passionate a love for the mysteries of nature that he forgets himself. The scientist is not the man who knows the instruments thoroughly; he is the man who knows nature. This sublime lover displays, as does a monk, the external signs of his passion. We call him a scientist who lives his life in his study quite oblivious of the outside world; who sometimes does eccentric things such as being careless about his dress, because he gives no thought to himself; who works so unremittingly with a microscope that he loses his eyesight; who inoculates himself with tuberculosis and who infects himself with cholera, in his anxiety to learn the carriers by which diseases are transmitted; and who knowing that a certain chemical substance may be explosive, yet carries out the preparation of it and is blown up.

That is the spirit of the man of science to whom nature reveals her secrets, crowning him with the glory of discovery.

There exists then a *spirit* in a scientist, surpassing any *mechanism* belonging to science. And a scientist has reached the height of his glory when the spirit has triumphed over the mechanism. For him science will not only have new revelations of nature, but also philosophic theories of thought.

I consider that we ought to infuse in teachers the spirit rather than the mechanism of the scientist; that is, the aim of training ought to be directed towards the spirit instead of towards the machinery. We must create in the soul of the teacher interest in the phenomena of nature in general, till he becomes one of those who love nature, and realizes the anxious expectation of the man who makes experiments and waits for the revelation which they may give.

Instruments are like the alphabet, and one must know how to use them in order to be able to read in nature. But as the book which contains the revelation of the greatest thoughts of a writer derives from the alphabets the means for composing words from letters, so nature, through the mechanism of experiments, reveals the infinite series of her secrets.

Anyone who could spell might be able to read laboriously the words in a spelling-book, as well as those in a work of Shakespeare, provided that in the last case the print was clear enough. The person who is initiated only into the crudity of experimenting is like the person who spells out the letter-sense of the words in a spelling-book; and it is at such a stage that we leave teachers if we limit their training to mechanical methods.

Instead of that we must make them interpreters of the spirit of nature, just as the man who, having once learnt to spell, may learn to read by means of graphic symbols the thoughts of Shakespeare, Goethe or Dante.

As we see, the difference is great and the way is long.

Yet our first mistake was natural. The child who has finished the spelling-book imagines that he can read; indeed he reads the shop-signs, the titles of newspapers and every word or sentence which comes under his eye. He would make a very simple mistake, if, on entering a library, he imagined that he could read the meaning of the books in it. If he tried, he would feel that he could only read mechanically, and would leave the library to go to school again.

The illusion is the same when it is attempted to train teachers for a new system of education by teaching them anthropometry and experimental psychology.

*   *   *   *

Let us put aside the difficulties of training teacher-scientists in that accepted sense; let us not even make an attempt at a programme, because otherwise we should have to deviate into a subject which lies outside our purpose. Let us suppose, instead, that we have already prepared the teachers, through prolonged practice in the observation of nature, and have raised them to the level of those zoologists who get up in the middle of the night to make tiresome journeys into the woods that they may be present at the awakening and the first doings in the daily life of some family of insects in which they are interested. Here we have the scientist who may be sleepy or weary of the way, but who is yet unrelaxing in his vigilance; he is not aware that he is muddy or dusty, he does not mind when the mists are soaking him or the sun is scorching him; he is intent solely on keeping his presence a dead secret, that, hour after hour, the insects may quietly perform their natural functions which he is keen to observe.

Let us suppose that they have reached the stage of that scientist who, already short-sighted, knowing how the work will tire his eyes, yet keeps under observation under the microscope the natural movements of some infusoria. He comes to the conclusion that in their mode of separating from one another and of selecting food they are endowed with a shadowy consciousness or instinct. He then disturbs this quiet life of theirs with an electric stimulus, noticing how some group themselves round the positive pole and some round the negative. Then he experiments with light stimulus and watches how some hasten towards the light whilst others avoid it. In this way he studies the phenomena of tropism, always keeping in the forefront the thought that what has to be decided is whether or not the attraction to or the avoidance of stimuli is of the same character as that of the natural separations and the choice of food; in other words, he wants to know if the movements are prompted by choice and a dawning conscious-ness, or better by natural instinct, rather than by some physical attraction and repulsion like that which exists between a magnet and iron. And let us suppose that this scientist, finding that it is two o'clock in the afternoon and that he has not yet had his lunch, is delighted to think that he has been working in a labo-ratory instead of in his home, where he would have been called two hours before and interrupted both in his interesting obser-vations and in his fast.

Let us suppose that the teacher has reached (independently of his scientific education) a similar feeling of interest, although in a lesser degree, in the observation of natural psychological phenomena in children. Well, such preparation would not be enough.

He is destined for his own special work—not that of observing insects or infusoria, but man.

And it is not man in the manifestations of his daily life, like those of a family of insects when they awake in the morning, but man at the awakening of his mental life.

For him who desires to cultivate it, interest in humanity must possess a quality which connects more intimately the observer and the observed than that which connects the zoologist or the botanist with nature; and that which is more intimate is necessarily more pleasant. Man cannot love the insect or the chemical reaction without becoming worn out; to anyone watching him without understanding, such attrition appears as suffering, as the exhaustion of life itself, as martyrdom. But the love of man for man may be sweeter, and may be so simple that not only those privileged in spirit but the masses may attain it without an effort.

Teachers, when they have been sufficiently imbued with the spirit of the scientists, must comfort themselves with the thought that very soon they will be able to experience *happiness* when they become observers of humanity.

In order to give an idea of this second form of preparation of the spirit, let us imagine that we are interpreting the sincere minds of those first followers of Jesus Christ who were listening to him speaking of a Kingdom of God which was greater than any which could be conceived of on earth. One of the disciples began to wonder how greatness would be assessed in this Kingdom, and asked Him with childish curiosity: "Who is the greatest in the Kingdom of Heaven?" Jesus called a little child to Him and said: " Whosoever shall humble himself as this little child, the same is the greatest in the Kingdom of Heaven."

Now let us imagine a mind filled with a mystic ardour which follows all the revelations of the little child's mind, in order that, with mingled feelings of respect and love, of sacred curiosity and of aspiration after the highest places in heaven, he may learn the way to his own perfecting, that he may carry his perfection into the beautiful work-room of a classroom peopled with little children.

Well, this would not be the new educator whom we wish to create!

Let us try to combine in one single mind the keen spirit of sacrifice which animates the scientist with the ineffable ecstasy of a mystic, and we shall have prepared completely the spirit of the teacher.

He will really learn from the child himself both the means and the manner of his own education; that is, he will learn from the child how to improve himself as a teacher.

Let us picture to ourselves one of our botanists or zoologists, skilled in the technique of observing and experimenting, who for example has made journeys to study the Peronospora in their natural surroundings, and who has followed up his operations in the field by microscopic and general work in the laboratory, conducting experiments in culture as part of his final research. Or let us think of another worker who has gone into the stables to study the ticks breeding in the excrements of animals. Or, finally, take one who understands what is meant by nature study, and who is familiar with all the means which modern experimental science offers for such work. Let us suppose that one of these men, selected because of his successful research, is given a scientist's post where he is required to carry out research work on the Hymenoptera. What would he feel if, when he took up his new post, there was placed in front of him a box, covered with clear glass, at the bottom of which were fastened with pins beautiful, preserved, dead butterflies, their wings outspread? The young student would say that this was a game for children and not material for study by scientists, that those preparations in the box were what followed

the performance of boys in the public garden when they caught
butterflies with a net fastened to a stick. The experimentalist
confronted with such material can do nothing.

The case would be the same if we placed a master who was a
scientist according to our definition in our present day schools,
where the children are repressed in all the spontaneous expressions of their individuality as if they were dead things, and are
fixed in their respective places on the benches like butterflies transfixed with a pin, whilst they spread abroad the wings of the knowledge
acquired in the driest fashion—knowledge which may be symbolized
by those wings which signify vanity.

It is not enough, then, to train the scientific teacher; we must
prepare the school for him.

The school must allow freedom for the development of the
activity of the child, if scientific education is to come into being;
this is the essential reform.

No one will dare to assert that such a principle already exists in
teaching or in the school. It is quite true that certain pedagogues
like Rousseau set out fantastic principles and vague aspirations
of liberty for the child, but the true conception of liberty is,
in fact, unknown to the pedagogues. Their conception of liberty
is often that which peoples set up for themselves in the hour
of their rebellion against slavery; or taking a higher level, people
have an idea of liberty which is always restricted because it means
a step to be mounted on a staircase, that is, it is the liberation of
something in a partial sense—of a country, of a caste, of a form
of thought.

On the contrary, the conception of liberty which ought to
inspire teaching is universal; it is the liberation of life imprisoned
by an infinite number of obstacles which are opposed to its
harmonious development, bodily and spiritual. This is a reality
of supreme importance, neglected up till now by the great crowd
of observers!

It is not merely a question the discussion of which should be
curtailed; it has to be proved.

Anyone who says that the principle of liberty permeates teaching and the school would raise a smile, just as if a child who saw placed before him a box of transfixed butterflies were to insist that they were alive and could fly.

A principle of repression which almost approaches slavery pervades a great part of teaching, and therefore the same principle animates the school.

One proof of that is the bench. Here is a shining example of the early scientific, meterialistic pedagogy which deluded itself by carrying its scanty stones for the rebuilding of the little, crumbling edifice of the school. The rough, dreary bench existed wherever scholars were gathered together; then science comes in and perfects the bench. All the contributions of anthropology are drawn upon to improve the bench; the age of the child and the length of his legs are used to make his seat of the right height; with mathematical precision is calculated the distance between the seat and the reading desk lest the child's back be deformed by spinal curvature; and finally (oh, the depths of insight and adaptation!) they separate the seats, measuring them in width so that once the child is seated he cannot stretch himself out to make the slightest lateral movement, and makes sure that he is separated from his neighbour; the bench is made in such a way that as far as possible the child is kept motionless. All this separation has for its hidden object the prevention of acts of sexual perversion in the class—and that even in infant schools!

What can one say of such prudence in a society in which it would be considered scandalous to enunciate principles of sexual morality in education, lest innocence should be contaminated? But here is science lending itself to this hypocrisy by making machines. Not only so; complacency goes further! Science perfects the benches so as to permit immobility to the child to the highest degree possible or, one may say, to spare him every movement; so that the pupil may be firmly fixed in his bench, so that the bench itself forces him to assume a hygienic position, with the seat, footrest and desk so arranged that the child can never rise to his feet. But, because the seat falls when a certain movement is made, the desk rises, the footrest is overturned and behold! the child has the exact space needed for standing erect.

Moving along this track the benches progressed towards perfection. All the followers of the so-called scientific pedagogy evolved a model one; not a few nations were proud of their *national bench*. In the competitive struggle, diplomas were awarded and patents were bought.

Undoubtedly this bench was based upon the findings of many sciences—anthropology, with the measuring of the body and the diagnosis of age; physiology, involving the study of muscular movements; psychology, in respect of precosity and perversion of instincts; and, above all, hygiene, in trying to prevent scoliosis.[1]

Here, then, was a really scientific bench, showing distinctly a morphological study of the child.

Here was an example of the literal application of science to the school.

But I believe that it will not be long before we shall be struck with wonder by what seems to be an incomprehensible fact, namely that so many students of child-hygiene, anthropology and sociology, in the course of the progress in thought made in the first decade of the twentieth century, in all nations where a movement for the protection of the child seems to have been revived, have failed to recognize the fundamental error of the bench.

I believe that not for long will people run their hands over those model benches wondering at their perfection, or study about them in books illustrated with words and figures, scarcely trusting their own judgment.

The bench—it was intended to prevent curvature of the spine in the pupils!

Yet the scholors were subjected to such a regime that, even if they had been born healthy their vertebral columns would have become contorted and they would have become hump-backed!

[1] Curvature of the spine.

The vertebral column, the fundamental, biologically primitive part, the oldest part of the skeleton; the most firmly fixed, since the skeleton is the hardest part of the organism! The vertebral column, which was able to resist without yielding in the fiercest struggle waged by primitive or civilized man, when he fought with the lions of the forest, when he subdued the mammoth, when he dug stone, when he bent iron, when he subdued the earth— that vertebral column does not resist but bends under the yoke of the school!

It is incomprehensible that so-called science should have laboured over the perfecting of an instrument of slavery in the school, without being penetrated in the slightest degree, by at least one ray of light, from the movement which was taking shape outside for bringing about social liberation.

The direction of reform is well known and is repeated by everybody. The underfed workman does not ask for restoratives but for an economic betterment which will prevent under-nutrition. The miner who, by carrying on his work extended on his stomach during too many hours of the day, is subject to hernia of the intestines, does not ask for abdominal belts which would keep the intestines in place, but asks for a reduction of hours and better working conditions that he may live a healthy life like other men.

And when, during this same social epoch we acknowledge that in the school the children work in conditions so adverse to the normal development of life that their skeletons may become deformed, then we respond to such a terrible revelation by giving them an orthopedic bench. It is like offering a hernia belt to the miner, or arsenic to the underfed man.

Some time ago a lady, imagining that I encouraged scientific innovations in the school, submitted for my judgment, with evident complacency, a corset for pupils, invented by herself, with which to complete the prophylactic work of the bench. It is true that we doctors use for the cure of deformities of the vertebral column means other than medicinal; we use orthopedic instruments, corsets, and the treatment by suspension—the latter means for the rickety child who is suspended periodically by the head and the top of the shoulders, so that the weight of the body draws down and thus straightens the spine. In the school the orthopedic instrument is in full action—the bench; today, some one suggests the corset; one step more, and we will have the suspension method advocated for scholars.

All this is the logical consequence of material scientific applications in the decadent school. The same might be said of the applications of anthropology and experimental psychology to education in our schools of today.

Obviously the rational way to prevent scoliosis among children is to change the form of their work, so that they are no longer compelled to remain for many hours in a harmful position.

It is a victory for liberty which is needed, not the mechanism of a bench.

Even if the bench did good service to the child's skeleton, it would make the room unhygienic, because of the difficulty of removing it to clean underneath; further, the board on which the child places his feet is not made to lift up, and so there accumulates under it the dust brought in by little feet which have been walking in the dirty streets.

Today the furniture of homes is being transformed so as to become lighter and simpler, so that it can be moved about easily and probably cleaned everyday, if not actually washed. But the school has remained blind to the transformations going on around it.

One must carefully consider what will happen to the spirit of the child when he is condemned to grow up in such an artificial and vicious manner that his very bones are deformed by it. When we speak of the redemption of the workers, we always have in mind that, underneath the surface evil, such as poverty of blood, hernia, etc. there exists another deeper trouble which attacks the human soul in the state of slavery, and this we refer to directly when we say that the labourer must be restored to liberty. We know very well that, when a man's blood becomes impoverished or his intestines get displaced, his mind gets depressed, stupified or perhaps killed. The moral degradation of the slave which is the main hindrance to our progress ought to be raised, and which cannot be done because of this dead weight. The call for redemption comes louder still from souls than from bodies.

What shall we say when it is a matter of educating children?

Here is a spectacle with which we are very familiar. In the classroom there is the interfering teacher who pours knowledge into the heads of the pupils. That his work may succeed, he must maintain the discipline of immobility, of forced attention on the part of his students; and the master must have power to use freely both rewards and punishments by which to restrain those who are condemned to be his hearers.

These external rewards and punishments, if I may be allowed the expression, constitute the *bench* of the soul, that is, the instrument by which slavery is inflicted on the spirit, except that here it is applied not to lessen deformities but to give rise to them.

In fact, rewards and punishments are adopted to compel children to obey the laws of the world rather than those of God. The laws of the world for the children are dictated almost always by the will of the adult man, who clothes himself with an exaggerated, unlimited authority.

Too often he commands because he is strong, and wishes the child to obey because he is weak. Instead of that, adult man ought to constitute himself as a loving and enlightened guide to the child and assist the new man to find the ways which lead to the Kingdom of Heaven. Of quite another character are the rewards and punishments promised by Jesus—the elevation of the good and the abyss of perdition into which the wicked must fall. Anyone who makes use of his talents may be exalted and the reward is accessible to all, whether their talents be many or few.

But, in the schools, there is only one reward available for all those who strive, a fact which gives rise to emulation, greed and vanity, instead of the upliftment which springs from effort, humility and love, which all may attain. In this way we create a conflict not only between the school and social progress, but also between the school and religion. Some day the child is bound to ask himself if the rewards obtained in school had not proved themselves obstacles to eternal life, or if the punishments which had humiliated him, when he could not defend himself, had not made of him the man who hungered and thirsted after justice, and whom Jesus defended from the summit of the mountain.

In social life, it is true, there do exist rewards and punishments different from those which are contemplated in a spiritual light, and the adult sets himself to force the child in a good time to accommodate itself to, and to restrain itself within the requirements of this world. The rewards and the punishments are designed to accustom him to a ready submission.

But if we bestow a comprehensive glance on social morality we see the yoke growing gradually less oppressive, that is, we see the gradual return in triumph of rational nature, of life governed by thought. The yoke of the slave gives place to that of the servant, and this in turn to the yoke of the workman.

All forms of slavery tend to disappear by degrees. The history of human progress is a history compounded of conquests and liberations, and we style that which does not come under these headings as retrogression. Now we must ask ourselves if the school has to be fixed in a permanent condition which society would consider retrogressive.

Something very similar to the school corresponds in the great government administrative departments and their employees. They also write all day long for some great distant result, the immediate advantage of which is not apparent. That means that the State carries on its great undertakings through their agency, and that the welfare of the people of the whole nation is dependent on their work. For them, the immediate object is promotion, as for the pupil it means promotion from class to class. The man who loses sight of his lofty destiny is like a degraded child, like a slave who has been deceived; the dignity of man is reduced to the level of the dignity of a machine, which needs to be oiled

if it is to work, because there is within it no breath of life. All
the very insignificant things like desire for decorations form the
artificial stimulus needed for his dry, dark journey; just so do we
give medals to scholars. The fear of missing promotion
hinders them from flight and binds them to monotonous and
assiduous labour, just as the fear of not passing into a higher class
forces the pupil to stick to his book. The censure of the superior
officer is exactly like the reproof of the teacher; the correction of
badly done letters is the equivalent of a bad mark on the badly
done exercise of the pupil.

If administrations do not adopt the excellent course which is
necessary for the greatness of the country, if corruption penetrates them with ease, it is because the greatness of the man has
been obliterated in the conscience of the clerk, his vision has
been restricted to the trifling matters which lie close to him and
which are considered by him as rewards or punishments. Power
allied with favouritism can do a great deal, because it acts on these
scholars of the State.

But the government of a country survives because the rectitude
of most of its employees is great enough to resist the corruption
of rewards and punishments, and this irresistible force of honesty
prevails. Thus life in social environment triumphs against every
cause of impoverishment and of death and marches on to new victories, and like the instinct of liberty it beats down all obstacles,
going from victory to victory.

It is this grand, inner force of life, a force often latent and
unsuspected, which is the driving force of the world.

No man who has really done great, successful work has ever
done it because he was animated by the sole attraction of what
we comprehensively call a reward, or only by the fear of the evil
which we call punishment. If there were a war in which a great
army of giants were fighting with no other motive than the lust
for winning promotion, epaulettes or medals, or were merely
driven by the fear of being shot, and if they were opposed by a
handful of pigmies burning with love of their fatherland, the

2

victory would smile on the latter. When heroism is absent from any work rewards and punishments will be able to do no more than complete the work of destruction, permeating it with corruption.

All victories and all human progress are dependent on the strength which comes from within.

Thus a young student may become a great doctor if he is inspired by the spirit of his vocation; but if he is influenced only by the hope of a legacy, or of a good match, or of any external advantage whatever, he will never become a true teacher and a great doctor, and the world will not move far ahead as the result of his work. If the rewards and punishments of the school and of ordinary life are essential to making a youth work up to a university degree, then it would be better that such an individual does not become a doctor. Everyone possesses some special bent, some latent vocation—modest, perhaps, but yet useful. Rewards may divert the vocational impulse into the false path of vanity, and in this way there may be disturbed or destroyed some human activity.

We are always repeating that the world is making progress, and that man must be urged to strive after progress. But progress is founded on new things which lie hidden, and most frequently upon things already in existence which are improved or perfected; and they not being visible are not prized, but often bring pioneers to martyrdom.

What a calamity it would be if poems were written solely from a desire to win laurels on the Campidoglio! [1] It would be better that the vision should remain buried in the mind of the poet, and that the muse of poetry should disappear. Poetry must be born in the mind of the poet when he is not thinking either of reward or of himself; and if he does win laurels, let him not grow vain.

There exists also an exterior reward for man. When the orator sees the faces of his listeners becoming charged with emotion, he

---

[1] The Capital Hill in Rome where in the days of the Roman Empire and in the Renaissance poets-laureate were created.

experiences a feeling so great that it can be compared only with
the intense joy of one who discovers that he is being loved. It
is always in touching and conquering the minds of others that
we derive the only reward which is a true recompense.

Sometimes it happens that we pass through some moments
of happiness vouchsafed to men that they may continue their
existence in peace. It may be satisfied love, or a son born to us,
or the publication of a book, or a great discovery, which per-
suades us that no one ever was as happy as we are. But, if at
that moment some legal authority, or one which is vested in
our teacher, comes forward and offers us a medal or a reward,
then he acts as the tiresome destroyer of our true reward. " Who
are you," our vanished illusion might say, " who has reminded
me that I am not superior to all others since some one is so much
higher than I that he can give me a reward? " The reward given
to a man should come only from God.

As for punishment, we do not mean to deny the social
function and the individual efficacy of it, but the moral adequacy
and the universal necessity for it. It is most useful when applied
to inferiors; but those are few, and social progress does not depend
on them. The penal code threatens us with punishment if we are
dishonest within the limits prescribed by the law. But we are not
honest merely through fear of the law; we refrain from stealing and
killing because we see the intrinsic sinfulness in doing them, which
perception is intended to make us feel sharply, because the tenure
of our existence influences us towards good conduct and is constantly and effectively restraining us from the danger of certain sins.

Without entering into psychological questions, it may be
affirmed that a delinquent, before he sins, knows of the existence
of a penalty and has felt the penal code weighing down on him. He
has challenged it, or he has entangled himself in it imagining that
he could set himself free; but there has ensued a struggle between
crime and punishment within his conscience. Whether or not this
penal code fulfills the purpose of preventing crime, undoubtedly
it has made for a single limited category of individuals—criminals.

The enormous majority of citizens are honest even when they are ignorant of the threats of punishment.

The true punishment for the normal man is to lose the consciousness of his own power and greatness, which constitute his quality of manhood; and such punishment often falls upon men when they are rejoicing in an abundance of what, in common language, are styled rewards. Unfortunately, man is not aware of the real punishment which threatens to overwhelm him.

Here there may be disclosed the remedy—education.

At the present time we keep the pupils in a school compressed between these instruments which degrade both body and spirit—the bench and external rewards and punishments—for the purpose of bringing them under the discipline of immobility and silence, and in order to lead them—where? Unfortunately, nowhere!

The object is to pour mechanically into their brain's programmes which are often drawn up by ministers and imposed by laws, alien to the trend of their time.

Confronted with such forgetfulness of life which flows on into our posterity, what can we do but hang our heads in confusion and cover our blushing faces with our hands?

Truly—" Today there stands forth one urgent need: the reform of methods in education and instruction; and he who struggles towards this end is struggling for the regeneration of man."

THE HISTORY OF METHODS

IN order to build up a scientific pedagogy, it is necessary to strike out in a direction different from that which has been in vogue.

The training of teachers must go on at the same time as the transformation of the school. If we have teachers trained in observing and in experimenting, it is right that they should be able to observe and experiment in the school.

A fundamental requisite for scientific pedagogy ought therefore to be a school which allows the spontaneous expressions and the individual vitality of the child to have free play. If a system of teaching is to be founded on the individual study of the child, it will have to be understood from the observation of free children, children who are studied and watched over, but not repressed.

In vain does one expect educational reform from the methodical examination of the children of today according to the guidance offered by experimental psychology and by anthropology. Every branch of the experimental sciences has arisen from the application of its own special method.

Generally speaking, it is important to define the method, the technique and after its application to wait for the results which will be disclosed by the experiment. It is also characteristic of experimental science that an experiment should be approached without preconceptions of any kind about the eventual issue of the experiment.

Anyone who experiments must for the moment get rid of all prejudices, and formal education forms part of these prejudices.

If then we wish to attempt experimental education, we must not have recourse to kindred sciences, but must almost forget them and clear the mind, so that it can proceed without any hindrance which will obscure the search for truth in the field belonging exclusively to teaching itself.

We must not, therefore, start from ideas already accepted about child psychology, but from a method which sets the child at liberty, so that we may deduce from observation of his spontaneous manifestations the real child psychology. Perhaps this method holds great surprises in reserve!

*　　*　　*　　*

This then is the problem—to establish its own method for experimental teaching.

It cannot be that of other experimental sciences. If to some extent scientific pedagogy is integrated with hygiene, anthropology and psychology, and even adopts in part the relative technique in method, that is, limited to details in the study of the individual to be educated, needing to be kept parallel to the very different work of education, it can only be a collateral contribution to pedagogy.

My present study treats of the method of experimental pedagogy. It is the result of the experience which I have obtained in infant schools, and in the first classes of elementary schools.

I offer really only the beginning of the method, as I have applied it to children between the ages of three and six, but I believe that this attempt, because of the surprising results which it has given, will be made to continue in an extended form.[1]

Although this educational system of which experience has proved the excellence is not yet definitely completed, nevertheless it already constitutes an entity sufficiently organic to be usefully adopted in infant schools and in the first classes in elementary schools.

I am not really exact when I say that the present work is founded on a few years' experience; I do not think that these last efforts of mine could have given rise to all that I am about to describe.

The educational system of the Children's Houses did not come into existence without prolonged preparations, and, though the present experience with normal children is so short, it has its origin in previous teaching experience with abnormal children, and this presents a very long course of thought.

About twelve years ago, when I was an assistant doctor in the Mental Clinic in the University of Rome, I had occasion to frequent the asylum to study sick people to be chosen for the purposes of clinical teaching, and in this way I became interested in the idiot children maintained there. At this time medical treatment of the thyroid was in full favour; therefore, in the midst of the confusion and exaggeration about therapeutic successes, the interest of doctors, to a greater extent than previously, was focussed on meantally afflicted children.

It was through my interest in deficient children that I came to know the special method of education devised by Edward Seguin, and also to investigate in a general way the treatments for various forms of abnormality such as deafness, paralysis, etc. The fact that teaching must be linked up with medicine in therapy

---

[1] The method has now been extended. and is largely experimented with in elementary classes: it is described in the book, *L'Autœducazione nelle scoule Elementari* (The Advanced Montessori Method). In more recent times it has extended backward to birth and forward to adulthood. Several secondary Montessori schools are in existence and have obtained State recognition.

forms the practical victory of the theories of the time, and under this guidance the treatment of kinesthesia in particular was extended.

However, thinking differently from my colleagues, I felt intuitively that the question of the defectives was definitely one of pedagogy rather than of medicine; and whilst many spoke in the medical conferences on the medico-pedagogical method for the cure and education of mentally defective children, I raised the question of their moral education at the Educational Conference in Turin in 1898; and I believe that I touched a very vibrant chord, for the idea, having passed from the doctors to the elementary teachers, spread in a flash as being a question of keen interest for the school.

Indeed I was given by the Minister of Education and by my teacher, Guido Baccelli, the work of conducting for the common teachers of the elementary schools in Rome a course of lectures on the education of mentally defective children. Later on, there was founded a Pedagogical Institute where gathered the idiots and mentally defective children who were at that time sheltered in the lunatic asylum in Rome together with adult lunatics, without any special care being given to them. In this new institution I proposed to carry out an educative experiment with these children applying the principles of Seguin. I also admitted many children who lived abandoned on the streets, and who on account of their mental deficiency had been eliminated from the public schools. In order, further, to orientate myself practically I stayed some time at the Salpetriere at Paris where the classes founded by Seguin himself for defective children were still in existence, and afterwards I went to London, where some private institutions for the education of this type of children existed.

Thus my interest in education was born. Nothing in fact is so facinating as to attend to the mental awakening of these children, enslaved by their own inferiority; and to witness this kind of liberation of the soul from extinction through spiritual poverty; to see them arise, reviving and opening up towards interests that give life to their intelligence; to witness the happiness that comes to them through every activity in which the hand becomes capable of achieving something. It is really *man* arising from death to the joy of living. This spectacle is so fascinating that it kept me for almost two years in daily contact with these children. I was with them from early morning till evening as if I were a real teacher, not a physician conducting an experiment.

These two years of practical work were my first approach to pedagogy, because never before had I taken any interest in education.

From the time when, in 1898-1900, I dedicated myself to the education of defective children, I had the intuition that the methods of Seguin were not merely an attempt at helping inferior beings, the mentally defective children, but that they were based on principles far more reasonable than those in use in ordinary education. Here indeed the result was not only that the pupils " learned something," but one witnessed an awakening of the personality.

It seemed to me and to many who took interest in my experiments that it was a matter of method being *different* from the ordinary methods, but not of methods particular to an inferior mind. On the contrary these different methods contained a system of mental treatment that was very logical and superior to that being empirically applied to normal children. Slowly I became convinced that similar methods to normal children would lead to a mental awakening and a beneficial modifying action in them also. I had in fact come upon an experiment of scientific pedagogy!

It was then that I began a really profound study of the so-called curative pedagogy, and consequently I wanted to undertake the study of normal teaching and the principles on which it is founded. Therefore I enrolled myself as a student of philosophy in the university. A great faith animated me. Although I did not know if I should ever be able to test the truth of my theory, yet I left every other occupation in order to fathom it, preparing myself almost as if for an unknown mission.

The methods for the education of defectives had their origin at the time of the French Revolution in the work of doctor J. M. G. Itard whose medical works have become historical, for he was the founder of that branch of medical science which specializes under the name of otiatry (diseases of the ear).

He was the first to attempt the methodical education of the sense of hearing, in the institute of deaf-mutes founded by Pereire in Paris; he succeeded in giving back hearing to those partially deaf. Later, having had in his charge for eight years an idiot boy who was known as the savage of Aveyron, he extended to all the senses the educational methods which had already given excellent results in hearing. Itard, a pupil of Pinel, was the first teacher to practise observation of the pupil, in a way similar to that which was done in the hospitals in the observation of the sick, especially of those suffering from nervous troubles.

The educational works of Itard are most interesting detailed descriptions of his teaching attempts and experiments, and anyone who reads them today will agree that they were the first attempts at " scientific pedagogy ". He, in fact, derived from scientific study a series of *exercises capable of modifying the personality*, of healing defects that kept the individual in a state of inferiority. Itard actually succeeded in rendering semi-deaf children capable of both hearing and speaking, whilst otherwise they would have remained deaf and dumb and consequently for ever abnormal. This is very different indeed from a simple *study of the individual* carried out by means of the tests of experimental psychology. They only lead to a statement on the mental personality; they do not modify it but leave the educational methods unchanged. Here, instead, the scientific means employed become the means by which education is given, so that pedagogy itself is changed.

Itard, therefore, may be called the founder of scientific pedagogy, not Wundt or Binet, who are the founders of a physiological psychology which can easily be applied also in the schools.

This is a fundamental point which well deserves to be made clear. Whilst Pestalozzi, in Switzerland, became the " father of a new affective education," in Germany half a century later Fechner and Wundt founded experimental psychology. The two currents grew and developed separately in the schools. Academic pedagogy continued to evolve on the old foundations, whilst side by side mental tests were given to the students which, however, did not affect education in the least.

The experiments of Itard on the contrary, carried out only slightly earlier, were a real beginning of scientific education, capable of modifying both educational methods and the pupils. As it came into being among deficient children, however, it was not taken into serious consideration in the educational world.

But the merit of having completed a real educational system for defective children belongs to Edward Seguin, who was first a teacher and then a doctor. Beginning with the experiments of Itard, he applied them, modifying and completing the method, during ten years of experience with children who had been taken from the asylum and brought together in a little school in the *rue* Pigalle in Paris. This method was published for the first time in a volume of about six hundred pages, published in Paris with the title, *Traitement Moral, Hygiene et Education des Idiots.*

Later on, Seguin emigrated to the United States of America, where there were founded many institutions for defectives, and where Seguin, after twenty years more of experience, published a second edition of his method which bore a different title, *Idiocy and its Treatment by the Physiological Method.* This volume was published in New York in 1866. In it Seguin defined clearly a method of education which he called a physiological method. He no longer refers in the title to the education of idiots almost as if it were special to them, but he speaks of idiocy as being treated by a physiological method.

If we remember that pedagogy had always been based on psychology and that Wundt postulated a physiological psychology, one must be struck by the coincidence of these conceptions and be led to suspect that the physiological method may have some connection with physiological psychology.

Whilst I was an assistant in the Mental Clinic, I had read with great interest Seguin's French work. But the English book published in New York twenty years later, although it was quoted in the works of specialized education of Bourneville, did not exist in any library. To my great astonishment, I could find no trace of it in Paris, where Bourneville told me that he did not know of its existence; Seguin's second book had never entered Europe. I hoped to find some copies of it in London, but I had to convince myself that even there the volume did not exist either in the public or in the private libraries. It was in vain that I made enquiries, visiting home after home of many English doctors who were well known as specialists for defective children, or who superintended special schools for them. The fact that this book was unknown even in England though it was published in English made me think that Seguin's system had not been understood. Indeed, in the publications relating to institutions for defectives, Seguin was constantly quoted, but the educational applications described were quite different from those advocated in Seguin's system. Almost everywhere there were applied more or less to defectives the methods used for normal children, and, especially in Germany, a German friend of mine who had gone there to help me in my researches noted how special didactic material existed here and there in the pedagogical museums belonging to schools for defectives. It was, however, never in practical use, whilst there the principle is defended that it is a good plan to adopt for slowly developed minds the same method as for normal, which is, however, more objective in Germany than with us.

At Bicetre also, where I remained to study for a long time, I saw that teaching mechanisms were adopted rather than Seguin's system; yet the French text was in the hands of the teachers. All the teaching there was mechanized, and every teacher followed the same routine to the letter. However, it was noticeable everywhere, in London and in Paris, that there was a desire to have fresh advice, to learn new experiments for the fact stated by Seguin that he had really succeeded in educating idiots with his methods, remained in practice a delusion. The cause of this lack of success is easily understood. Everybody only retained the idea that the deficient children, inferior beings, should ultimately be educated like normal, superior, children. The conception that a " new education " was born in the pedagogic world had not penetrated, neither the fact that it was that new education which could raise the deficient children to a higher level. Much less was there an intuition that a method of education which raised defectives could also raise normal children.

I carried out my experiments on the defectives in Rome and carried on their education for two years. I followed Seguin's book and I also found a treasure in the admirable experiments made by Itard. Besides that, I had made for myself, following the guidance of these texts, a rich stock of teaching material.

This material, which I did not see in its entirety in any other institution, was a marvellous instrument, excellent in the hands of anyone who knew how to use it, but by itself could pass unnoticed among the defectives. I understood why teachers had become so discouraged, and why the method had been abandoned. The theory, that the teacher must place himself on the level of the pupil, plunged the teacher of defectives into a kind of apathy; he knew that he was educating inferior intellects and therefore he did not succeed in educating them. So it is with the teachers of little children who think of educating them by placing themselves on their level with games and often with nonsensical talk.

Instead of that, what we must aim at doing is to awaken in the mind of the child the man who is asleep there.

I was possessed by this inspiration, and I believed that at the start the teaching material had to be associated with the voice of the teacher which called and roused the children and induced them to use the material and educate themselves. I was guided by my great respect for their misfortunes, and the love which these unhappy children were capable of kindling in all who came near them. Seguin also expressed himself in a similar way on the subject; reading his patient attempts I understood well that the first teaching material used by him was spiritual. Because at the end of the French volume, the author, giving a review of his work, sorrowfully comes to the conclusion that it will be lost if the teachers are not prepared. He holds an entirely original idea about the training of teachers for defectives; it looks like advice given to a woman who is preparing herself to be an enchantress. He would like them to be beautiful, to have fascinating voices, and thinks that they should take the utmost pains to make themselves attractive. Their bearing and the modulations of their voices should be studied with the same care as that taken by great dramatic artists who prepare themselves for the stage, because they have to conquer minds which are weak and weary, by stirring up the great emotions of life.

This kind of secret key, which turns upon the action of the spirit, opened the long series of educational experiments so admirably analysed by Edward Seguin and really most efficacious in the education of idiots. I obtained surprising results from them, but I must confess that whilst my efforts were producing intellectual progress, I was prostrated by a kind of exhaustion— I felt that I was being drained of some of my strength. What we call encouragement, comfort, love, respect, are drains on the human mind, and the more lavishly one spends oneself in this way, the more does one renew and re-invigorate the life around.

Without that, the most perfect external stimulus passes unnoticed, as did the sun for Saul, when he exclaimed that there was thick darkness.

I could write more about the new experiments, but it is not opportune here. I will only mention how at this stage I tried out a system for reading and writing which was quite original; these subjects of education were not treated at all either by Itard or Seguin.

I taught reading and writing, including penmanship, to some defectives of my institution who became fit to be presented at an examination for the public schools along with normal children, and who passed the test.

These marvellous results seemed to be almost miraculous to those who observed them. But, in my opinion, the children from the institution equalled the normal children in the public examinations only because they had followed a different path. They had been assisted in their mental development whilst the normal children had been stifled and repressed. I thought that if one day the specialized education which had so marvellously improved the idiots could be applied to the development of normal children, the miracle would disappear from the world, and the abyss between the inferior mentality of idiots and normals would never be lessened. Whilst everyone was admiring the progress of my defectives, I was thinking of the reasons which might have reduced the healthy, happy pupils of the ordinary schools to a level so low that it could be reached in intelligence tests by my unhappy pupils.

One day one of my mistresses in the institute for defectives made me read Ezekiel's prophecies which had made a deep impression on her, because it seemed to her a prophecy about the education of defectives:

" The hand of the Lord was upon me, and carried me out in the spirit of the Lord, and set me down in the midst of the valley which was full of bones,

" And caused me to pass by them round about: and, behold, there were very many in the open valley; and lo, they were very dry.

" And he said unto me, Son of man, can these bones live? And I answered, O Lord God, thou knewest.

" Again he said unto me, Prophesy upon these bones, and say unto them, O ye dry bones, hear the word of the Lord.

" Thus saith the Lord God unto these bones; Behold, I will cause breath to enter into you, and ye shall live:

" And I will lay sinews upon you, and will bring up flesh upon you, and cover you with skin, and put breath in you, and ye shall live; and ye shall know that I am the Lord.

" So I prophesied as I was commanded: and as I prophesied, there was a noise, and behold a shaking, and the bones came together, bone to his bone.

" And when I beheld, lo, the sinews and the flesh came up upon them, and the skin covered them above: but there was no breath in them.

" Then said he unto me, Prophesy unto the wind, prophesy, Son of man, and say to the wind, Thus saith the Lord God; Come from the four winds, O breath, and breathe upon these slain, that they may live.

" So I prophesied as he commanded me, and the breath came into them, and they lived, and stood up upon their feet, an exceeding great army.

" Then he said unto me, Son of man, these bones are the whole house of Israel: behold, they say, Our bones are dried, and our hope is lost: we are cut off from our parts."

Indeed the words, " I will cause breath to enter into you, and ye shall live," seem to refer directly to the individual work of the teacher, who encourages, incites, and helps the pupil and prepares him for education.

And the other words—" I will lay sinews upon you, and will bring up flesh upon you, and cover you with skin," recall the fundamental sentences in which is summed up Seguin's method: " To lead the child as it were by the hand of the education of the muscular system and that of the nervous system and the senses," with which Seguin teaches idiots to walk, to keep their balance in the most difficult movements of the body, like mounting a staircase, jumping, etc.; and at last, teaching them to feel, beginning with the education of the muscular, tactile and heat sensations, and ending with those of the special senses. But these are simply made adaptable to the physical life. " Prophesy unto the wind," says the prophet; " and the breath came into them and they lived." Seguin indeed led the idiot from the physical life to the life of the spirit, " from the education of the senses to notions, from notions to ideas, from ideas to morality ". But when such a marvellous work is accomplished, and by means of detailed physiological analysis and a gradually progressive method the idiot has become a man, he is always only an inferior among other men, an individual

who will never be able to adapt himself to his social surroundings.
" Our bones are dried, and our hope is lost; we are cut off from
our parts."

The principle that the teacher must undergo a special training
which touches her sentiment and does not consist merely in an
intellectual study, and again that education is fundamentally a
" contact of souls " and that the teacher must feel " respect and
sympathy " for the children she educates, is the characteristic contribution given by Pestalozzi in his schools. This, however, is
only a first step essential in order that the child's soul be awakened.
Afterwards the activity of the child must find means (and scientific means for that matter) which lead to development. This
second part is the contribution of scientific pedagogy. That is
why we affirm today, in virtue of our experience, that the teacher
is the *trait-d'union* between the child—distracted, lulled or repressed—and the educative environment prepared for his activity.
Very often this contact between the child and the environment
cannot be established, unless he be delivered first from the burden
of previous repression and its fatal consequences. In that case
a healing, or as we say, a normalizing process has to be initiated
before the means of development can be offered. Many of our
teachers suffered great disappointment at their lack of success,
because they started their work as if this process had taken place,
and overlooked the necessity of this readjustment.

Seguin's wearisome method, however, was laid aside, because
this enormous expenditure of effort was not justified by the poverty
in the final results.

Everyone said the same thing: there was still so much to
be done for normal children!

*   *   *   *

Having acquired faith in Seguin's method through my experience, after I had retired from active work among defectives,
I set myself to study the works of Itard and Seguin. I felt the
need for meditating over them. So I did what I had never done,
and what very few perhaps repeat—I copied out in Italian, from

3

beginning to end, the writings of these authors by hand, almost producing books as the Benedictines did before the introduction of printing. I wrote them by hand in order to have time to weigh the value of every word and to grasp the spirit of the authors. I was on the point of finishing the copying of the 600 pages of Seguin's French work, when I received from New York a volume of the second edition, that is the English book published in 1866. This old volume had been found among the books discarded from the private library of a New York doctor and had been readily given over to the person who sent it to me. I translated it with the help of an English lady. This volume did not offer a great contribution of later teaching experiments, but rather the philosophy of the experiments described in the first volume. The man who had studied abnormal children for thirty years expounded the idea that the physiological method—a method which had as a base the individual study of the pupil, and as part of its educational procedure, the analysis of physiological and mental characters—ought to be applied to normal children, thus leading to the regeneration of all humanity. Seguin's voice seemed to me to be that of the prophet crying in the wilderness and my mind was overwhelmed with the immensity of the importance of a work which might reform the school and education.

At that time, as a student of philosophy at the university, I was following the course in experimental psychology which had just been founded in Italian Universities—in Turin, Rome and Naples. I was also carrying out, at the same time, in elementary schools research work in pedagogic anthropology and used the opportunity to study the methods and theories in use for the education of normal children. These studies led me to the teaching of Pedagogic Anthropology in the University of Rome.

This then was my preparation. I had grown up intellectually in contact with the scientific problems of my time and was finding my way towards new branches which were coming into existence in the field of mental medicine. I understood, as others did not, that scientific education cannot be based on studying and measuring the individual to be educated, but on permanent treatment which is capable of modifying them. Hence Itard's education was scientific, because the measurement of hearing was only a means leading up to the transformation of the partially deaf into individuals who could hear. In the case of the " Savage of Aveyron," scientific methods very similar to those used by the founders of experimental psychology had succeeded in restoring to social life an individual so far removed from society that he appeared as a deaf-mute, an idiot; and in changing him into a person who heard and understood language as we speak and write it.

Similarly Seguin, with analytical methods very similar to those of Fechner, but more ample, not only studied hundreds of defective children assembled in the mad house in Paris, but transformed them into men able to do useful work in the community, fit to assimilate mental and artistic instruction.

I myself, using only what was called the study of the individual by means of scientific instruments and mental tests, had transformed the defectives expelled from the schools as being unfit for education, into individuals who entered into competition with the normal pupils in the schools. They were changed into persons socially useful and educated like intelligent children. *Scientific education, therefore, was that which, while based on science, modified and improved the individual.*

Scientific education, depending on objective research on the fundamentals of psychology, ought to be capable of transforming normal children. How? Certainly by raising them above the normal level, *making them better men.* A science of education has not the purpose of merely " observing," but that of " transforming " children.

These were the conclusions I arrived at: not only to observe, but to transform. Observation had founded a new psychological science, but it had transformed neither the schools nor the scholars. It had added something to the ordinary schools though it had left those schools in their original condition, neither the methods of instruction nor those of education having varied.

The new methods, if they were run on scientific lines, ought *to change completely both the school and its methods,* ought to give rise to a new form of education.

The central fact in the scientific education of defectives had been that the idiots and those below normal did not respond to teaching and could not execute orders. Hence it was necessary to have recourse to other means which would be adjusted to the capacity of each individual.

Education of this type had been a piece of research, a scientific experiment, an attempt to investigate the possibilities inherent in the scholar, and to offer him means, stimuli, which might awaken whatever energy was left in him and employ it in a permanent fashion, augmenting it with and co-ordinating it by individual exercises.

The teacher when faced with a deaf person, with an idiot, as with a new-born child, is powerless. Only experimental science can point the way to a new practical education.

My desire had been to experiment with the methods elaborated with so much success by Seguin on children in the first elementary classes when they presented themselves in school, undisciplined and illiterate, at the age of six.

But I had never thought of applying them in infant schools. It was chance which shed a ray of light into my mind. We are generally hampered by habits and prejudices, and our logical power is left unused.

Perhaps it was logical to apply methods used for defectives to little children when these also were regarded as being impossible to educate, inaccessible to teaching because the mind had not yet reached a high enough level of maturity.

It is possible to draw comparisons between defectives and normal children if we consider children of different ages. Compare those who have not the power to develop (defectives) with those who have not yet had time to develop (very small children). Backward children are judged mentally as being children whose mentality closely resembles that of normal children some years

younger than them. In spite of the fact that in such a comparison
there is lacking the consideration of initial force innate in such
differing degrees in the two natures, the comparison is not illogical.

Small children have not yet acquired definite co-ordination of
the muscular movements, hence their unsteady walk, their inability to perform the usual acts of daily life like putting on
clothes and stockings, fastening up, buttoning, putting on gloves,
etc. The organs of the senses, for example the power of accom-
modation in the eye, are not yet completely developed. Language
is rudimentary and shows the well-known defects of child-speech.
The difficulty of concentrating, instability, etc. are other characters
of the same kind.

Prayer, in his studies on infant psychology, has at great length
illustrated the comparison between the pathological defects of
language and those normal to the child who is in the course of
development.

The methods which are effective in helping the mental development of backward children might be of service in helping the
development of all children, thus constituting a healthful course
for the normal human being.

Many defects like those of language, which become permanent,
are acquired because we neglect the child during the most important period of his life—between three and six years of age when
his principal functions are formed and fixed.

This ambitious idea of being able to assist through scientific
methods of education the actual development of man during the
period of life when intelligence and character are being built
up had not struck me in spite of the interest which I had in
the question.

That is why the story of this kind of " psychological discovery " and of this scientific method of education became a story
of interest.

Chance played its part, as it had done in so many discoveries,
like that of electricity. In fact, chance, that is the environment,
must almost always apply the spark to intuition; it is the environment

which reveals what is new, and after that intuition and awakened interest are able to pursue a new path of progress.

In my case the story is interesting because, independently of studies and preconceptions, it offered a complex environment in which not only the education of the child but the social life of men and their feelings combined into one whole.

HISTORY OF THE DISCOVERY OF A SCIENTIFIC EDUCATION
FOR NORMAL CHILDREN

It was the end of the year 1906. I was returning from Milan where I had been elected to take part in the adjudication of prizes at the International Exhibition, in the section of scientific pedagogy and experimental psychology. I was invited by the Director-General of the Roman *Instituto dei Beni Stabili* (Association for Good Building), to assume the organization of infant schools in tenement houses.

The magnificent idea was to reform a Quarter like that of San Lorenzo in Rome, which was filled with refugees and wretched people, and where a population of about 30,000 was crowded together, living in conditions beyond all civil control. There were work-people without work, beggars, prostitutes, convicts just released from prison, all of whom had taken refuge within the walls of houses which had not been completed because of the economic crisis which had suddenly caused the suspension of building in the whole Quarter. The project conceived by Engineer Talamo had been to buy up those walls, those skeletons of houses, and complete by degrees, making them into permanent homes for the people. Along with this plan was coupled the truly admirable idea of gathering together all the little children under school age (from three to six years of age) in a kind of " school in the house ".

Every tenement was to possess its own school, and as the Institute already owned more than four hundred blocks in Rome, the work presented magnificent possibilities for development. Meanwhile the first school was to be opened in January 1907, in a large tenement house in the San Lorenzo Quarter. In the same Quarter the Institute already possessed fifty-eight buildings, and the Directors' plans provided there for coming into existence soon about sixteen schools in the houses.

This special type of school was christened with the charming name " Children's House ". The first of them was opened, under this name, on January 6th, 1907, in the Via dei Marsi, 53, and I was entrusted with the responsibility of directing it. The social and pedagogic importance of such an institution became apparent to me at once in all its greatness and I indulged in what seemed to be then exaggerated visions of its triumphal future; but today many are beginning to understand that I foresaw the truth. January 6th, in Italy, is the children's festal day, corresponding to the Epiphany in the Catholic calendar. It is exactly like Christmas Day in Protestant countries, when there is a Christmas tree, and gifts and toys are given to the children. On the 6th of January then there assembled the first group of little children, rather more than fifty of them. It was interesting to watch these little creatures, so different from those who are to be found in the usual charity schools. They were timid and clumsy, apparently stupid and un-responsive. They could not walk together and the mistress had to make each child take hold of the pinafore of the one in front, so that they walked in a kind of Indian file.

They wept and seemed to be afraid of everything—of the beautiful ladies present, of the tree and of the objects on it. They did not take the presents and they did not eat the sweets; they did not answer when spoken to. They were really like a set of wild children. They certainly had not lived, like the wild boy of Aveyron, in a wood with animals, but they had lived in a forest of people, lost and beyond the bounds of civilized society. At the sight of this touching spectacle many ladies said that only by a miracle could these children be educated, and that they would like to see them again in a year or two.

I was invited to speak, but not being able to enter into the details of structural and economic work, after a general reference to the work which was beginning, I read part of a prophecy which in the Catholic church forms part of the service of Epiphany on the 6th of January, because this corresponded to the feast day chosen for the inauguration of the Children's House.

Isaiah, Chapter 60. " Arise, shine; for thy light is come, and the glory of the Lord is risen upon thee.

" For, behold, the darkness shall cover the earth, and gross darkness the people: but the Lord shall arise upon thee, and his glory shall be seen upon thee.

" And the Gentiles shall come to thy light, and kings to the brightness of thy rising.

" Lift up thine eyes round about, and see: all they gather themselves together, they come to thee: thy sons shall come from far, and thy daughters shall be nursed at thy side.

" Then thou shalt see, and flow together, and thine heart shall fear, and be enlarged; because the abundance of the sea shall be converted unto thee, the forces of the Gentiles shall come unto thee.

" The multitude of camels shall cover thee, the dromedaries of Midian and Ephah; all they from Sheba shall come: they shall bring gold and incense; and they shall show forth the praises of the Lord."

" Perhaps," I added as a conclusion, " it may be that this Children's House may become a new Jerusalem, which, as it is multiplied among abandoned people, will bring light into education."

The newspapers of the day criticized these words as being an exaggeration when applied to an enterprise still so small.

So it was that when, a year later, there was opened another tenement with its Children's House, the *Instituto dei Beni Stabili* thought it best to suggest a serious speech which would give the Italian public a clear idea of the truly valuable character of this civic work of reform, and of its economic and social foundation.

This speech is reproduced in full in the next chapter, that it may afford inspiration to those who are engaged in the problem of the " *house* " for those unfortunate people sunk in the misery of exceptional conditions, as these were, for the San Lorenzo Quarter came into existence as a consequence of the displacement of population which had followed the War of Independence in Italy, when crowds flocked unexpectedly into Rome as being the capital.

Here we have then the meaning of my teaching experiment, carried on for two years in the Children's House. It represents the results of a series of trials made by me in educating young children according to new methods. It certainly is not a matter of the pure and simple application of Seguin's method to infant schools, such as anyone could find out by consulting that author's works; it is nevertheless true that under these two years of experimenting there lies an experimental basis which goes back to the time of the French Revolution and which includes the assiduous labours of Seguin and Itard. As for me, thirty years after Seguin's second publication, I took up again the ideas, and, if I may venture to say so, the work of this author, with the same enthusiastic feeling with which he had inherited the ideas and the work of his master Itard, who died in his filial care. For ten years I experimented practically and meditated on the work of these distinguished men who had sacrificed themselves, leaving to humanity the most fruitful proofs of their obscure heroism. To my ten years of study there may also be added the forty years of the work of Itard and Seguin. There had already been spent fifty years of active preparation, distributed over more than a century of time, before this trial was attempted, so short apparently, of only two years; I do not think that I am making a mistake in saying that it represents the succession of labours of three doctors who, from Itard to myself, took the first steps in the paths of psychiatry.

NOTE—This group of children not only received an education but they furnished surprising revelations which roused interest throughout the whole world, and the Children's House became a centre of pilgrimage for people from all countries, especially from America. Today there have been founded in India Children's Houses in the desert of Rajputana, where camels and dromedaries are numerous and still form the only means of communication between the villages, and carry visitors to the Children's Houses.

INAUGURAL ADDRESS
DELIVERED ON THE OPENING OF ONE OF
THE " CHILDREN'S HOUSES " IN 1907

IT may be that the life lived by the very poor is a thing which some of you here today have never actually looked upon in all its degradation. You may have only felt the misery of deep human poverty through the medium of some great book, or some gifted actor may have made your soul vibrate with its horror.

Let us suppose that in some such moment a voice should cry to you: " Go, look upon these homes of misery and blackest poverty. For there have sprung up among the terror and the suffering, oases of happiness, of cleanliness, of peace. The poor are to have an ideal house which shall be their own. In Quarters where poverty and vice ruled, a work of moral redemption is going on. The soul of the people is being set free from the torpor of vice, from the shadows of ignorance. The little children, too, have a ' House ' of their own. The new generation goes forward to meet the era, the time when misery shall no longer be deplored but destroyed. They go to meet the time when the dark dens of vice and wretchedness shall have become things of the past, and when no trace of them shall be found among the living." What a change of emotions we should experience! and how we should hasten here, as the wise men guided by a dream and a star hastened to Bethlehem!

I have spoken thus in order that you may understand the great significance, the real beauty, of this humble room, which seems like a bit of the house itself set apart by a mother's hand for the use and happiness of the children of the Quarter. This is the second " Children's House " which has been established within the ill-favoured Quarter of San Lorenzo.

The Quarter of San Lorenzo is celebrated, for every newspaper in the city is filled with almost daily accounts of its wretched happenings. Yet there are many who are not familiar with the origin of this portion of our city.

It was never intended to build up here a tenement district for the people. And indeed San Lorenzo is not the People's Quarter, it is the Quarter of the *poor*. It is the Quarter where lives the underpaid, often unemployed, working-man, a common type in a city which has no factory industries. It is the home of him who undergoes the period of surveillance to which he is condemned after his prison sentence is ended. They are all here, mingled, huddled together.

The district of San Lorenzo sprang into being between 1884 and 1888 at the time of the great building fever. No standards, either social or hygienic, guided these new constructions. The aim in building was simply to cover with walls square foot after square foot of ground. The more the space covered, the greater the gain of the interested Banks and Companies. All this with a complete disregard of the disastrous future which they were preparing. It was natural that no one should concern himself with the stability of the building he was creating, since in no case would the property remain in the possession of him who built it.

When the storm burst, in the shape of the inevitable building panic of 1888 to 1890, these unfortunate houses remained for a long time untenanted. Then, little by little, the need of dwelling-places began to make itself felt, and these great houses began to fill. Now, those speculators who had been so unfortunate as to remain possessors of these buildings could not and did not wish to add fresh capital to that already lost. So the houses constructed in the first place in utter disregard of the laws of hygiene, and rendered still worse by having been used as temporary habitations, came to be occupied by the poorest class in the city.

The apartments not being prepared for the working class, were too large, consisting of five, six, or seven rooms. These were rented at a price which, while exceedingly low in relation to the size, was yet too high for any one family of very poor people. This led to the evil of subletting. The tenant who has taken a six-room apartment at eight dollars a month sublets rooms at one dollar and a half or two dollars a month to those who can pay so much, and a corner of a room, or a corridor, to a poorer tenant, thus making an income of fifteen dollars or more, over and above the cost of his own rent.

This means that the problem of existence is in great part solved for him, and that in every case he adds to his income through usury. The one who holds the lease traffics in the misery of his fellow tenants, lending small sums at a rate which generally corresponds to twenty cents a week for the loan of two dollars, equivalent to an annual rate of 500 per cent.

Thus we have in the evil of subletting the most cruel form of usury: that which only the poor know how to practice upon the poor.

To this we must add the evils of crowded living, promiscuousness, immorality, crime. Every little while the newspapers uncover for us one of these *interieurs*: a large family, growing boys and girls sleep in one room; while one corner of the room is occupied by an outsider, a woman who receives the nightly visits of men. This is seen by the boys and girls; evil passions are kindled that lead to the crime and bloodshed which unveil for a brief instant before our eyes, in some lurid paragraph, this little detail of the mass of misery.

Whoever enters, for the first time, one of these apartments is astonished and horrified. For this spectacle of genuine misery is not at all like the garish scene he has imagined. We enter here a world of shadows, and that which strikes us first is the darkness which, even though it is midday, makes it impossible to distinguish any of the details of the room.

When the eye has grown accustomed to the gloom, we perceive, within, the outlines of a bed upon which lies huddled a figure—some one ill and suffering. If we had come bringing money from some society for mutual aid, a candle must be lighted before the sum can be counted and the receipt signed. Oh, when we talk of social problems, how often we speak vaguely, drawing upon our fancy for details instead of preparing ourselves to judge intelligently through a personal investigation of facts and conditions!

We discuss earnestly the question of home study for school children, when for many of them home means a straw pallet thrown down in the corner of some dark hovel. We wish to establish circulating libraries that the poor may read at home. We plan to send among these people books which shall form their domestic literature—books through whose influence they shall come to higher standards of living. We hope through the printed pages to educate these poor people in matters of hygiene, of morality, of culture, and in this we show ourselves profoundly ignorant of their most crying needs. For many of them have no light by which to read!

There lies before the social crusader of the present day a problem more profound than that of the intellectual elevation of the poor; the problem, indeed, of *life*.

In speaking of the children born in these places, even the conventional expressions must be changed, for they do not " first see the light of day "; they come into a world of gloom. They grow among the poisonous shadows which envelop over-crowded humanity. These children cannot be other than filthy in body, since the water-supply in an apartment originally intended to be occupied by three or four persons, when distributed among twenty or thirty is scarcely enough for drinking purposes!

We Italians have elevated our word " casa " to the almost sacred significance of the English word " home," the enclosed temple of domestic affection, accessible only to dear ones.

Far removed from this conception is the condition of the many who have no " casa," but only ghastly walls within which the most intimate acts of life are exposed upon the pillory. Here there can be no privacy, no modesty, no gentleness; here there is often not even light, nor air, nor water. It seems a cruel mockery to introduce here our idea of the home as essential to the education of the masses, and as furnishing, along with the family, the only solid basis for the social structure. In doing this we should be not practical reformers but visionary poets.

Conditions such as I have described make it more decorous, more hygienic, for these people to take refuge in the street and to let their children live there. But how often these streets are the scene of bloodshed, of quarrel, of sights so vile as to be almost inconceivable. The papers tell us of women pursued and killed by drunken husbands! Of young girls, with the fear of worse than death, stoned by low men. Again, we see untellable things—a wretched woman thrown forth by the drunken men who have preyed upon her into the gutter. There, when day comes, the children of the neighbourhood crowd about her like scavengers about their dead prey, shouting and laughing at the sight of this wreck of womanhood, kicking her bruised and filthy body as it lies in the mud of the gutter!

Such spectacles of extreme brutality are possible here at the very gate of a cosmopolitan city—the mother of civilization and queen of the fine arts—because of a new fact which was unknown to past centuries, namely *the isolation of the masses of the poor.*

In the Middle Ages, leprosy was isolated; the Catholics isolated the Hebrews in the Ghetto; but poverty was never considered a peril and an infamy so great that it must be isolated. The homes of the poor were scattered among those of the rich, and the contrast between these was a commonplace in literature up to our own times. Indeed, when I was a child in the school, teachers, for the purpose of moral education, frequently resorted to the illustration of the kind princess who sends help to the poor cottage next door, or of the good children from the great house who carry food to the sick woman in the neighbouring attic.

Today, all this would be as unreal and artificial as a fairy tale. The poor may no longer learn from their more fortunate neighbours lessons in courtesy and good breeding, they no longer have the hope of help from them in cases of extreme need. We have herded them together far from us, without the walls, leaving them to learn of each other, in the abandon of desperation, the cruel lessons of brutality and vice. Any one in whom the social conscience is awake must see that we have thus created infected regions that threaten with deadly peril the city which, wishing to make all beautiful and shining according to an aesthetic and aristocratic ideal, has thrust without its walls whatever is ugly or diseased.

When I passed for the first time through these streets, it was as if I found myself in a city upon which some great disaster had fallen. It seemed to me that the shadow of some recent struggle still oppressed the unhappy people who, with something very like terror in their pale faces, passed me in these silent streets. The very silence seemed to signify the life of a community interrupted, broken. Not a carriage, not even the cheerful voice of the ever-present street vendor, nor the sound of the hand-organ playing in the hope of a few pennies, not even those things, so characteristic of poor quarters, enter here to enlighten this sad and heavy silence.

Observing these streets with their deep holes, the door-steps broken and tumbling, we might suppose that this disaster had been in the nature of a great inundation which had carried the very earth away; but looking about us at the houses stripped of all decorations, the walls broken and scarred, we are inclined to think that it was perhaps an earthquake which has afflicted this Quarter. Then, looking still more closely, we see that in all this thickly settled neighbourhood there is not a shop to be found. So poor is the community that it has not been possible to establish even one of those popular bazaars where necessary articles are sold at so low a price as to put them within the reach of any one. The only shops of any sort are the low wine-shops which open their evil-smelling doors to the passer-by. As we look upon all this, it is borne upon us that the disaster which has placed its weight of suffering upon these people is not a convulsion of nature, but poverty—poverty with its inseparable companion, vice.

This unhappy and dangerous state of things, to which our attention is called at intervals by the newspaper accounts of violent and immoral crime, stirs the hearts and conscience of many who come to undertake among these people some work of generous benevolence. One might almost say that every form of misery inspires a special remedy and that all have been tried here, from the attempt to introduce hygienic principles into each house, to the establishment of creches, " Children's Houses," and dispensaries.

But what indeed is benevolence? Little more than an expression of sorrow; it is pity translated into action. The benefits of such a form of charity cannot be great and, through the absence of any continued income and the lack of organization, it is restricted to a small number of persons. The great and widespread peril of evil demands, on the other hand, a broad and comprehensive work directed towards the redemption of the entire community. Only such an organization as, working for the good of others, shall itself grow and prosper through the general prosperity which it has made possible, can make a place for itself in this Quarter and accomplish a permanent good work.

It is to meet this dire necessity that the great and kindly work of the Roman Association of Good Building has been undertaken. The advanced and highly modern way in which this work is being carried on is due to Edoardo Talamo, Director-General of the Association. His plans, so original, so comprehensive, yet so practical, are without counterpart in Italy or elsewhere.

This Association was incorporated three years ago in Rome, the plan being to acquire city tenements, remodel them, put them into a productive condition, and administer them as a good father of a family would.

The first property acquired comprised a large portion of the Quarter of San Lorenzo, where today the Association possesses fifty-eight houses, occupying a ground space of about 30,000 square metres, and containing, independent of the ground floor, 1,600 small apartments. Thousands of people will in this way receive the beneficent influence of the protective reforms of the Good Building Association. Following its beneficent programme, the Association set about transforming these old houses according to the most modern standards, paying as much attention to questions of hygiene and morals as to those relating to buildings. The constructional changes would make the property of real and lasting value, while the hygienic and moral transformation would, through the improved condition of the inmates, make the rent from these apartments a more definite asset.

The Association of Good Building therefore decided upon a programme which would permit of a gradual attainment of its ideal. It is necessary to proceed slowly because it is not easy to empty a tenement house at a time when houses are scarce, and the humanitarian principles which govern the entire movement make it impossible to proceed more rapidly in this work of regeneration. So it is that the Association has up to the present time transformed only three houses in the Quarter of San Lorenzo. The plan followed in this transformation is as follows:

(a) To demolish in every building all portions of the structure not originally constructed with the idea of making homes, but from a purely commercial standpoint, of making the rent-roll larger. In other words, the new management tore down those parts of the building which encumbered the central court, thus doing away with dark, ill-ventilated apartments, and giving air and light to the remaining portion of the tenement. Broad airy courts took the place of the inadequate air and light shafts, rendering the remaining apartments more valuable and infinitely more desirable.

(b) To increase the number of stairways, and to divide the room space in a more practical way. The large six or seven room suites are reduced to small apartments of one, two, or three rooms, and a kitchen. The importance of such changes may be recognized

4

from the economic point of view of the proprietor as well as from the standpoint of the moral and material welfare of the tenant. Increasing the number of stairways diminishes that inevitable abuse of walls and stairs where so many persons must pass up and down. The tenants more readily learn to respect the building and acquire habits of cleanliness and order. Not only this, but in reducing the chances of contact among the inhabitants of the house, especially late at night, a great advance has been made in the matter of moral hygiene.

The division of the house into small apartments has done much towards this moral regeneration. Each family is thus set apart, *homes* are made possible, while the menacing evil of subletting, together with all its disastrous consequences of over-crowding and immorality, is checked in the most radical way.

On one side this arrangement lessens the burden of the individual lease-holders, and on the other increases the income of the proprietor, who now receives those earnings which were the unlaw-ful gain of the system of subletting. When the proprietor who originally rented an apartment of six rooms for a monthly rental of eight dollars, makes such an apartment over into three small, sunny and airy suites consisting of one room and a kitchen, it is evident that he increases his income.

The moral importance of this reform as it stands today is tremendous, for it has done away with those evil influences and low opportunities which arise from crowding and from promiscuous contact; and it has brought to life among those people, for the first time, the gentle sentiment of feeling themselves free within their own homes, in the intimacy of the family.

But the object of the Association goes beyond even this. The house which it offers to its tenants is not only sunny and airy, but in perfect order and repair, almost shining, and as if perfumed with purity and freshness. These good things, however, carry with them a responsibility which the tenant must assume if he wishes to enjoy them. He must pay an actual tax of *care* and *good-will*. The tenant who receives a clean house must keep it so, must respect the walls from the big general entrance to the interior of his own little apartment. He who keeps his house in good condition receives the recognition and consideration due to such a tenant. Thus all the tenants unite in the ennobling welfare of practical hygiene, an end made possible by the simple task of *conserving* the already perfect conditions.

Here indeed is something new: So far only our great national buildings have had a continued *maintenance fund*. Here, in these houses offered to the people, the maintenance is confided to a hundred or so working men, that is, to all the occupants of the building. This care is almost perfect. The people keep the house in perfect condition, without a single spot. The building in which we find ourselves today has been for two years under the sole protection of the tenants, and the work of maintenance has been left entirely to them. Yet few of our houses can compare in cleanliness and freshness with this home of the poor.

The experiment has been tried and the result is remarkable. The people acquire, together with the love of home-making, that of cleanliness. They come, moreover, to wish to beautify their homes. The Association helps this by placing growing plants and trees in the courts and about the halls. Out of this honest rivalry in matters so productive of good, grows a species of pride new to this Quarter; this is the pride which the entire body of tenants takes in having the best-cared-for building and in having risen to a higher and more civilized plane of living. They not only live in a house, but they *know how to live*, they *know how to respect* the house in which they live.

This first impulse has led to other reforms. From the clean home will come personal cleanliness. Dirty furniture cannot be tolerated in a clean house, and those persons living in a permanently clean house will come to desire personal cleanliness.

One of the most important hygienic reforms of the Association is that of *the baths*. Each remodelled tenement has a place set apart for bathrooms, furnished with tubs or shower, and having hot and cold water. All the tenants in regular turn may use these baths, as for example, in various tenements the occupants go according to turn, to wash their clothes in the fountain in the court. This is a great convenience which invites the people to be clean. These hot and cold baths *within the house* are a great improvement upon the general public baths. In this way we make possible to these people, at one and the same time, health and refinement, opening not only to the sun, but to progress, those dark habitations, once the vile caves of misery.

But in striving to realize its ideal of a semi-gratuitous maintenance of its buildings, the Association met with a difficulty in regard to those children under school age, who must often be left alone the entire day while their parents went out to work. These little ones, not being able to understand the educative motives which taught their parents to respect the house, became ignorant little vandals, defacing the walls and stairs. And here we have another reform, the expense of which may be considered as indirectly borne by the tenants as was the care of the building. This reform may be considered as the most brilliant transformation of a tax which progress and civilization have as yet devised. The " Children's House " is earned by the parents through the care of the building. Its expenses are met by the sum that the Association would have otherwise been forced to spend upon repairs. A wonderful climax, this, of moral benefits received: Within the " Children's House," which belongs exclusively to those children under school age, working mothers may safely leave their little ones and may proceed with a feeling of great relief and freedom to their own work. But this benefit, like that of the care of the house, is not conferred without a tax of care and good-will. The regulations posted on the walls announce it thus:

" The mothers are obliged to send their children to the Children's House clean, and to co-operate with the directress in the educational work."

Two obligations, namely the physical and moral care of their own children. If the child shows through its conversation that the educational work of the school is being undermined by the attitude taken in his home, he will be sent back to his parents, to thus teach them how to take advantage of their good opportunities. Those who give themselves to low-living, fighting and brutality, shall feel upon them the weight of those little lives, so needing care. They shall feel that they themselves have once more cast into the darkness of neglect those little creatures who are the dearest part of the family. In other words, the parents must learn to *deserve* the benefit of having within the house the great advantage of a school for their little ones.

"Good-will," a willingness to meet the demands of the Association is enough, for the directress is ready and willing to teach them how. The regulations say that the mother must go at least once a week to confer with the directress, giving an account of her child, and accepting any helpful advice which the directress may be able to give. The advice thus given will undoubtedly prove most illuminating in regard to the child's health and education, since to each of the "Children's Houses" is assigned a physician as well as a directress.

The directress is always at the disposition of the mothers, and her life, as a cultured and educated person, is a constant example to the inhabitants of the house, for she is obliged to live in the tenement and to be therefore a co-habitant with the families of all her little pupils. This is a fact of immense importance. Among these almost savage people, into these houses where at night no one dared to go about unarmed, there has come not only to teach, *but to live the very life they live*, a gentlewoman of culture, an educator by profession, who dedicates her time and her life to helping those about her: a true missionary, a moral queen among the people, she may, if she be possessed of sufficient tact and heart, reap an unheard of harvest of good from her social work.

This house is verily *new*; it would seem a dream impossible of realization, but it has been tried. It is true that there have been before this attempts made by generous persons to go and live among the poor to civilize them. But such work is not practical, unless the house of the poor is hygienic, making it possible for people of better standards to live there. Nor can such work succeed in its purpose unless some common advantage or interest unites all the tenants in an effort towards better things.

This tenement is new also because of the pedagogical organization of the " Children's House ". This is not simply a place where children are kept, not just an *asylum*, but a true school for their education, and its methods are inspired by the rational principles of scientific pedagogy.

The physical development of the children is followed, each child being studied from the anthropological standpoint, being given linguistic exercises, a systematic sense-training, and exercises which directly fit him for the duties of practical life, from the basis of 'the work done. The teaching is decidedly objective, and presents an unusual richness of didactic material.

It is not possible to speak of all this in detail. I must, however, mention that there already exists in connection with the school a bathroom, where the children may be given hot or cold baths, and where they may learn to take a partial bath—hands, face, neck, ears. Wherever possible the Association has provided a piece of ground where the children may learn to grow the vegetables in common use.

It is important that I speak here of the pedagogical progress attained by the " Children's House " as an institution. Those who are conversant with the chief problems of the school know that today much attention is given to a great principle, one that is ideal and almost beyond realization—the union of the family and the school in the matter of educational aims. But the family is always something far away from the school, and is almost always regarded as rebelling against its ideals. It is a species of phantom upon which the school can never lay its hands. The home is closed not only to pedagogical progress, but often to social progress. We see here for the first time the possibility of realizing the long talked-of pedagogical ideal. We have put *the school within the house*; and this is not all. We have placed it within the house as the *property of the collectivity*, leaving under the eyes of the parents the whole life of the teacher in the accomplishment of her high mission.

This idea of the collective ownership of the school is new and very beautiful and profoundly educational.

The parents know that the " Children's House " is their property, and is maintained by a portion of the rent they pay. The mothers may go at any hour of the day to watch, to admire or to meditate upon the life there. It is in every way a continual stimulus to reflection, and a fount of evident blessing and help to their own children. We may say that the mothers *adore* the " Children's House," and the directress. How many delicate and thoughtful attentions these good mothers show to the teacher of their little ones! They often leave sweets or flowers upon the sill of the schoolroom window as a silent token, reverently, almost religiously, given.

And when after three years of such a novitiate, the mothers send their children to the common schools, they are excellently prepared to co-operate in the work of education, and will acquire a sentiment rarely found even among the best classes, namely the idea that they must *merit* through their own conduct and with their own virtue, the possession of an educated son.

Another advance made by the " Children's House " as an institution is related to scientific pedagogy. This branch of pedagogy, heretofore being based upon the anthropological study of the pupil whom it is to educate, has touched only a few of the positive questions which tend to transform education. For a man is not only a biological but a social product, and the social environment of individuals in the process of education is the home. Scientific pedagogy will seek in vain to better the new generation if it does not succeed in influencing also the environment within which this new generation grows. I believe, therefore, that in opening the house to the light of new truths and to the progress of civilization we have solved the problem of being able to modify the *environment* of the new generation, and have thus made it possible to apply, in a practical way, the fundamental principles of scientific pedagogy.

The " Children's House " marks still another triumph; it is the first step towards the *socialization of the house*. The inmates find under their own roof the convenience of being able to leave their little ones in a place, not only safe, but where they have every advantage.

And let it be remembered that *all* the mothers in the tenement may enjoy this privilege, going away to their work with easy minds. Until the present time only one class in society might have this advantage. Rich women were able to go about their various occupations and amusements, leaving their children in the hands of a nurse or a governess. Today the women of the people who live in these remodelled houses may say, like the great lady, " I have left my son with the governess and the nurse." More than this, they may add, like the princess of the blood, " And the house physician watches over them and directs their sane and sturdy growth." These women, like the most advanced class of English and American mothers, possess a " Biographical Chart," which, filled for the mother by the directress and the doctor, gives her the most practical knowledge of her child's growth and condition.

We are all familiar with the ordinary advantages of the social transformation of the general environment. For example, the collective use of railway carriages, of street lights, of the telephone, all these are great advantages. The enormous production of useful articles, brought about by industrial progress, makes possible for all to have clean clothes, carpets, curtains, table delicacies, better table-ware, etc. The giving of such benefits generally tends to leave social caste. All this we have seen in its reality. But the social-izing of *persons* is new. That the collectivity shall benefit from the services of the servant, the nurse, the teacher—this is a modern ideal.

We have in the " Children's Houses " a demonstration of this ideal which is unique in Italy or elsewhere. Its significance is most profound, for it corresponds to a need of the times. We can no longer say that the convenience of leaving their children takes away from the mother a natural social duty of first importance,

namely that of caring for and educating their tender offspring.
For today the social and economic evolution calls the working-
woman to take her place among wage-earners, and takes away
from her by force those duties which would be most dear to her.
The mother must, in any event, leave her child, and often with
the pain of knowing him to be abandoned. The advantages furnished by such institutions are not limited to the labouring classes,
but extend also to the general middle-class, many of whom work
with the brain. Teachers, professors, often obliged to give private
lessons after school hours, frequently leave their children to the
care of some rough and ignorant maid. Indeed, the first an-
nouncement of the "Children's Houses" was followed by a
deluge of letters from persons of the better class demanding that
these helpful reforms be extended to their dwellings.

We are, then, socializing a "maternal function," a feminine
duty, within the house. We may see here in this practical act the
solving of many of the woman's problems which have seemed to
many impossible of solution. What, then, will become of the home,
one asks, if the woman goes away from it? The home will be
transformed and will assume the functions of the woman.

I believe that in the future of society other forms of socialized
life will come to be a practical necessity.

Take, for example, the infirmary: woman is the natural nurse
for the dear ones of her household. But who does not know how
often in these days she is obliged to tear herself unwillingly from
the bedside of her sick to go to her work? Competition is great,
and her absence from her post threatens the tenure of the position
from which she draws the means of support. To be able to leave
the sick one in a "house infirmary," to which she may have access
at any free moment she may have and where she is at liberty to
watch during the night, would be an evident advantage to such a
woman.

And how great would be the progress made in the matter of
family hygiene, in all that relates to isolation and disinfection.
Who does not know the difficulties of a poor family when one

of the children has some contagious disease, and needs to be isolated from the others? Often such a family may have no kindred or friends in the city to whom the other children may be sent.

Much more distant, but not impossible, is the community kitchen, where the dinner ordered in the morning is sent at the proper time, by means of a dumb-waiter, to the family dining-room. Indeed, this has been successfully tried in America. Such a reform would be of the greatest advantage to those families of the middle class who must confide their health and their pleasures of the table to the hands of an ignorant servant who ruins the food. At present, the only alternative in such cases is to go outside the home to some cafe where a cheap *table d'hote* may be had.

Indeed, the transformation of the house must compensate for the loss in the family of the presence of the woman who has become a social wage-earner.

In this way the house will become a centre, drawing unto itself all those good things which have hitherto been lacking: schools, public baths, hospitals, etc.

Thus the tendency will be to change the tenement houses, which have been places of vice and peril, into centres of education, of refinement, of comfort. This will be helped if, besides the schools for the children, there may grow up also *clubs* and reading-rooms for the inhabitants, especially for the men, who will find there a way to pass the evening pleasantly and decently. The tenement-club, as possible and as useful in all social classes as is the "Children's House," will do much towards closing the gambling-houses and saloons, to the great moral advantage of the people. And I believe that the Association of Good Building will before long establish such clubs in its reformed tenements here in the Quarter of San Lorenzo: clubs where the tenants may find newspapers and books, and where they may hear simple and helpful lectures.

We are, then, very far from the dreaded dissolution of the home and of the family, through the fact that the woman has been forced by changed social and economic conditions to give

her time and strength to remunerative work. The home itself
assumes the gentle feminine attributes of the domestic housewife.
The day may come when the tenant, having given to the proprietor
of the house a certain sum, shall receive in return whatever is
necessary to the *comfort* of life; in other words, the administration
shall become the *steward* of the family.

The house, thus considered, tends to assume in its evolution
a significance more exalted than even the English word " home "
expresses. It does not consist of walls alone, though these walls
be the pure and shining guardians of that intimacy which is the
sacred symbol of the family. The home shall become more than
this. It lives! It has a soul. It may be said to embrace its inmates
with the tender, consoling arms of woman. It is the giver of moral
life, of blessings; it cares for, it educates and feeds the little ones.
Within it, the tired workman shall find rest and newness of life.
He shall find there the intimate life of the family and its happiness.

The new woman, like the butterfly coming forth from the chry-
salis, shall be liberated from all those attributes which once made
her desirable to man only as a source of the material blessings
of existence. She shall be, like man, an individual, a free human
being, a social worker; and, like man, she shall seek blessing and
repose within the house, the house which has been reformed and
socialized.

She shall wish to be loved for herself and not as a giver of
comfort and repose only. She shall wish a love free from every
form of servile labour. The goal of human love is not the
egotistical end of assuring its own satisfaction—it is the sublime
goal of multiplying the forces of the free spirit, making it almost
divine, and, within such beauty and light, perpetuating the species.

This ideal love is made incarnate by Frederick Nietzsche, in
the woman of Zarathustra, who conscientiously wished her son to
be better than she. " Why do you desire me? " she asks the man.
" Perhaps because of the perils of a solitary life? "

" In that case go far from me. I wish the man who has conquered himself, who has made his soul great. I wish the man who

desires to unite with me, body and soul, to create a son: A son better, more perfect, stronger, than any created heretofore! "

To better the species consciously, cultivating his own health, his own virtue, this should be the goal of a man's married life. It is a sublime conception of which, as yet, few think. And the socialized home of the future, living, provident, kindly, educator and comforter, is the true and worthy home of those human mates who wish to better the species, and to send the race forward triumphant into the eternity of life.

ANALYSIS OF THE CONDITIONS OF THE FIRST EXPERIMENT

HISTORY OF ITS PROPAGATION

The environment in which the first Children's Houses sprang up must have been extremely favourable to education, for the first group of children attained such success in their surprising transformation that no other group ever reached their level.

For that reason it is worth while to analyse the elements concerned in these ventures.

First there must have been created among the inhabitants and the families of the children a sense of peace and well-being, of cleanliness and intimacy which hitherto had been unknown to them. Besides, the people concerned represented a *moral selection*. They were poor, honest people, without profession, who depended from day to day on casual labour, some as porters, some as laundresses, some as gatherers of seasonal flowers in the fields (like violets). They had lived mixed up in the same surroundings with coarse and immoral people. All these people, gathered together in the reconstructed Houses, were without exception illiterate.

The children lived in a kind of Paradise, which was the same for all of them. The stolid ignorance of their parents precluded any possible educational influence in the family; there was no contrast there with what the children benefitted from education in the school. The person who held office as a mistress was not a real teacher, but a woman having a small amount of education who busied herself with domestic affairs and helped with the field-work from which they derived their means of existence. This mistress had no educational ideas, no scholastic principles; she was responsible to no authority, was criticized by no inspector of schools.

During the day-time, the children were abandoned by the father and the mother, who both went out to look for a chance of employment.

These conditions, which might seem to be most adverse to the success of a school, represented as it were a void, a zero, as far as the arbitrary influence of education was concerned. Scientific procedure in the school reached full efficiency because there were no obstacles to oppose it.

This contributed to the success of an experiment which was unmixed and isolated from other conceptions, carried on in a laboratory of psychology, which was what the Children's House actually became.

It was here that there occurred surprising manifestations like "the explosion of spontaneous writing and reading," "spontaneous discipline," "free social life," which have roused the curiosity and the admiration of the world.

It was this very group of children, callous and half-wild, which became a centre of interest so noted that from every part of the world, and especially from the United States of America, there came visitors as to a Mecca of education.

Because of this attraction the San Lorenzo Quarter was over-run with sovereigns, ministers, scientists, aristocrats, all of them desirous of seeing the wonderful children at close quarters. From that centre Children's Houses have spread throughout the whole world.

After the first Children's House was opened on January 6th, others were opened in other re-conditioned houses of the *Beni Stabili*, a few months later, on April 7th; and on October 18th, 1908, under the direction of Miss Anna M. Maccheroni, there was opened the Children's House in the *Umanitaria* of Milan, which was the largest social institution in Italy, founded by Socialist Jews for the elevation of the people. It was a centre composed of model workmen's dwellings, but at the same time a centre of propaganda, in which there was working—a matter worth mentioning—a gloomy, severe journalist, whose name was to become famous and fatal in the world, namely Benito Mussolini.

It was the *Umanitaria* which organized a general move forward, undertaking the manufacture of material, that is, the scientific apparatus I designed for the first Children's House.

After this the *Beni Stabili* opened schools in the tenement buildings which existed in various parts of Rome, this time for middle-class people, who had asked for the privilege of Children's Houses for their children also. Then there was founded the first Children's House for the aristocracy, opened by the English ambassador in Rome and accommodating children from the highest ranks of society.

After a disastrous earthquake which destroyed the city of Messina in Sicily, there were gathered together in Rome 60 children found wandering among the ruins, and for this group of little unknown creatures, now orphans, bewildered and stupified by the terrible shock, was founded the Children's House in the Via Giusti, kept by the Franciscan sisters Missionaries of Mary. The Children's House in the Via Giusti became celebrated because of the transformation wrought on these little ones, to whom was restored the joy of life; it inspired novels and poetry, like the *Montessori Mother* of the American authoress Dorothy Canfield-Fisher. Children's Houses were opened in various places, after Baron and Baroness Franchetti provided a first course of training for teachers, which was originally intended for the preparation of Italian teachers for rural schools, but which in that first session included teachers from nine European nations. After that in 1913, on the very eve of the first world war, there was organized, on the initiative of Americans, a first international course in Rome, which was attended by students from European countries, from America, Africa and India.

Scientific pedagogy for children had come into existence with immense energy to modify education.

The Children's Houses spread rapidly over the world, in spite
of the difficulties due to the war and to prejudices.   And today,
during the second world war, the Children's Houses are multiplying in India.

The history of the movement shows us that the same education is possible, though with some degrees of adaptation, in all
social grades of society, with happy children, as with children
shattered by the shock of a disaster, and among all races of the
world.   The Child is the driving force which is manifested in our
time, bringing new hope to men in nations wrapt in obscurity.

The Children's House is endowed with double importance: its
social importance is wrapt up in its form of a " school in a house ";
its purely educational importance depends on the methods for
child education with which I experimented.

As a factor of civilization affecting the people directly, the
Children's House deserves to be illustrated in a separate volume.
It indeed solves many social and educational problems which
seemed Utopian, and it forms part of the modern transformation
of the home; that is, it touches directly the most important side of
the social question, that which concerns the intimate life of men.

GENERAL SECTION

TEACHING METHODS USED IN THE CHILDREN'S HOUSES

As soon as I knew that I had at my disposal a school of little children, I made up my mind to study their education from the scientific point of view, and to abandon the methods followed more or less by others who confused the study of children with their education, and who gave the name of scientific pedagogy to the study of children taught in the ordinary schools which remain unaltered by it. The new pedagogy, founded on precise and objective studies, ought, on the contrary, to transform the school and act directly on the scholars, bringing new life to them.

As long as science confined itself to getting to know the children better, without rescuing them in a practical manner from the many evils which it has been discovering in the ordinary schools and in the old methods of education, no one had any right to proclaim the existence of a ' scientific pedagogy '. As long as research did nothing beyond propounding new problems there was no ground for declaring that a scientific pedagogy had been evolved, since it is the solution of problems which it ought to accomplish, not just the exposition of the difficulties and the dangers which exist in the ordinary schools, both those which are hidden and those which obviously permeate the education of children in these schools. To have discovered and demonstrated a hitherto unsuspected evil is a work founded on hygiene and experimental psychology, but it is not the building up of a new pedagogy.

As for child psychology itself, it cannot have discovered the natural characters and therefore the psychological laws which govern child development, because in schools there exist conditions of life so abnormal that they give rise to characters of defence and weariness instead of revealing the expression of creative energy which belongs to life.

Wundt himself, the founder of psychological physiology, agreed that " the psychology of the child is unknown ".

I had thought of taking into account other research work, whilst keeping myself independent of it. I retained as essential only the affirmation, or rather the definition made by Wundt: " All the methods of experimental psychology can be reduced to one single method, that is, to observation which is regulated with precision."

When it is a question of children, another factor must certainly come in—the study of development. Here also I retained the general rule, but without confining myself to dogmas relative to the activity of children as depending on age.

MORPHOLOGICAL GROWTH

In my schools I have taken great care from the very beginning to follow the growth of the child's body, studying and measuring it in accordance with the practice fixed by anthropological research. However, I simplified the measurements considerably and adopted an order which made it easier to record data. I tried also to interest the children directly in the proceedings. There were sent out periodically to the families the measurements relating to their own children, together with the average normal measurements according to age; and the result of this was that the parents followed intelligently the physical development of their children.

I caused to be constructed a measuring machine for children which had a metric scale ranging between 0.50 m. to 1.50 m.;

on the platform of the machine was arranged a small movable
stool 30 cms. high, for measuring the height when seated. Today I
suggest that the machine be made with a double platform; on one
side to measure the full height and on the other the height when seated. In the second case, the zero is at 30 cms. level, that is, it
corresponds with the height of the seat, which is fixed. The pointers
running in a groove on the vertical pole are independent of each
other; they can, however, take two measurements at the same
time, that is, they measure two children together. In any case
the inconvenience and the loss of time involved in removing
and putting back the seat and in calculating the difference on
the metric scale is avoided.

Having thus prepared the technique of the research, I arranged
to take measurements, both standing and sitting, every month;
and, in order to bring together the most exact measurements
relative to development and to make the research more regular,
I made it a rule that the height should be taken on the day on which
the child completed a month of its age.

To secure this, I planned a register as follows:

Day of the month	September		October	
	Height		Height	
	Standing	Seated	Standing	Seated
1				
2				
3				
4				
etc.				

The spaces relating to every number serve for registering the name of the child born on any day of the month. Thus the teacher knows what pupils she ought to measure on a particular day of the calendar, and she writes down her measurements in correspondence with the month. In this way the most accurate registration is secured without the teacher being aware of it in the sense that she does not feel the work and fatigue of it to any great degree.

As for weight, I planned that it should be taken every week by means of a weighing machine placed in the dressing-room adjoining the bathroom. Choosing the day of the week on which he was born, the child is weighed; this is done when he is undressed, previous to his bath. In this way the bathing of the children (perhaps 50 of them) is spread out over seven days, and about three to five children come to the bath every day. In practice, the weekly bath presents no few difficulties, and it is often necessary to make this theoretical. In any case, I planned the weekly weighing in the manner specified with the intention of regulating and making sure of weekly baths also.

The registration of weight is made very simple. There are set out in a register the days of the week in a vertical column, and corresponding to each one are drawn lines intended for the names of the pupils born on that day.

I am of the opinion that these are the only anthropological measurements with which the mistress need concern herself and are the only ones which directly affect the school.

I planned that the other measurements should be taken by a doctor who had specialized in child anthropology, or who intended to specialize in this branch of pedagogic anthropology. In the meantime, I myself undertook these duties.

The work of the doctor is bound to be complicated and to make the arrangement of it easier, I had printed biographical forms, specimens of which I reproduce here:

	SEPTEMBER [1]			
	1st week kg.	2nd week kg.	3rd week kg.	4th week kg.
Monday ...				
Tuesday ...				
Wednesday ...				
etc.				

N. . . . Date of entry . . . .

Christian name and Surname . . . . Age . . . .

Names of parents . . . .

Father's age . . . . . Mother's age . . . .

Profession . . . . . .

Hereditary antecedents . . . . . .

Personal antecedents . . . .

---

[1] Every page of the register corresponds to one month.

ANTHROPOLOGICAL NOTES

Height standing	Weight	Chest measurement	Height seated	Index of height	Index of weight	Head			
						Circumference	Diameter f to b	Transverse diameter	Head Index

Physical constitution . . . . . .

State of nourishment of the muscles . . . . . .

Colour of the skin . . . . . .

Colour of the hair . . . . . .

NOTES

. . . .

. . . .

. . . .

It will be seen that the scheme is quite simple; that is because I intend that the doctor and the teacher be guided by the conditions in which they are carrying on their observations.

The anthropological investigations are carefully fixed in order that the plan should be respected, and that the fundamental anthropological research should be secured. I then advise that every year the following measurements should be taken for every child: the circumference of the head, the two maximum diametres of the head, the circumference of the chest, the index figures for head, weight and height, and such others, selected as opportunity arises, as may be suggested by modern treatises on pedagogic anthropology. The doctor is urged to carry out such investigations within the week, or at least within the month in which the child completes his first year, and if possible on the anniversary of his birth. So, by observing this rule, the doctor lessens his task; in the 365 days of the year only 50 children at the most complete one year of their existence; this allows the doctor to make his observations from time to time without his being overburdened with work in the slightest degree. It is the teacher's duty to inform the doctor of the various birthdays of the children.

Conducted in this way anthropometry has also educational applications.

Children, on leaving the Children's House, will certainly be able to answer the following questions: On what day of the week were you born? On what day of the month? When does your birthday come?

And in addition to that they would have acquired orderly habits, and above all they would get accustomed to observing themselves. (I may say here that little children take great pleasure in measuring themselves. At the first glance which a teacher turns on a child and the word ' height,' he kicks off his shoes quickly with a joyful laugh, runs and places himself on the machine, taking up of his own accord the correct position so perfectly that the teacher has only to lower the pointer and take the reading.)

Besides the measurements which the doctor takes with the ordinary instruments (callipers, metallic tapes), he makes observations on the pigmentation, on the trophic condition of the muscles, on the state of the lymphatic glands, on the blood supply, etc. He makes a note of malformations, and occasional pathological conditions, which have to be carefully described (rickets, infantile paralysis, squinting, etc.). Such an objective study will also enable the doctor to frame the questions about the history of the case which are sent to the parents.

In addition the doctor pays the usual health visits, diagnosing cases of eczema, ear trouble, conjunctivitis, feverish conditions, intestinal disturbances, etc. The importance of this is completed by medical service dispensed in the house which secures immediate attention and continued supervision, as could be seen in the *Casa Moderna dei Beni Stabili* at Prati di Castello in Rome.

From my work in these Children's Houses of the *Beni Stabili*, I have come to the conclusion that the usual enquiries into case histories which are taken directly from clinics are not suitable for the school, because for the most part the family history is generally perfectly normal. Hence I exhorted the teachers to obtain through conversations with the mothers information which was rather of a social character—such as the education of the parents, their habits, earnings, expenses, etc. in order to compile a family monograph in the style of Le-Play. I consider that this suggestion is practical only where the teacher dwells among the families of her pupils, and not elsewhere.

However, it would be most beneficial everywhere if the advice of the doctor could be passed on to the mothers through the medium of the teacher, advice respecting the individual hygiene of every child as well as child hygiene in general. To the advice the teacher might also add her own suggestions about the individual education of the child; but, on that point, the hygienic-social side of the Children's Houses, I cannot dwell here.

The observation method is based on one foundation only— that children are permitted to express themselves freely, and thus reveal to us needs and aptitudes which remain hidden and repressed when there does not exist an environment which allows free scope for their spontaneous activity. It is essential that together with an observer there should exist something to be observed; and if it is necessary that the observer should be trained to see and to recognize the truth, it is, on the other hand, also necessary to prepare conditions which render possible the manifestation of the natural characteristics of the children.

This last part of the problem, which no one had yet taken into consideration, seemed to me the one which was supremely important, and the one most directly connected with education, seeing that it relates to the active life of the child.

I began then by getting manufactured school equipment which was made in proportion to the child and which provided for his need to move about intelligently.

I had constructed little tables of various shapes, which would be quite steady but which would be extremely light so that two children, four years old, could carry them easily. I had also made small seats, some straw-bottomed, others of wood, light and with some attempt at elegance; they were not a small version of seats for adults but were made in proportion to the child's body. In addition I ordered little wooden armchairs with wide arms, and also wicker-work armchairs. There were also included small square tables for one person, as well as tables with larger dimensions, which were covered with little white cloths and decorated with vases of flowers and foliage. Part of the equipment consisted of a wash-bowl placed so low down that it was accessible to a child three or four years old; it had its side ledges, all white and washable, to hold soap, brushes and towels. The side-boards were low, light and very simple. Some were closed in by a simple curtain, others had doors each of which closed with a different key, the fastening being within the reach of the child's hand so that he can open and close them and place objects within the compartments. On the top of the long, narrow side-board was spread a white linen cloth, on which was placed a bowl containing live fish, or other ornaments.

All round the walls, low enough to be within easy reach of little children, were arranged black-boards, and many small pictures representing pretty family scenes, or objects of nature like animals or flowers, as well as historical or sacred pictures which could be changed from day to day.

A large coloured picture, a reproduction of Raphael's *Madonna of the Chair*, hung high up on the wall. We had chosen it to stand as the emblem, the symbol of the Children's Houses. Indeed the Children's Houses represent not only social progress but also the progress of humanity; they are intimately bound up with the elevation of motherhood, with the advancement of women, and with the protection of posterity. The Madonna idealized by the divine Raphael is not only lovely and sweet, a sublime virgin and mother with her adorable baby, but beside this perfect symbol of real, living maternity, was the figure of John the Baptist, who represents for us in the fresh beauty of babyhood the cruel sacrifices of him who went before to prepare the way. Further, it introduced a work of art by the greatest Italian artist, and if, some day, Children's Houses are scattered throughout the world, Raphael's picture will be there to speak eloquently of the land of its origin.

The little ones may not be able to understand the symbolic meaning of the *Madonna of the Chair*, but they would see in it something greater than in other pictures which show fathers, mothers, grandparents and babies. They would enfold it in their hearts with religious feelings.

That is the teaching equipment.

PRACTICAL OBSERVATIONS

Let us begin with the first objection which presents itself to the minds of followers of the old methods of discipline. The children, as they move about, will overturn chairs and tables, producing noise and disorder; but this prejudges the matter. Thinking in the same way, most people believed that the new-born baby should be wrapped in swaddling clothes, and that children

A Municipal Montessori School built according to original plans. The classroom is octagonal in shape. Amsterdam, Holland.

learning to walk need little closed ' cages.' So, in the schools, it is considered necessary to have heavy benches almost nailed to the floor. All these ideas are based on the conception that the child ought to grow up into immobility and on the strange prejudice that the educational benefit depends upon a special position of the body.

The tables, seats and armchairs, all light and portable, will allow the child to choose the position which pleases him best; he will be able to make himself comfortable as well as to seat himself; and that will be both an external sign of liberty and a means of education. If an awkward movement of the child upsets a chair noisily, he will get an evident proof of his incapacity; the same movement, made among benches, would have passed unnoticed. The child will thus have means of correcting himself, and when he has corrected himself, he will have the proof of it plainly in evidence; chairs and tables will remain quiet and steady in their places; that will mean that the child has learnt to move about. With the old method, instead of this result, the very contrary was aimed at and achieved—that is, the immobility and the silence of the child himself. It was an immobility and silence which hindered the child from learning to move about with grace and judgement, so that when he found himself in surroundings where benches did not exist, he was prone to overturn light articles. In our schools, on the contrary, the child acquires deportment and control over movement which will be of service to him outside school; whilst still a child, he will become a person of free but correct behaviour.

The mistress of the Children's House in Milan had constructed a long shelf beside a window, on which were set out the supports for the choice of the metal insets necessary for the first drawing exercises (vide later: Teaching material in the preparation for writing). But the ledge, being too narrow, was very inconvenient for the children when they were choosing their pieces, and they often let a case fall to the ground, scattering with a great amount of noise the metal insets which it contained. The mistress planned to have the shelf altered, but the carpenter delayed his coming, and

in the meantime the children learnt to carry out their performances
so cleverly that no more cases fell to the ground in spite of their
uncertain balance. The children's skill in moving things had made
good the defect in the furniture.

The simplicity and the imperfection of external objects are
helpful in developing the activity and the dexterity of the pupils.

All this is logical and simple; and now, having been enunciated and experimented with, it seems to be as evident to everybody
as the egg of Christopher Columbus.

DISCIPLINE AND LIBERTY

We have to deal with another difficulty frequently raised by
those who practise the usual methods of discipline, namely how
can discipline be maintained in a class of children free to move
about?

Certainly in our system we have a different conception of
discipline; we regard discipline as being an active state of things.
We do not consider that discipline has been achieved when an
individual has been rendered by artificial means as silent as a mute
and as motionless as a paralytic. Such an individual is annihilated,
not disciplined.

We claim that an individual is disciplined when he is master
of himself, and therefore is capable of controlling himself when
it is necessary to comply with a law of life.

This idea of active discipline is neither easy to understand nor
to obtain, but it certainly embodies a lofty principle of education;
it is very different from the absolute and undisputed compulsion
which produces immobility.

The teacher must be equipped with a special technique if she
is to guide the child along this path of discipline in which he ought
to walk throughout his life, continually moving onwards towards
perfection.

Thus whilst the child is learning to move about with ease and
certainly, he is preparing himself not only for school but also for
life, so that he grows up into an individual habitually correct in

his behaviour in his usual everyday life. He becomes accustomed to a form of discipline which is not limited to school surroundings, but extends outwards into society.

The liberty of the child ought to have as its limit the collective interest of the community in which he moves; its form is expressed in what we call manners and good behaviour. It is our duty then to prevent the child from doing anything which may offend or hurt others, and to check behaviour which is unbecoming or impolite. But as regards all else, every action which has a useful purpose in view, whatever it may be and in whatever form it shows itself, ought not only to be permitted, but it ought to be kept under observation; that is the essential point. By means of scientific preparation the teacher must not only become equipped with observing powers, but must acquire an interest in the observation of natural phenomena. According to our system she ought to fill a passive role in a much higher degree than an active one. Her patience, her inactivity, will be compounded of keen scientific curiosity and respect for the phenomena which she wishes to observe. The teacher must understand and feel her position as an observer.

Such is the test which should be applied in the school for little ones who are giving the first revelations of their lives. We cannot possibly estimate the consequences of preventing a spontaneous action when the child is just beginning to do things; perhaps we may be destroying life itself. The humanity which manifests itself in its intellectual splendour in the sweet and tender age of childhood, as the sun shows itself at dawn and the flower when it first opens its petals, ought to be respected with religious veneration; and if an educational act is to be efficacious it will only be so if it tends to help towards the complete unfolding of life.

In order to do this it is necessary to avoid rigorously the arresting of spontaneous movements and the imposition of doings dictated by the will of others. From this ruling there must be excepted useless or dangerous actions, because these ought to be prevented.

The Difficulty of Class Discipline

In order to carry out my plans I generally had to make use of mistresses already experienced in the old methods of the ordinary schools. That convinced me of the radical difference between the two systems. Even an intelligent mistress who had grasped the principle found great difficulty in putting it into practice. She could not understand her apparently passive role, one like that of the astronomer, who sits motionless before the telescope, whilst worlds are wheeling through the universe. This idea that life and all pertaining to it go on by themselves, and that in order to study life, to enquire into its secrets and to direct it, one must observe it and get to know it without interfering with it, is really very difficult to assimilate and put into practice. The mistress has accustomed herself too completely to being the only freely active person in the school, which results in the extinction of the activity of the children. When she fails to obtain order and silence she looks at people in dismay protesting that she cannot help it; in vain does one repeat to her that disorder at the start is unavoidable. And when she is obliged to do nothing but look on, she asks herself if she ought not to send in her resignation, seeing that she is no longer a teacher.

But when she begins the task of distinguishing between those acts which have to be prevented and those which should be observed, the old-fashioned teacher discovers something to be lacking in herself and suddenly begins to ask herself if she will be equal to her new duties.

In fact, anyone who is not trained will find herself for a long time helpless and bewildered; similarly, a mistress will be the more intensely interested in proportion to her scientific education and her practical experience.

In a novel called *My Millionaire Uncle*, there is a very eloquent example of the old methods of discipline. The uncle is evidently a very difficult child, and after he had done enough mischief to upset a city he is, as a despairing resort, shut up in a school. Here the uncle, Fufu by name, performs his first kindly act and experiences his first stirring of emotion when, on finding himself near pretty little Fufetta, he notices that she is hungry and has no lunch.

"He glanced round him, looked at Fufetta, got up, took his lunch basket and without saying a word placed it on her lap.

"Then he drew back a few steps, and without knowing why he did it, he bowed his head on his chest and burst into sudden tears.

"My uncle could not explain the reason for this unexpected outburst of weeping.

"He had seen for the first time two gentle eyes filled with sorrowful tears; suddenly his feelings had been stirred, and at the same time he had been filled with shame that he should be eating whilst somebody near by was going hungry.

"Not knowing how to express what he was feeling, nor yet what to say in making the offering of his basket as an excuse for doing so, he had been completely overcome by this first disturbance of his childish soul.

"In great agitation Fufetta ran quickly to him. With the utmost gentleness she drew aside the elbow in which he had hidden his face.

"'Do not cry, Fufu,' she said in a low entreating tone. The face which showed itself was gloomy and bashful, but the countenance which she bent over him was full of motherly concern, as if she were talking to one of her rag dolls.

"Then she kissed him, and my Uncle, yielding again to the impulse which agitated his heart, threw his arms round her neck, put forward his lips, and without thinking or looking, still silent and sobbing, kissed her on the chin.

"Then he drew a long sigh, passed his sleeve across his face to wipe from his eyes and nose the moist traces of his emotion, and recovered his serenity.

"A harsh voice shouted from the far end of the court—'Here, you two down there, hurry up, get inside.'

"It was the guardian. She killed that first right impulse in the soul of a rebel, with the same blind brutality which she would

6

have employed if they had been beating each other. It was now time to go back to school, and all had to obey."

This illustrates the unthinking manner in which my young teachers behaved at first; almost involuntarily, they reduced the children to immobility without taking enough pains to discriminate between their movements. There was, for example, one baby who gathered her companions round her in a group, and then, in the middle of it, moved about talking and making quiet gestures. The mistress at once hurried up, stilled the waving arms and exhorted her to keep quiet. But, watching the child, I saw that she was pretending to be the teacher and the mother of the others, that she was teaching them their prayers, with wide gestures, invocations to the saints and the sign of the Cross; already she was showing herself to be a leader. Another small boy, who was in the habit of making purposeless movements and was regarded as being almost abnormally unstable, one day set himself, with intense concentration, to displacing the small tables. At once they put a stop to his doings because he was making too much noise. But that proceeding of his was really a first manifestation of movements co-ordinated towards an end; in it he was showing his tendencies, and therefore it was an action which should have been respected. In fact, after this he began to be as tranquil as the other children on every occasion when he had to move about some small object on his table.

Sometimes it happened that, whilst the mistress was replacing in the boxes objects that had been used, a child would draw near and take up something with the obvious intention of imitating her. The first impulse of the teacher was to send her back to her place with the usual admonition—" Let them alone, go to your place." The child was really expressing by her action an inclination to do a useful action; she would have succeeded well, for example, in exercises demanding arrangement. On another occasion the children were crowding together in the room round a basin of water in which small objects were floating about. We had in the school a little one of just two and a half years old; he had remained alone at the back and was evidently filled with the greatest curiosity. I watched him from a distance with much interest; he drew close up to the group, pushed them aside with his tiny baby hands, realized that he had not the strength to make room for himself, and then stopped and looked round. Most interesting was the picture of thought shown on that small childish face; if I had had a camera I would have captured that expression. He spied an armchair, and evidently thought of carrying it to a place behind the group of boys and mounting it. He turned a countenance beaming with hope on the armchair. But at that moment the teacher took him up brutally (or perhaps kindly, according to her thought) in her arms and let him see the basin over the heads of his companions, saying—" Come, dear, come poor little fellow, you shall see too." Certainly the baby, on seeing the toys floating about, did not experience the joy which was about to be his from overcoming an obstacle by his own efforts, and seeing these objects brought him no advantage, whilst his own intelligent effort would have developed his mental powers. The teacher hindered the child from educating himself, without giving him any compensating benefit. He was on the eve of feeling himself to be a conqueror, and instead of that he found himself borne aloft in two arms as if he were impotent. From his face there faded out that expression of joy, of anxiety, of hope which had interested me so much, and there remained only the stupid expression of the child who knows how others will act for him.

When mistresses grew tired of my making observations they began to let the children do whatever they wanted to do. I saw some with their feet on the table and with their fingers in their noses without the mistress interfering to correct them. I saw others pushing their companions about, looking very truculent, without the mistress taking the slightest notice. Then I had to interfere, trying patiently to point out how essential it was to be absolutely rigorous in preventing and by degrees eradicating all actions which should not be practised, with a view to the child's learning the exact difference between right and wrong.

This is the starting point for discipline, and it is the most wearisome time for the teacher. The first truth which children have to grasp before they can be actively disciplined is the difference between right and wrong and the duty of the educator is to see that the child does not confuse goodness with immobility and naughtiness with activity, as happened in the old style of discipline. Hence our duty is to discipline for activity, for work, for well-doing; not for immobility, for passivity.

A room in which all the children are moving about purposefully, intelligently, and voluntarily, without creating confusion, would seem to me to be very well disciplined.

To arrange the children in lines as in an ordinary school, to assign a place to each little one, and to expect the children to remain still observing some order agreed upon—that may be carried out as a special practice for the purpose of collective education.

It happens also in ordinary life that people have to remain seated together quietly, when they are present, for example, at a concert or a lecture. And we adults know that this involves no small sacrifice of our inclinations.

It is permissible then to arrange the children in order in their places. To get them to understand such an idea so that they learn, they assimilate the principle of collective order—that is the important point.

If, after having understood this idea, they get up, talk, change their positions, they are not doing so as at first, without knowing it and without thinking about it, but they are doing it because they want to rise up, to talk, etc.; that is, from that well-known state of repose and order, they set out to engage on some activity of their own; and knowing that certain acts are forbidden, they will be forced to remember the difference between right and wrong.

The way in which the children change over from the ' ordered' position becomes better co-ordinated as the days pass; they really learn to consider their own actions. Observatory notes of the manner in which children's early, disorderly movements are gradually replaced by those which are spontaneously regulated constitute a book for the teacher, a book which should inspire her own doings, the only one in which she can read and study if she is to become a good teacher. Since the child with similar exercises makes a kind of selection of his own tendencies, at first he is confused in the unintentional disorder of his doings.

It is marvellous to find how individual differences manifest themselves in the most striking fashion when this procedure is followed; every child reveals himself.

Some there are who stay quietly in their places, apathetic, sleepy; others stand up, shout, bang, overturn things; others again set about a definite action such as putting a chair crossways and trying to sit down in it, displacing a table, looking at a picture, and so on. In some cases children are revealed as being slow in their mental development, or perhaps sickly; sometimes character develops late; finally they may turn out to be intelligent, adaptable to their surroundings, capable of expressing their tastes, their inclinations, their power of spontaneous attention, the limits of their endurance.

INDEPENDENCE

The concept of liberty for the child cannot be simple like that which is associated with the observation of plants, insects, etc. The reason is that the child, owing to its characteristic helplessness when born and its position as a social individual, is fettered by many bonds which restrict its activity.

An educational method which is based on liberty must intervene in order to help the child to regain it; that is, to lessen as far as possible the social bonds which limit his activity. By degrees, as the child proceeds on his way, his spontaneous demonstrations will become more instinct with truth, will reveal his character more clearly. That is why the first form of educational intervention ought to have as its object the leading of the child along the paths of independence.

One cannot be free without being independent; hence, in order to attain independence, the *active* manifestations of personal liberty must be guided from the earliest childhood. Little children, from the moment when they are weaned, are travelling along the hazardous road of independence.

What is meant by a weaned child? A baby who has become independent of the mother's breast. In place of this single nourishing breast he will be able to choose from a hundred dishes of soft stuff, that is, his means of existence is extended; he will even be able to choose his 'pap,' whereas at first he had been limited to a single form of nutriment.

Yet he is still dependent, because he is unable to walk, cannot wash or dress himself, cannot ask for what he wants in intelligible language; he is the slave of everybody. At the age of three, however, the child should have made himself to a great extent independent and free.

We have not yet realized properly the lofty conception of independence, because the social conditions in which we live are still servile. In a period of civilization in which servants exist, the conditions cannot nurture the idea of independence, just as in the days of slavery the idea of liberty was obscured.

Our servants are not our dependents; rather are we their dependents. It is not possible to tolerate in a social structure so radical a human error without its leading to general effects of moral inferiority. We very often think we are independent because no one gives us orders or because we give orders to others, but the man who is dependent on a servant is dependent on his own inferiority. The paralytic who cannot lift his shoes owing to a pathological cause, and the prince who cannot lift his because of a social idea, are practically in the same condition.

The people who admit servitude, who believe that it is to the advantage of a man to be 'served' in everything rather than be 'helped' by another, regard servility as an instinct. In fact, we are very ready to rush to serve, as if we were likely to fail in perfect courtesy, politeness or kindliness.

He who is served instead of being helped, in a certain sense, has injury done to his independence. Here is a conception which forms the foundation of man's future dignity: I do not wish to be waited on because I am not impotent, but we must help one another, because we are members of a community. This indicates what we must attain to before we feel ourselves really free.

— Teaching, if it is to benefit the tender children, must be such as will help them to advance along the road to independence. Helping them to walk alone, to run, to mount and descend staircases, to lift up fallen objects, to dress and undress themselves, to wash themselves, to speak so as to state their needs clearly, to make attempts to satisfy their desires—that is what constitutes education in independence.

We wait upon children; and a servile act which affects them is no less fatal than an act which kills one of their useful natural actions. We believe that children are like inanimate puppets; we wash them, we feed them as if they were dolls. We never think that the baby who does nothing, does not know how to do anything; but he ought to do things, and nature has given him all the means whereby he may learn to do them. Our duty towards him is, without exception, to help him to perform useful acts. The mother who feeds the baby without making the slightest effort to teach him to hold the spoon and to find the way to his mouth, or who, whilst eating herself, does not at least invite him to watch how it is done—she is no good mother. She offends the human dignity of her son, treats him like a puppet, whilst he is a man entrusted to her care by Nature. Who is there who does not understand that to teach a child to eat, to wash himself, to dress himself, constitutes a task much longer, more difficult and more tedious than feeding, dressing and clothing him?

The first is the work of an educator; the second is the easy, inferior work of a servant.

The second is not only inferior and easier work but it is dangerous, for it closes outlets, erects obstacles in the way of the life which is unfolding, and besides the immediate consequences, it gives rise to graver consequences in the future. The gentleman who has too many servants not only becomes more and more completely their dependent and their slave, but his muscles weaken through lack of exercise and at last lose their natural power of action. The mind of anyone who, in order to get what he needs, does not work but gives orders atrophies and grows weak. In such a manner do we inoculate the mind of childhood with the deadly sin of laziness.

Supposing that one day, his mind having been suddenly enlightened, the man accustomed to be served should wish to regain his independence, he would perhaps discover that he no longer possessed the strength needed to be independent. These criticisms ought to be made known to parents of the privileged classes.

Just in proportion as it is useless, assistance forms an impediment to the development of natural strength.

The danger of servility is not confined to the useless waste of life which leads to helplessness, but includes the development of reactions which also are characterized by perversion and lack of strength, and may be compared with the outbursts of the hysterical person or the convulsions of the epileptic.

They are the actions of unbridled power. Such violent exhibitions of strength run parallel with lack of strength; they rise from the rage which springs from laziness.

Let us imagine a skilful and sensible workman, not only capable of producing much excellent work but of exercising a healthy influence in his workshop by the calm judgment with which he manages everything. Often he will act as a peace-maker, be the one who smiles when others are in a bad temper. It would not, however, astonish us to learn that at home this workman scolds his wife if the soup is not tasty enough or is not ready in time, or to find that he readily breaks out into anger. At home he is no longer the skilful operator; the skilful worker is the wife who serves him and who pities him. Here we have then an example of a man who is calm where he is the master of his work, and is overbearing where he is waited upon. Perhaps if he learnt how to prepare soup he might become a perfect man.

The man who acts by himself, who expends his strength on his own actions, conquers himself, increases his power and perfects himself.

The men of future generations must be made *strong men*, that is, independent and free.

REWARDS AND PUNISHMENTS FOR OUR CHILDREN

We have only to apply the principles set out above to find that there is born in the child a peacefulness which characterizes and almost illumines all his doings. Truly there is born a new child morally superior to the one who is treated as a helpless and incompetent being. A sense of dignity accompanies this new-found feeling of inward liberation; henceforth the child interests himself in his own conquests, remaining indifferent to the many small external temptations which would have excited his lower feelings irresistibly.

I must confess that this experience filled me with astonishment. I also had been under the delusion of one of the most absurd proceedings of ordinary education, that is, I also believed that in order to foster in the child a strong sense of work and tranquillity it was necessary to encourage by means of an external reward his lower feelings such as greed, vanity and self-love. And I was also astonished when I found out that the child who is allowed to bring himself up abandons these lower instincts of his. I then exhorted the teachers to discard the usual rewards and punishments, which were no longer adapted to our children, and to confine themselves to directing them gently in their work.

But nothing is more difficult for the teacher than giving up old customs and old prejudices. One of them especially employed herself in my absence in improving on my ideas, introducing a little of the methods to which she had been accustomed. One day, on an unexpected visit, I surprised a child, one of the most intelligent, wearing on his breast a large silver Greek cross suspended from a handsome white ribbon; another child was seated in a chair in the middle of the room.

The first had been rewarded, the second was in disgrace. The mistress, at least in my presence, did not interfere with any action, and things remained as I had found them. I said nothing and set myself to watch. The child wearing the cross moved backwards and forwards carrying things from his little table to that of the teacher and *vice versa*, quite busy and intent on his own doings. As he moved about he passed close to the culprit's chair. His cross dropped to the ground, the child in the chair picked it up, looked at it well on all sides and then said to his companion—" Do you see what you have let fall?" The child turned and looked at the thing indifferently; his expression seemed to say—" Do not interrupt me," his voice said, " What does it matter to me?" " It does not matter to you," replied the one undergoing punishment, " then I will put it on." And the other replied—" Yes, yes, you put it on," in a tone which seemed to say, " But leave me alone." The small boy in the armchair fixed the cross on his breast, looked at it well and settled down in his seat more comfortably, extending his arms along the arms of the chair. Things remained so and it was quite right. This pendant could satisfy the naughty one, but not the child contented with his work!

One day I brought on a visit to another Children's House a lady who praised the children highly and finally in my presence opened a box from which she took out many little brass medals bright and shining, attached to red ribbons. " The mistress will fix them on the breasts of the best and cleverest children," she said. Seeing that I was not obliged to inform this lady about my methods, I was silent; the mistress took the box. Then a little one, four years old, a most intelligent child who was sitting quietly at the first table, wrinkling his forehead and making a gesture of protest, shouted out several times—" Not to the boys though, not to the boys."

What a revelation! The little one already was conscious of being among the best and cleverest, though no one had made it known to him, and he did not want to be offended by this reward. Not knowing how to defend himself, he appealed to his standing as a boy!

As for punishments, we have often found ourselves faced with children who continue to disturb others without paying any attention to our reproofs. They were at once examined carefully by the doctor, but very often they were quite normal children. Then we placed a small table in a corner of the room and isolated the child at it, making him sit down in an armchair in front of the class and giving him all the objects he wanted. This isolation always succeeded in calming the child. He saw from his position the whole band of his companions and their way of behaving was an object lesson in behaviour more efficacious than any words of the teacher could have been. Little by little he realized the advantages of being in company with others and began to want to do as they did. We have brought under discipline in this way all the children who at first seemed to be rebels. The isolated child was made the object of special care as if he were helpless or sick. I myself, when I entered, went first of all straight to him, caressing him as if he were a baby; afterwards I turned to the others, interesting myself as if they were men. I do not know what passed through their minds, but certainly the ' conversion ' of the isolated individuals was always decided and thorough. They then became proud of being able to work and of behaving properly; generally they displayed tender affection for their teacher and for me.

LIBERTY OF DEVELOPMENT

From a biological point of view, the conception of liberty in the education of the youngest children should be understood, as a condition suited to favourable development, both on the physical side and on the intellectual side. Were the teacher possessed of a profound reverence for life she would respect, whilst observing with human interest, the unfolding of infant life. The life of the child is not an abstraction; it is the life of every single child. There exists only one real biological revelation—the living individual; and towards these single individuals, observed one by one, education ought to be directed, that is to say the help required for

the normal expansion of life. The child is a body which grows
and a mind which unfolds; the double physiological and psychical
form springs from one eternal fount-life. Their mysterious potentialities ought not to be either dissected or crushed out by us;
we must wait for the succession of events in which they show
themselves.

The environment factor is without a doubt subsidiary to the
phenomena of life. It can modify, as it can help or destroy, but
it can never grow. The origins of development are internal. The
child does not grow because he is nourished, because he breathes,
because he lives in suitable climatic conditions; he grows because
the potential life within him pursues its course, becomes effective;
because the fruitful germ from which life springs is developing.
Puberty does not come because the child laughs, or dances, or
does gymnastics, or is nourished better than usual, but because
some physiological change has happened. It is life which is manifested; life which creates; life which gives; and life is confined
within limits and controlled by insuperable laws.

When therefore we speak of liberty for the small child we do
not mean to countenance the unregulated external actions in which
children, left to themselves, indulge as a relief for their aimless
activity; we assign to the word the profound sense of liberation
of its life from obstacles which might hinder its normal
development.

The child has a great mission which is all the time urging him
onwards—that of growing and becoming a man. Because the
child is unconscious of his internal needs, and because adults are
far from being able to interpret them, there are created around
the child, in the social life of the family and the school, many
mistaken conditions which hinder the expansion of child-life. To
remove as far as possible these circumstances through a thorough
study of the intimate and hidden needs of early childhood in order
to accommodate our help to those needs, is to liberate the child.

This idea demands on the part of the adult greater care and
finer observation of the real needs of the child; and, as the first

Exercises of Practical Life, done with great precision and perfection of
technique, satisfy the need for intelligent activity and lead to independence
and co-ordination of movements.   A. M. I. Montessori Schools in Adyar
and Bombay, India; and Karachi, Pakistan.

practical act, it leads to the creation of an environment in which
the child can employ himself in a series of interesting objectives
to be attained—thus directing into orderly and well-executed
actions his unbridled activity.

EXERCISES IN PRACTICAL LIFE

In the environment described above, bright and gay and furnished according to the proportions of the child, there exist objects
which are designed through their use to achieve some definite
purpose, as for example, certain simple pieces of cloth which the
child can learn to button up, to lace up, to hook up, to tie, etc.
Or there are wash-basins in which the child may wash his hands;
brooms with which to sweep the floor, dusters and other things
suited for removing dust from furniture, various brushes for cleaning shoes and garments—all objects which invite the baby to do
something, to carry out a real piece of work having a practical
goal to be aimed at. To spread out carpets and roll them up
again after they have been used; to spread the tablecloth for the
actual setting of the table at the dinner hour, and to fold it up and
replace it accurately when the meal is over, or to lay the table
completely and afterwards clear away, to wash up the dishes and
replace every item in its own place in the cupboards—these are
pieces of work which are planned and arranged in an order not only
as regards successive difficulties of execution, but which demand a
gradual development of character because of the patience which
is necessary for carrying them out and the responsibility which
they involve in order that they should be carried into effect.

The activities which I have just indicated are called " exercises
in practical life," because in the Children's Houses real everyday
life is carried on in which all housework is entrusted to the little
ones, who execute with devotion and accuracy their domestic duties,
becoming singularly calm and dignified.

Besides those objects which introduce into the instruction all
the doings of practical life, there are many others (*vide* following

pages) which lend themselves to a gradual development of intelligence leading on to culture, such as sets of material for the
education of the senses and others for learning the alphabet,
numbers, and writing, reading and arithmetic. Such objects are
called " material for development " to distinguish them from those
which are used in practical life.

When we speak of environment we include the whole assem-
blage of things from which the child is free to choose for using just
as he pleases, that is to say, in conformity with his inclinations and
his need for action. The teacher does nothing beyond helping him
at first to get his bearings among so many different things and to
find out the precise use of them; that is to say, she initiates him
into the ordered and active life of the environment. But after
that she leaves him free to choose and carry out his work.
Generally the children have different desires at the same moment,
and one is busy with one thing and one with another, without
disputes arising. In this way there moves along an admirable
social life full of energy and vivacious activity; one in which with
quiet delight the little ones solve for themselves the various
problems of social life which the free and many-sided activity
raises up from time to time. Educational influence is diffused
through all the surroundings, and persons, children and teacher,
come to take their share in it.

Preparing and serving meals are efficient factors in social education. The concentration show by the face, the hands and the general attitude of the body reveals interest and satisfaction. Montessori School, Gwalior, India.

NATURE IN EDUCATION

ITARD, in his classic book, *Des premiers developments du Jeune Sauvage de l'Aveyron* (Of the first developments of the young Savage of Aveyron), describes in detail the drama of the extra-ordinary education which was directed towards dispelling the mental darkness of an idiot and rescuing a man from a state of savagery.

The savage of Aveyron was a child who had grown up in a state of abandonment in the environment of Nature. After being abandoned in a wood by assassins who thought they had killed him, the boy was cured by natural means and lived for many years in a state of freedom and nakedness in the forests. At last he was captured by hunters and was carried into the civilized life of Paris; the scars on his small body were evidence of his struggles with wild beasts and of the wounds sustained in his falls from heights.

The child was mute when found and remained a mute; his mentality, diagnosed by Pinel as that of an idiot, proved almost incapable of assimilating intellectual education.

Yet scientific pedagogy owes to this child the first advances made in it. Itard, a physician specializing in the infirmities of deaf-mutes and a student of philosophy, embarked upon his education with methods which he had already partially tested in restoring hearing to partly deaf individuals. At first, he was of the opinion that the wild boy's inferior traits were due to lack of education rather than to organic defects. He was a believer in the principles of Helvetius, " Man is nothing without the work of man "; that is to say, he believed education to be all-powerful. He was an opponent of the pedagogic principle, enunciated by Rousseau before the Revolution—" *Tout est bien sortant des mains de l'Auteur des choses, tout degenere dans les mains de l'homme* "; briefly: The work of education is harmful and injures man.

The wild boy, according to Itard's first illusion, demonstrated experimentally through his characteristics the truth of the first assertion. When, however, helped by Pinel, he became aware that he had to deal with an idiot, his philosophic theories gave place to a most admirable trial treatment in experimental pedagogy.

Itard divides the education of this boy into two parts. In the first, he tries to bring him within the bounds of ordinary social life; in the second, he attempts the intellectual education of the idiot. The boy, whilst living his life of terrible abandonment, had found happiness in it; he had almost been absorbed as part of Nature in which he delighted; rain, snow, tempest, boundless space had formed his spectacles, his companions, his love. Civilized life means renunciation of all this, but it carries with it a conquest which furthers human progress. In the pages of Itard there is described vividly the moral work through which the savage was guided into civilization, involving the multiplication of the needs of the child and surrounding him with loving care. Here is an example of the admirably patient work done by Itard as an observer of the spontaneous manifestations of his pupil; it is certainly capable of giving teachers who have to prepare themselves for using experimental methods an idea of the patience and the self-abnegation demanded when phenomena have to be observed.

" When, for example, observation was kept on him in his room, he was seen to be swaying himself to and fro with wearying monotony, his eyes always looking towards the window and staring into empty space. If a storm of wind arose suddenly, or if the sun all at once emerged from the clouds and lit up the heavens with brilliance, the boy broke out in shouts of laughter, as if almost convulsed with joy. Sometimes the moments of joy were replaced by a kind of frenzied rage; he twisted his arms, drove his clenched hands into his eyes, grinding his teeth and becoming dangerous to all around him.

"One morning the snow was falling abundantly, whilst he was still in bed; on waking up he uttered a cry of joy, leapt from the bed, ran to the window, then to the door; back and forth he went impatiently between the two; then dashed out undressed into the garden. There, giving utterance to his delight in shrill cries, he raced about, rolled in the snow, gathered up great handfuls of it and swallowed it with incredible avidity.

"But his sensations were not always shown in such a lively and noisy manner when he was affected by the great displays of Nature. It is worth noting that in certain cases they assumed a calm form of regret and melancholy. Thus when severe weather drove everybody else from the garden, the savage of Aveyron chose that time to wander into it. He used to make a tour of it several times and then seat himself on the border of the fountain.

"I have spent *whole hours*, with intense pleasure, watching him in this position, noting how insensibly that face of his, vacant and twisted into grimaces, assumed an expression of sadness and melancholy reminiscence, whilst his eyes gazed fixedly at the surface of the water, on which from time to time he would throw some dead leaves.

"When, during the fine night of full moon, a beam of silvery rays penetrated into his room, rarely did he fail to wake up and station himself at the window. During a *great part* of the night he would stand there motionless, his head thrust forward, his eyes dwelling on the moonlit landscape, immersed in a kind of ecstasy of contemplation, the immobility and the silence of which were interrupted only at long intervals by a breath long as a sigh, dying away in a plaint of lamentation."

7

In other passages, Itard relates how the boy was not able to *walk* in a civilized manner, but could only *run*; and tells how he, Itard, used to run after him at first when he was taking him for a walk in the Paris streets rather than put a violent check on the boy's speed.

The gradual, very gentle introduction of the little savage to the ways of social life, the way in which the master at first adapted himself to his pupil rather than the pupil to the master, the subsequent attraction to a new life which was to win the child over by its charms instead of being imposed harshly in such a way that it caused oppression and torture to the pupil—all these constitute so many precious educational principles which may be generalized and applied to child education.

I believe that there exists nothing written which offers us so eloquent a contrast between the natural and the social life, and which shows so clearly how the latter consists entirely of renunciations and restrictions. It suffices to think of the run reduced to a walk, and of the ringing shout brought down to the modulations of the usual speaking voice.

In our time and in the civilized environment of our society, children however live very far distant from Nature, and have few opportunities of entering into intimate contact with it or of having direct experience with it.

For a long time the influence of Nature on the education of the child was considered only as a moral factor. What was sought for was the development of special sentiments aroused by the wonderful objects of Nature—the flowers, the plants, the animals, the landscape, the wind, the light. Later, the attempt was made to apply the activity of the child to nature by initiating him into the cultivation of the so-called " education plots ". The idea, however, of *living* in Nature is the most recent acquisition in education. Indeed the child needs to live naturally and not only to know Nature. The most important fact really is the liberation of the child, if possible, from the bonds which isolate him in the artificial life created by living in cities.

It was only a short time ago that, under the form of *Infant Hygiene*, there came into practice that part of physical education which meant giving children a closer acquaintance with the open air in the public gardens, and leaving them exposed for some time to water and sunshine on the sea-shore. Simpler and scantier garments, sandals in place of shoes, the bareness of little feet, are also timid attempts at liberation from the heavy restrictions which quite needlessly bind children to so-called civilized life. If we think, however, of the much greater extent to which weak, tuberculous and rickety children are exposed to Nature in modern sanatoria because experience has taught us that the only means of restoring them to health is to make them sleep in the open air and to live in the sun, it ought to be perfectly evident that all the more would strong, normal children be able, not only to endure but to be invigorated by being exposed more freely than they are at present to the natural elements. But there still exist too many prejudices about the matter, for we have all made ourselves prisoners voluntarily, and have finished up by loving our prison and transferring our children to it. Nature has, little by little, been restricted in our conception to the little growing flowers and to the domestic animals on which we depend for food, for labour or for defence. Besides that, our minds have been shrunken, have adapted themselves to harbouring contrasts and contradictions, have even confused the pleasure of looking on animals with that of being near the poor creatures destined to die in order to feed us, or that of admiring the song and the beauty of birds imprisoned in little cages—a kind of nebulous " love of nature ". Does there not also exist the belief that by transporting a little sea-sand to some receptacle like a tray one is giving immense assistance to children? Very often it is imagined that the sea-shore is educational because sand is found there as in the receptacle. And so, within the confusion of this world prison of ours, we arrive at the most unnatural conclusions.

Nature, to tell the truth, frightens most people. They dread air and sunshine as if they were deadly enemies. They fear the hoar-frost of the night as they would a serpent hidden in the vegetation. They fear rain as much as a conflagration. If nowadays, urged on by the talk about hygiene, civilized man—that complacent prisoner—makes a move to free himself in Nature, he does it timidly, with the most meticulous precautions.

Sleeping in the open air, exposing himself to wind and rain, defying the sun, plunging into water, are all things about which we may talk at length but which we do not always practise. Who is there who does not make haste to close a door for fear of a draught? And how many do not close the windows before going to sleep, especially if it is winter and it is raining? Almost everybody believes that to take very long walks in the open country, whether it is sun or rain, taking advantage of all natural shelter, is a heroic effort, a *hazard*. One must grow accustomed to these things, they say; but they make no move. How is one to get accustomed, then? Perhaps the little children ought to get accustomed; but no! They are even more sheltered than the adults. Even the English, with their sporting bent, do not subject their little ones to the tests given by Nature and hard work. Even there, the good nurse draws them, when they are already well grown, in their little carriages, into the shade when the weather is good, and does not allow them to run about and do as they choose. No! Sport, where it is born, is born as a veritable battle between the most robust and the boldest youths, those very individuals who are called to arms to fight the enemy.

It would be premature to say: "Set the children free, let them have fair play, let them run out when it is raining, take off their shoes when they find pools of water, and when the grass of the meadows is damp with dew let them run about with bare feet and trample on it; let them rest quietly when the tree invites them to sleep in its shade; let them shout and laugh when the sun wakes them up in the morning, as it wakes up every other living creatures which divides its day between waking and sleeping." Instead of that, we ask ourselves anxiously how we can make the children sleep after daybreak, and how we can train them not to take off

Nature-study has great interest and reveals a remarkable power
of observation. Refined movement, trained senses, intelligence
developed on a basis of ordered ideas find unlimited scope for
exploration. Top: Shishu Vihar, Dadar, Bombay, India.
Bottom: Montessori Centre, Laren N. H., Holland.

their shoes and not to wander over the fields. When, having been kept in restraint by us, having been degraded and irritated by the prison, the child kills insects or little harmless animals, it seems to us natural; we do not realize that this mind has already become estranged from Nature. What we are really asking from our babies is that they adapt themselves to prison without bothering us.

The muscular energy of the children, of even the smallest, is greater than we imagine, but in order that this is revealed to us it must have free play.

The city child says he is tired after a short walk, making us think that he has no strength. But his weariness is caused by his unnatural surroundings—by the monotony, the unsuitable clothing, by the torture which the soft little feet cramped up in leather shoes suffer through contact with the bare pavement of the city streets, by the enervating example of the people round him, all of them silent, indifferent, without a smile. The attractions of fashionable clothes to be admired, of a club to join, are worldly matters which have no existence for him. He is on a leash. Laziness lays hold of him and he demands to be dragged along.

But when children are placed in natural surroundings, then there is the revelation of their strength. Normal babies, even when less than two years of age, if they are strong in constitution and well nourished, can walk for miles. The tireless little legs will climb long, steep slopes in the sunshine. I remember how a child of about six years old disappeared for several hours. He had gone on walking up a hill thinking that if he could reach the top he would see the world which lay on the other side. He was not tired, but he was disillusioned at not finding what he was in search of. I once knew a young couple who had a baby barely two years old. Father and mother, wishing to go to a place a good distance away, had thought of taking turns in carrying the little one in their arms, but it was an exceedingly tiring job. It happened that the child, full of enthusiasm, walked all the way by himself, and repeated the journey every day. Instead of carrying him in their arms, the parents forced themselves to walk very slowly, and stopped when he stopped to gather some little flower, or, when discovering the beauty of a donkey which was eating grass in a field, he sat down, serious and thoughtful, to keep company for a moment with this humble and privileged creature. Instead of carrying their baby, these parents had solved their problem by learning from the baby.

Only the poets feel the fascination of a tiny rivulet of water trickling over the pebbles as it is felt by the child, who grows enthusiastic over it, laughs and wants to stop and touch it with his hand as if to caress it. No one of whom I know, except St. Francis, has admired the modest insect and the perfume of unattractive little plants, as does one of our little ones.

But I suggest that you take up in your arms an infant which has not yet learned to walk; hold him on a country road from where is there a wide magnificent view, in such a way that his back is turned to the scene. You will see him making efforts to turn round and look at the panorama. Stop with him! He enjoys that beauty even when he is not able to stand upright and when his tongue cannot yet ask you to stop. Yes, let us say it with a paraphrase—" He does not live by milk alone."

Have you never seen children standing serious and much affected round the body of a nestling which had fallen from the nest, or watched them moving back and forth, talking about what has happened, asking questions, grieving very sincerely about what has happened? Well, these are the children who, in their next period of degeneration, might be capable of going out to rob birds' nests.

The feeling for Nature grows with exercise, like everything else; it is certainly not strengthened by us through descriptions or exhortations made pedantically to a child who is listless and bored by being shut within walls and who is accustomed to see and hear that cruelty towards animals is a necessity of life. It is experience which brings things home to him. The death of the first dove killed intentionally by a member of the family is a black spot in the heart of almost all children. We have to cure the unsuspected wounds, the spiritual maladies which already exist in these gracious little sons of the prisoners of our artificial environment.

NATURE IN SCHOLASTIC EDUCATION

Education in the school will be able to fix the attention of the child on particular objects which will show precisely how far he has been able to develop feelings for Nature, and which will awaken in him latent or almost lost sentiments. To supply him with incentives to activity and at the same time information which interests him constitutes, as is true for every other activity, the function of scholastic education.

The child, who is the greatest spontaneous observer of Nature, undoubtedly needs to have placed at his disposal material on which to work.

SOLICITUDE FOR OTHERS

Solicitous care for living things affords satisfaction to one of the most lively instincts of the child mind. It is easy, therefore, to organize an active service for the care of plants and, more particularly, of animals. Nothing is better calculated than this to awaken an attitude of foresight in the little child who lives through his fleeting moments without thought for the days to come. When he knows that some animals need him, that the little plants will dry up if he does not water them, his love binds together with a new thread the passing moments and the day which is to follow.

Watch the little ones as on one morning, after they had for many days, with loving care, placed food and water near the brooding doves, they discover the nestlings! Another day, it is a number of delightful chickens which are there, where before there had been the eggs which the hen had been keeping under her wings for so long. What tenderness and what immense enthusiasm! There is born in the children the desire to give further help; they collect little bits of straw, threads of old cotton material, wisps of cotton-wool, for the birds which are building their nests under the roof or on the trees in the garden. And a chorus of chirping, growing all round about, gives them thanks.

The metamorphosis of insects, and the care which mothers bestow on their offspring, form subjects of patient observation by the children, and often give rise to reasoning which surprise us. There was one small child who was so struck by the metamorphosis of tadpoles that he followed up their development, recording the various phases of the frog, like a small scientist.

The plant world also calls to them. In one Children's House in Rome, as they had no ground which could be cultivated, they had placed jars of flowers, round a large *terrazza*.[1] The children never forgot to water the plants with a small watering-can. One morning I found them seated on the ground, all in a circle round a splendid red rose which had opened during the night—silent and tranquil, completely absorbed in mute contemplation.

Once a little girl who had grown up with a love for the flowers and gardens which her mother and her teachers had never allowed her to lack, was looking down from a terrace evidently greatly excited. "Down there," she said to her mother, "there is a garden growing things to eat." It was an orchard which, to the mother, did not seem worth admiring, but which filled the child with enthusiasm.

PREJUDICE IN THE GARDEN

Even into the midst of Nature we cannot help carrying prejudices about which it is very difficult to ascertain the truth. We have made for ourselves too symbolical an idea of flowers; we try to adapt the activity of children to our own ideas instead of following the child in order to interpret his real tastes and needs. So it is that in the garden the child has been forced into activity artificially created by the adult. The act of placing a seed in the ground, and then of waiting for the seedling to grow from it is work on too small a scale and involves too long a wait for children.

---

[1] See footnote in Chapter XVI, " The Mechanism of Writing ".

They want to do big things, and to bring their activity into immediate connection with the products of Nature. Without a doubt children love flowers, but they are very far from being satisfied with remaining among flowers, with brooding for long over their coloured blossoms. Children are profoundly content if they can act, make discoveries, explore, even apart from external beauty.

FAVOURITE WORK

As the result of experiments which we have made, various conclusions, different from those with which I myself had begun, have been demonstrated by children left with free choice.

The work which pleases children most is not so much that of sowing seed as that of harvesting: work, as one knows, not less intense than the other. It is harvesting, one might say, which intensifies the interest in seed-sowing. Anyone who experiments with gathering in the crops will feel more keenly the hidden fascination of sowing.

One of the most brilliant experiments was that of harvesting grain and grapes. The reaping of a field of corn, the making up of this into sheaves to be bound together with bright-coloured ribbons has had great success and can be made the occasion of delightful field festivals. The care of the vines, the cleansing of the grapes, as well as the collecting of the beautiful fruit in baskets may also be turned into gala days of all kinds.

All the fruit trees lend themselves to work of this kind. The gathering in of the almonds interests even the smallest children, who do a really useful bit of work, so diligent are they in seeking out the hidden almonds and gathering them into baskets. Hunting out the strawberries lurking under the leaves is work not less pleasing than that of seeking for sweet violets.

There follows from these experiments an interest in seed-sowing on a large scale, as for example in a corn-field, with all its operations. Only the adult can prepare the furrows, but the children can pile up the various heaps of grain to be sown, which are placed in separate baskets; they then cast the seed diligently along the furrows. The springing up of so many rows of tender pale-coloured little plants gives intense satisfaction to both eye and mind. The growth seems to be made more striking by the uniform quantity, by the patterns of long, parallel lines which are coloured in themselves. It seems that the magnificence is derived from the massing together of single items which by themselves are without much interest. The yellow stems as they sway about in the wind, and as they grow up and up even to the child's shoulders, fill with enthusiasm the little band waiting to harvest them. Although our field-work had a religious purpose [1] we were able to reach the conclusion that the life of the field is better adapted to the child than philosophy and symbolism of flowers.

The little plots of fragrant herbs are also full of practical interest. The activity of the child is then directed to searching for, identifying and choosing herbs of various scents. The exercise of recognizing similar things and of looking for a perfume rather than a flower, demands intense effort and arouses the feeling of making a discovery of something which is hidden.

Naturally the flowers also are of interest, but gathering flowers is rather more contrary to nature than gathering the fruits offered by the earth through the medium of the flowers. These by their fleeting beauty seem to call to themselves insects more than man, in order that they may be helped to carry out their mission of eternal life. It is true that children brought up so that their needs are satisfied, often sit down beside flowers and admire them; nevertheless they get up very soon and go off in search of something to do; the reason is that it is through activity that they themselves can stimulate into unfolding those buds of theirs which are instinct with beauty.

SIMPLICITY

The work must be such as possesses variety within itself. The end operations of sowing and reaping are not essential for rousing the child's interest. He adapts himself cheerfully to the

[1] See Chapter XXIII, " Religious Education ".

simplest doings which have an immediate end in view, and allow him bring into play some purposive effort—as for example, clearing away weeds from paths and furrows, sweeping up dried leaves, cutting off some old branch. In a word, to have a wide field for activity and to have opportunities for new experiences and for engaging in difficult enterprises, brings satisfaction to the spirit of animation which prompts the child to make its way in the world.

Our experience reminds us of quite small children who wander fearlessly among cows, or children who are making friends with flocks of sheep. Others are preparing soil with a sieve and carrying it away in barrows or building up great beds with branches of trees.

The care of the greenhouses and the preparation of water for acquatic plants, the arranging of the nets which protect the water from insects and such things, are work which it is perhaps rarely possible to carry out, for the environment does not generally provide for them; but they would never be outside the strength and the good-will of the child.

Our Garden

Another conclusion we arrived at by placing the child in conditions in which his needs could be demonstrated was that of limiting the field or the garden to its spiritual needs. It is a common belief, on the contrary, that it is desirable to give children unlimited space. In that case the child was being considered mainly in the matter of his physical life; the limits were to be determined by the nimbleness with which his legs could run. However, even considering the ' racecourse ' as the limit of the ground, we will find it to be decidedly more restricted than we had imagined it to be, provided that we are willing to determine that limit with precision. In an immense field, children play and race about in some well-defined space. All living things tend to localize themselves and to keep themselves within boundaries.

This deduction applies also when we consider the mental life. The limits must be sought for in that right measure which lies between excess and insufficiency of space and things, a miserable affair which does not even satisfy his own sense of importance. Whether it is his own property or not does not matter to the child whose needs are satisfied. He must be able to survey just as many plants as he can get acquainted with, just as many as he can fix in his memory in such a way that they are familiar to him.

Even for us, a garden with too many plants, too many flowers, is a place full of ' unknowns,' which live outside our consciousness. Lungs will breathe well in such places, but the mind will remain without kindred attachments. But a very small patch of ground cannot satisfy us either; what it contains is a mere nothing, does not fulfil our needs, does not satisfy the hunger of the spirit which longs to enter into communication with other spirits. There are then limits—the limits of *our garden*—in which every plant is dear to us and gives us help which, we feel, aids us in maintaining our intimate personality.

The decision respecting limits has raised great interest, and has been applied in many countries as the practical definition of the garden as being what responds to the needs of the child's spirit. Today, the lay-out of our gardens proceeds step by step along with the building up of the Children's Houses.[1]

---

[1] In later experiments, planned by Mr. Mario Montessori, scientific education in nature subjects is being carried out more extensively. It is impossible to describe here the great amount of work and the ample and striking material which have been suggested exclusively by the interest and the activity shown by the children. It is enough to mention that they include a great part of the morphology and the classification of the animal and the vegetable kingdoms, preparing for and beginning the experimental study of physiology. Precise and scientific attention is also given to the preparation of aquaria and terraria which should not lack in any school. Spontaneous and purposeful exploration of Nature followed this preparation in the school and led to a host of discoveries made by the children themselves. On this basis, responding to the characteristic needs of the young child for sensorial and motor activity applied to the absorption of fundamental knowledge, the ground was prepared for a vast and far-reaching development in the elementary school. It provided the solution for the problem of satisfying the interests of the older child without burdening his mind with a preliminary and boring effort to master terminology and static notions, when the interest for them has disappeared. It is the younger child who spontaneously and enthusiastically prepares the foundations, which the older child then uses to satisfy his own superior interest.

EDUCATION IN MOVEMENT

THE RED MAN AND THE WHITE MAN

ONE point which I think it is well to clear up for teachers is the distinction to be drawn between the nutritive part of the bodily system and the part which functions in bringing us into relationship with the environment and the organs with one another. The former depends on the circulation of the blood, the latter on the nervous system.

The nervous system can be distinguished as consisting of the main sympathetic nervous system, which specially controls the visceral functions and which is closely linked up with emotional states; and the central nervous system with its infinite ramifications of nerves which, proceeding from the sense organs, place these centres in communication with the external world, and by terminating in muscles establish the dependence of these on the will. We need no other indications than those of the emotions and the will to convince us that the sympathetic system is subordinate to and dependent on the other. And that, above all, ought to be considered by anyone whose aim is education.

The question which occupies us at the moment, however, is to bring for a moment under our attention, in their entirety and in outline, the two great systems—that of the circulation, which, having for its centre the heart, permeates the whole body with its extremely minute system of capillary vessels, and the nervous system, which, having its principal centre in the brain, sends out an infinite number of branches which break up into the microscopic ramifications of the periphery.

As is well known, capillary vessels and ultimate nerve-endings are to be found in all the most minute parts of the body, the blood supplying the material nourishment, and the nervous element maintaining the vital tone even in histological places. In order to obtain a clear impression of the distribution of the capillary system and of the peripheral nervous system, it is enough to remember that the prick of a pin in any part of the body whatever (external or internal) causes bleeding and gives rise to pain. If, speaking theoretically, we could dissect out in a complete manner the circulatory system and the nervous system, the result would be a reproduction of the body in all its details: in the first case a ' red man ', and in the second, a ' white man '.

To the ' red man ' belongs the life of nutrition, since in him are linked up the systems which serve to gather in from the outside world the material necessary for sustaining the body—food and oxygen—as well as the organs intended to get rid of refuse. On the other hand, embodied in the ' white man ' are the organs of the senses, which serve to collect sensations from the external world, and the immense muscular system which carries out motor activity. Although the two ' men ' are quite distinct one from the other and are clearly separated in their functions (one takes in material for the body, the other food for the spirit), yet they are interlocked so closely and are in such intimate reciprocal relationship that no part of the organism could function without their mutual action. The heart beats and drives the blood onward, because it is enervated; the nerve centres and the nerves carry out their work because they are fed by the blood.

The muscles form the most massive part of the bodily structure. They are attached to the skeleton, which exists in order to provide them with points of support, as well as to protect the centres of the nervous system and of the circulation. To them belongs all activity relating to the external world and expression. The small organs of the senses are almost the breathing pores by which the mind takes in the images necessary for mental impressions; but to the muscles is reserved the practical work of life. All the work of the will is carried out by these marvellous instruments of movement. The function of the mind is just to possess all these means of expression with which the idea is changed into action; feeling is realized in work.

Whilst the muscles exercise an important a function and in order to fulfil it carry out operations most complicated in their co-ordination, at the same time they assist the circulation of the blood in such a pronounced manner that they lend the greatest assistance to the heart. This, however, happens as a material consequence of that movement designed to further relationships.

It has happened, however, that man (especially the children) has been condemned to an inactive existence, to carry on mental work dissociated from the organs with which it ought to be bound up, which include not only the brain but the organs of the senses and the muscular system. Physical degeneration has been the consequence of this, because even nutritional life forms part of the individual unity. The educational consequences of this fact have been demands on the ' active life,' that is to say the motor life, principally with the object of reviving and intensifying the ' nutritive life,' in which languor accompanies physical weakness, the alteration of the building-up processes and a predisposition to diseases. This muscular system, to which belong the lofty functions of the life of relationships, has therefore been degraded to the mere task of helping the blood to travel more quickly on its difficult and complicated journey; the organs for the expressions of the mind will then form a kind of suction pump acting on the liquid of the blood.

Such a reversal of functions certainly cannot restore man to normal activity; to the error of apathy, there has been added a functional error. One mistake tries to remedy another mistake. And the mental is always more damaged by it, even in its moral expression. For acrobatism is a physical struggle. Games and similar activities dissipate the higher qualities of man.

What does one do when a joint is dislocated and causes deformities and pain and ailments of so many kinds? One puts the bone back into its place to restore it to normal functioning. This being done, all the consequences which were the effects of a single cause disappear of themselves. The educational error then was to let thought and fancy wander about vaguely allowing the senses to remain unused and the muscles inert, whereas senses, nerve centres and muscles constitute one whole. The correction needed is to put into an active state the functioning of the organs connected with the mental life. Mental work ought to be accompanied by sensations of truth and beauty, which reanimate it, and by movements which bring ideas into play and leave their traces in the external world, where men ought to be giving each other mutual help. Muscular exercises ought always to be at the service of the mind, and should not abdicate in order to make themselves servants of the material part of the nutritive life in what is called the ' physical life '.

For example, work is a physical exercise which is at the service of the mind, and when man works, it helps indirectly to make the blood circulate and the lungs to breathe.

The problem of health is also, therefore, a problem of work.

To work in the open air, when conditions of nutrition are good, within the limits which the higher functions of the human mind permit, is to live normally and to attain perfect health.

GYMNASTICS AND BEHAVIOUR

In the ordinary schools it is usual to call by the name " gymnastics " a kind of collective muscular discipline the aim of which is to carry out movements under commands given to a whole class. This work in the gymnasium is often a first step towards acrobatics.

These different kinds of movement have been found useful in order to counterbalance the muscular inertia of pupils who have to follow a sedentary life in their studies, whilst keeping themselves in a prescribed position imposed by class-discipline, that is to say, seated stiffly on wooden benches. So gymnastics represent a remedy necessitated by an evil inflicted on the children; and nothing is more characteristic and almost symbolical of the old regime than this action and counter-action enforced by the teacher, who dictatorially increases evils and remedies for the passive, *disciplined* child.

The modern tendencies which place gymnastics on different levels, as for example, games in the open air which come to us from England or the rhythmical gymnastics of Dalcroze, consider the child in a more human fashion. They give him an opportunity for loosening his muscles from their enforced positions with a greater regard for his personality. All these methods, however, are reactions from a life which has been wrongly understood and have no modifying influence on life itself. They lie, like amusements, outside the usual existence.

Making muscular education penetrate into the very life of the children, connecting it up with the practical life of every day, formed a main part of the practical side of our method, which has introduced education in movement fully into the indivisible whole of the education of the personality of the child.

The child, as all agree, must be continually on the move; the need for movement, which is irresistible in childhood, apparently lessens as the inhibitory powers develop, during the time when these, harmonizing with the motor impulses, are building up machinery for bringing them into subjection to the will. Thus the more advanced child possesses more obedient motor tendencies, and when an outside will influences his he can dominate impulses. This, however, always remains as the foundation of the life of relationship, for this is precisely the characteristic which distinguishes not only man but all the animal kingdom from the vegetable world. Movement is therefore the essential of life and education cannot

8

be conceived of as a means to moderate or worse to inhibit movement; it should only function as an aid to a better expenditure of
energy, whilst allowing it to develop normally.

In nature children possess a guide which leads them to modify
their way of moving about; this does not need to be demonstrated.
The infant's movements are ceaseless and unco-ordinated like those
of a puppet; the child of three is always on the move, often throw-
ing himself on the ground, running about and touching everything;
the child of nine walks and moves about no longer feeling the
need to stretch himself on the ground or to lay hold of everything
with which he comes in contact. These modifications develop by
themselves, independently of any educational influence. They are
associated with an external transformation of the proportions of
the body, between the length of the trunk and that of the lower
limbs. In the new-born child the length of the trunk from the
top of the head to the hollow of the groin is equal to 68% of the
total length of the body; this means that the legs represent 32%
of the length. On the other hand, in the adult man, bust and
legs are about equal in length. The change in these proportions
forms part of growth. When the child enters our schools at three
years of age, his legs correspond to 38% of his height; and then
they grow, relatively to the trunk, until they exceed by a great deal
the proportions in the adult; already at seven years of age the legs
are 75% of the height. It is known that after puberty it is the
trunk which grows mainly, until it attains the usual adult proportions. It is worth while to consider such an elementary detail
of growth in order that we may understand that children's needs
in respect to movement must vary, and that we must observe
them as they move about spontaneously if we are to be able
to help them to grow up to their fullest possible measure. It is
enough to point out some fundamental characteristics. Children
with their short legs are making great efforts to establish perfect
balance, and with a little run they mask the difficulty of simply
walking, whilst they feel the need for resting themselves by extending their trunk on the ground and raising their legs in the air.

Whilst the infant assumes almost as a natural position that in which the trunk is supine and the feet turned up into the air to meet the extended hands, the child between three and five years of age seeks a resting position by stretching himself prone on the ground and often elevating his shoulders by supporting himself on his elbows; that is, he assumes the position, *ventre a terre*. He has also to find positions of rest different from that of sitting on a chair. Children love to sit on the ground, using as a base the whole length of the crossed legs or the length of one leg placed alongside; in doing so they give themselves a wider base of support. Considering this natural need for a period of rest to break the continuous movement, we have provided in the Children's Houses small rugs, which usually are rolled up and kept in a part of the room set apart for the purpose; children who want to work on the ground rather than seated at a table must first of all take a mat, spread it out on the ground and then work on it there. No adult tells them to change these positions, so the child quietly follows the dictates of its nature.

GYMNASTICS AND WORK

The exercises of practical life, when one thinks of it, constitute real and proper gymnastics; the gymnasium in which they are fostering all movements is just the environment in which one lives. Here we have something which is quite different from the labour which produces new things. Instead of that it preserves things as they exist; it is a continual displacing of objects under the direction of intelligence which sets before it an aim to be reached. Rolling up a rug, brushing a pair of shoes, washing a wash-basin or floor, laying the table, opening and closing boxes or doors or windows, arranging a room, setting chairs in order, drawing a curtain, carrying furniture, etc.—all these are exercises in which the whole body is engaged, sometimes one, sometimes another movement being perfected. By means of habitual work the child learns to move its arms and hands and to strengthen its muscles in a better way than by the usual gymnastics. But the exercises of practical life cannot be regarded as simple muscular gymnastics; they are part of the work. It is the restful work of muscles which function without growing tired because interest and variety renew them with every movement. It is the exercise natural to man who, when he moves, ought to have an object in view; muscles ought always to serve the intelligence and thus remain in functional unity with the human personality. If man is an intelligent creature and is muscularly active, then his rest lies in intelligent activity, as the rest of every other creature lies in the normal exercise of its functions. We must, then, offer to the child means within his surroundings by which to exercise his activity, remembering that the Children's House includes children of various ages—from three to six years—who all live together like members of a family and who, therefore, require different occupations.

The objects which we use for practical life have no scientific signification; they are the objects in use where the child lives and which he sees being used in his home; they are made, however, in sizes adapted to the little man. The quantity is not fixed by the method, but depends on the resources of the school, and above all on the length of time which the child spends in school each day. If the school has a garden attached to it, there will form part of the practical operations such work as taking care of the paths, tidying up the plants, gathering fruit when it is ripe and so on. If the day's time-table is very long, dinner will form part of the occupations; it introduces effort and action more difficult and more interesting than any other kind of practical work; it includes laying the table with the utmost care, serving at table, eating properly, washing plates and cups, carrying away and storing pots and pans, and so on.

THE WORK

When the child arrives in school, he takes off his own garments. Little hooks, fixed to the wall at such a height that the arm of the child can reach them comfortably, are at his disposal.

Little water-taps, placed so low that they do not reach the knee of an adult: minute appurtenances like bits of soap, nail brushes, small hand-towels are within the reach of the child. Or, failing the water-tap and basin, there will be some sort of wash-basin, were it only a small bowl set on a low table together with a little jar and a receptacle into which used water can be poured. A box containing shoe brushes, a few bags hung on the wall in which are kept clothes-brushes so narrow that a tiny hand can grasp them easily, form other practical objects. And, where it is possible, there ought to be kept a small dressing-table with a small mirror, placed so low that it reflects perhaps no more than the space between the feet and the knees of an adult. The little one will be able to look at himself when he is seated and should his hair become untidy by taking off his hat or through the wind in the street he will be able to put it in order; there will be at hand a little hair-brush and a tiny comb. The child then puts on his pinafore and working blouse, and he is now ready to make his entry.

If the school is not in order, then there is work to be done. Perhaps there are vases of rather faded flowers which it is well to throw away, or the water needs to be changed. The statue of the baby Jesus, so dear and pretty, has not been dusted; that must be done. Cloths of various kinds and colours hang from hooks, together with a bright-coloured feather duster; the article most suit-able is chosen and the cleaning begins. A table has a spot on it! It must be removed: soap and a brush. If a little water has fallen on the floor it must be wiped up at once. Or if a piece of bread or a dry leaf has fallen on the floor, the broom is there, small, light, so inviting with the pretty colours and pictures which adorn a handle shining with polish and cleanliness! What is there more pleasing than the dust-pans all green with red spots, or what as white as a wash-tub? Similar occupations are engaged in as often as occasion arises; we have no time-table either for forenoon or afternoon. The child is all the time inspecting his surroundings minutely, his ' House '; and when any chair is out of place, making things look disorderly, we may be certain that it will be the smallest children who will take notice of it. Before the age of three the work of arranging furniture and putting everything in order forms the highest and most improving work, and for that reason also, it makes the loudest calls for action.

THE VOICES OF THINGS

The teacher superintends, it is true; but it is the things of various kinds which call to children of various ages. Truly the brilliancy, the colours, the beauty of gaily decorated objects are no other than *voices* which call the attention of the child to themselves and urge him to do something. Those objects possess an eloquence which no mistress can ever attain to: "Take me," they say, "see that I am not damaged, put me in my place." And the action carried out at the instigation of the things gives the child that lively satisfaction, that access of energy which prepares him for the more difficult work of intellectual development. Very often there is more than one voice of things which is calling; the call gives a complicated order; some important pieces of work require not one child but an organized band of them and require long training and preparation. Such are the tasks of laying the table, serving dinner and washing up pots and pans.

THE TALENTS

It would be a mistake, before testing it, to make an estimate of the capability of children as based on their ages and to exclude any of them helping on the supposition that they are not capable of giving help. The teacher ought always to open the doors of opportunity, never discourage anyone by lack of trust. Even the tiniest children want to be doing things and are possessed of an urge to exert themselves, more vigorously than the bigger ones. The wise mistress will therefore be on the look-out for any contribution which even the smallest child can give. Perhaps the little one of two and a half will be able to carry the bread, whilst the child of four and a half will manage to carry the pan of hot soup. The importance of the work does not concern the children; they are satisfied when they have given the maximum of which they are capable, and when they do not see themselves excluded from the possibilities which the surroundings offer for doing something. The most favoured work offers the greatest scope to each of them. They possess a kind of inward ambition which is directed in bringing into full play the 'talents' which God has given to them, as in the Gospel parable; and when they do succeed in it, they attract the liveliest interest of many admirers. The children when invited to table do not think only of eating; they love this splendid chance of showing their inner powers and often their fine feelings (as in waiting for companions, in saying their prayers). They waste no time, and they know how to take advantage of opportunities. Look at this minute waiter, covered up in his white apron, as he stands there thoughtfully before the table on which he has just spread the table-cloth so carefully, and thinks over the number of the guests, and then about the best arrangement of the places which presently will have to be laid. That laughing baby who pours the water into the glasses so slowly, guiding her hand so that the bottle shall not touch the edge of the glass and shall not let the last drop of water fall on the table-cloth! Moving swiftly and gaily there arrives a band of little serving-maids, each one carrying a pile of plates, the crockery for every separate table. It is satisfaction which has given lightness to these bodies and stimulated them like music.

PRECISION

Anyone who comes much into contact with these children finds out that underlying the active force which directs them to carry out certain practical matters, there exists a secret of success; it is the precision, the exactitude with which the acts must be done. The obvious aim of pouring into a glass interests them much less than the pouring of it without touching the edge of the glass with the bottle and without spilling on the cloth the last drop of water. Washing the hands is a more attractive proceeding if one has to remember the exact place where the soap has to be put and where the towel must be hung up.

Movement in itself is a crude affair, but if it is actuated by a desire for perfection, its value is increased. The hands, for instance, are washed not only to get them clean, but that there may be acquired the ability to wash oneself perfectly. By washing one's hands in this way one is left not only with clean hands, but one becomes more skilful, gaining a certain refinement which makes one superior to the child with dirty hands. This revelation made by the children of loving not only activity directed to a purpose, but of being attracted by special details and therefore by precision of execution, has opened up a wider field to education. It is the education of movements which surges into the front rank, whilst learning practical things is only an external call, the apparent motive which stimulates a profound need of organization.

THE SENSITIVE AGE

Children are then at an age in which movements possess fundamental interest; they seem to be most anxious to know how they ought to move about. They are passing through that period of life in which they must become masters of their actions. Without our looking beyond the intimate physiological reasons, we note that the muscular and nervous organs are passing through the stage when the co-ordination of movements is established. They are in the critical and transitory stage of definite construction. To initiate perfection at this time of life is an immensely productive piece of educational work; the teacher reaps a wonderful harvest after a minimum of trouble given to sowing the seed. She is teaching people to be avid for this definite knowledge.

She gets the impression of giving rather than of teaching, of performing an act of charity. When she is casting among the

With what care do these three little girls perform their self-chosen task! Polishing brass is a delightful and serious occupation.   Montessori School, Gwalior, India

crowd of little ones the seed which is *necessary* for that age, she feels that she is doing a work of the most worthy charity, like that of giving food to the starving.   Later on, these same children will tend to become careless about precision of movement; the constructive period of muscular co-ordination will begin to decline. The mind of the child will pass onward; he will no longer have that love of his.   His mind is compelled to follow a definite course, which is as independent of his own will as it is of the power of his teacher.   Later on, duty will make him preserve, by an effort of his will, what he had created lavishly in the stage of love, that is, at the time when he had to create within himself new aptitudes. It is, then, at this stage that there is a possibility of initiating children into the analysis of movements.

THE ANALYSIS OF MOVEMENTS

Every complex action is made up of successive incidents, one quite distinct from the other; one act follows another.   Trying to recognize and to execute exactly and separately these successive acts is the analysis of movement.

In dressing and undressing are performed very complicated actions, which we adults, except in special social conditions, carry out very imperfectly.   The imperfection consists in mixing up together several of the successive movements of the action.   It is something which resembles the jumbled up pronunciation of long words, in which several syllables are run together into an indistinct and sometimes incomprehensible sound.   The person speaks badly; he does not analyse the word into the sounds of which it is composed.   The elimination of or the confusion of sounds has nothing to do with the slowness or the rapidity of speech.   One can speak both clearly and rapidly; indeed the person who distorts his words is often slow of speech.   It is not a question of speed, but of exactitude.   Now we, generally speaking, display in many of our movements an inexactitude which springs from lack of education and which clings to us, though we may not be conscious of it, as a real mark of inferiority. Let us suppose, for example, that we want to button a jacket! After having more or less got the button through, we begin to thrust the thumb through the button-hole, and to grab at the opposite side in search of the button, ignorant of how the button should be directed to put it in place. On the other hand, what is necessary to do first of all is to bring the two edges of the jacket close together and then to direct the button into the line of the hole and push it through, finally straightening it up. This is in fact how it is done by servants and tailors when they are dressing their masters or customers. The garments are then kept uninjured for a long time, whereas by the other method three or four buttonings put them out of shape and deprive the garment of its elegant fresh look. By similar stupid procedure we spoil locks, by putting the keys into them blindly, and mixing up the two successive motions by turning the key and pulling the door at the same time. Often we pull the door half shut with the key even when it is not intended for that purpose, as is indicated by the more or less handsome door-handles. In the same way we ruin our best books as we turn over the leaves, because our movements are not adapted to the purposes. The results of the wrong treatment given to objects reflect back on ourselves, for our movements become habitually so rough and clumsy that the harmony of the body is spoilt. If we observe the movements of an aristocrat, of one of those people spoken of as ' distinguished,' we find that the distinction is due to their actions being carried out in the proper consecutive order. This is just the kind of person who moves easily and gracefully.

ECONOMY OF MOVEMENT

The analysis of movement is bound up with economy of movement; to perform no movement unnecessary for the purpose is really the highest degree of perfection. There follow as a consequence aesthetic movement, artistic attitudes. Greek movements and those which today resemble them most, like those in the

buttoning frames are
...urce of great delight
...bling the child to con-
... independence in car-
... for his own person.
... the two girls below
... enjoying an activity
... proves their indepen-
...ce from the help of
...ing adults. It is not
...ty, but this vital urge
... prompts them.

...: Photo by Mrs. V. A.
...er in an English Mon-
...ori School.   Bottom:
...I.I. Montessori School,
...a, Bombay, India.

Japanese dance, are none other than a selection of the movements absolutely necessary in the analytical succession of actions. But all this is not confined to art; it is a general principle which concerns every act of life. A clumsy, ungraceful movement is generally overburdened by acts unnecessary for its object. Anyone who, when about to get out of a carriage, opens the door a little before the carriage has stopped and extends his foot towards the step, is unconsciously doing two or three useless things, because he cannot alight yet. But all that is not only useless for the purpose of alighting, but it is a sign of an uneducated person.

These seem to be difficult things for us to teach. But there is an age when movements possess a fascinating interest, when the muscular and nervous apparatus responds to exercise, and when are laid down for the future the differences between a cultured and an uncultured individual—it is the age of infancy.

BUTTONING FRAMES

Pieces of cloth which can be fastened together serve the child as objects for practising analysis of movement; they are fixed on a frame which carries two rectangles of material which can be joined together. Every frame illustrates a different kind of joint—buttons, hooks, laces, ribbons, buckles, patent fasteners, etc. These objects of development enter into the dressing of ourselves. The two pieces of stuff must be placed edge to edge so that the things to be used for joining them lie immediately opposite each other. These may be eyelets into which a lace has to be threaded, or a button and button-hole, or ribbons to be tied—all needing manipulations diverse and complicated enough to enable the child to distinguish the succession of acts, each one of which has to be completed before proceeding to the next. For example: The button must be tilted with one hand, whilst the other hand moves the button-hole till it lies over the button held edgewise; then the button is passed through; after that it is made to lie horizontally. After the teacher has demonstrated with the utmost exactitude the mode of procedure, the child tries again and again indefinitely, buttoning and unbuttoning a great many times until he acquires skill and speed.

OTHER MEANS

The following list may supply examples of similar activities: One is locking and unlocking doors, distinguishing between the acts of inserting the key, which should be held horizontally, of turning it, then drawing it out of the box or the door. Another is opening a book properly and then turning over the pages one by one, touching them delicately. Others are—rising from and sitting down on a chair; carrying things (stopping before putting them down); avoiding obstacles while walking, that is, not knocking against people or things. These form a set of the examples which are in use in the Children's Houses.

Besides these, another series of actions is introduced in the course of the everyday life of the child—those relating to formalities in social intercourse, such as saluting, picking up and holding out to others an object which has been dropped, avoiding passing in front of anyone, giving way to others, and so on.

THE LINE

In everything there exists the multiple expression of one single idea; it is this unique and fundamental thought which must be sought for as being the key to a general problem. The perfecting of the most varied movements also has its key, the governing essential with which all perfection is bound up. This is the equilibrium of the body. We have therefore thought out a method for helping little children to maintain their balance safely, whilst at the same time perfecting the movement which above all others is essential, that is walking.

A line in the shape of a long ellipse having been drawn on the floor (either with chalk or painted to make it more durable) the

Walking on the line—an exercise in balance. The face and outstretched arms betray effort and concentration. Montessori School in England. Photo by Mrs. V. A. Baker

child walks on it, placing the foot completely on the line, so that the line lies along the axis of the flat part of the foot. The exact placing of the foot is the first point which has to be shown; the toe and the heel must both be on the line. Moving the feet forward in this position, as anyone can prove, gives the impression of falling. That means that an effort has to be made in order to preserve equilibrium. When the child is beginning to be sure of his walking power, he is taught to overcome another difficulty; the feet have to advance in such a way that the foremost is planted with the heel in contact with the toe of the other foot. The exercise not only demands an effort to maintain balance, but it exacts from the child the closest attention in order that the feet may be placed in the position required. There results from this the ordinary utilization of that instinct which everyone has noticed in children, the desire to walk on a plank or any narrow bar; and that explains the keen interest which little children take in our exercises on the line, and in the development of them which has taken place in our schools.

A mistress plays the pianoforte or a violin or a small organ; not to get the children to walk according to a musical rhythm, but to give some animation to the movement, so useful when one has to make an effort.

CONCURRENT EXERCISES

In all our schools there is today, as part of the standard apparatus, a stand to which are attached many different little banners, all attractive because of their bright colours. It is well known how much the children like to hold them in their hands. Those walking on the line, directly after they have overcome their first difficulties and acquired equilibrium, may take one of the little flags, provided they can hold it aloft. If they do not pay great attention to controlling the arm, the flag will drop little by little. Attention therefore has to be divided between controlling the feet, which have to be placed without fail on the line, and guiding the arm which holds up the banner.

The next difficulties are found in exercises which are more and more exacting in their control of movements. One is worked with a set of glasses which contain coloured liquids; the liquid reaches nearly to the brim, and the child has to walk holding the glass quite upright so that the liquid is not spilt. The whole hand must therefore be controlled by that will which is at the same time keeping the feet from straying from the line.

Other objects consist of bells which have to be carried whilst the child is walking and must be kept quite upright, that is, perpendicular. As he walks all round the line, not a sound must be heard; whenever the attention wanders, the fact is loudly announced by the bell.

At this stage there comes into existence an interest in overcoming greater and greater difficulties. The child launches himself into joyous activity which little by little makes him master of all his movements. He is often most audacious in his belief in himself. I have seen children holding in their hands several cubes placed one on top of the other in a column, and carrying this erection on their walk without letting them fall. Others place little baskets on their heads and proceed with the greatest care.

IMMOBILITY AND SILENCE

Quite another kind of exercise in the control of movement is that which makes it possible (as far as it concerns children) to create absolute silence. This does not mean the approximation given by sitting still and saying nothing, but is a perfect condition to be arrived at gradually. It involves not uttering a single sound, not producing the slightest noise such as might be made by moving a foot or by a hand slipping, or by noisy breathing. Absolute silence is the equivalent of absolute immobility. But we will discuss silence along with exercises of the senses; it is simply mentioned here in order to complete the picture which helps in analysing and co-ordinating movements.

OPEN ROADS

The final object of such exercises is the perfecting of the individual who practises them. But the ways which open up and lead to new possibilities are multitudinous; the individual who has gone far forward along the path leading to perfection becomes capable of many things and perfection is not barren of practical results.

The child who has become master of his actions through long and repeated exertion, and who is satisfied through the employment of those motor acts of his which he has used in such interesting and pleasing fashion, is a child filled with joy and health, who is distinguished by his calmness and his discipline.

He has also prepared himself to acquire many practical accomplishments. His body is ready to respond to musical vibrations; he is admirably prepared for rhythmical gymnastics. In the second stage, music does not continue to be an indifferent incitement to effort, but becomes an inner director of movements which are obedient to its rhythm.

Let us review matters. These little ones of ours are prepared for entering a sacred building, where silence and stillness are obligatory for those who are worthy to enter it. You see them there paying attention to the movements of every muscle. They can walk about without making a noise, stand up and sit down, carry chairs without disturbing the peace of the holy place. We certainly do not say that the child is religious because he does this, but in practice he is ready to enter with dignity into the place where religion is practised. He is a child refined and perfected and therefore he is capable of entering upon every road which may lead to his advancement.

THE FREE LIFE

Those conquerors of themselves are also conquerors of liberty, for there disappear from their constitutions so many disorderly and ignorant tendencies which of necessity place children under the continuous and rigid control of the adult. They can scatter themselves in a garden without damaging paths or flowers, can run about in a meadow without tumbling down in wrong positions. Dignity and graceful bearing, easy movement, are gifts superadded to their patient and laborious fundamental acquisitions. Using a word which translates the English idea, they are " controlled " beings; and directly they become capable of controlling themselves they are freed from the control of others. Those who familiarize themselves with the theoretical study of our method receive an impression that in the beginning it runs contrary to the preconception which they had formed of it—that the child is free to do what he pleases. Instead, they begin to fear for this little one who is supposed to be free, yet who is obliged in his walking to place his feet exactly on a line, who is drilled into reducing his small body to sheer immobility, who toils with the patience of a servant and who analyses every movement. Only practical experience can show him children who delight in immersing themselves in these " sacrifices," and convince him that the needs of very small children who in the course of development are fundamentally governed by the need for being developed.

THE REALITY

The exercises in equilibrium and analysis, by stabilizing the body in its mechanism of equilibrium and accustoming the attention to follow every action, encourage perfection in the execution of every act. The doings of everyday life divert the lively intelligence of the child to the many actions which he carries out during the day, and a reciprocal influence is the result; analysis helps synthesis and its applications, and *vice versa*. The secret of perfection lies in repetition, and therefore in connecting up the exercises with the usual doings of real life. If the child does not lay the table for a company of people who really dine, if he has not at his disposal real brushes to clean, and real carpets to clean every time they are used, if he does not himself have to wash and dry plates and glasses, etc. there will never be born in him any real ability. And if he does not live a social life in which he observes the rules of education he will never acquire that graceful naturalness which is so attractive in our children. We know what a perpetual struggle it is to prevent ourselves from falling into that depth of indolence which is always hindering us on our journey towards perfection, just as the force of gravity in the end stops the smoothest, most polished sphere from running on the most level surface. To have reached the highest refinement would matter nothing, if that were not linked up with daily life, where various motives urge us never to relax and where the fruits of dexterity acquired are transmitted reciprocally. Roughness, inexactitude, spring up like those herbs which grow even among dry stones, on a rock which, from its very nature, would seem to be protected from them.

GIVING ACTIONS THEIR PEACE

One detail usually very little understood is the distinction between teaching how one ought to act—leaving free, however, the practical applications of it—and the other plan (which is done by other methods) of guiding the child in every action and imposing the power and the will of the adult on the child. Those who teach in the old style suppose that we, while defending the liberty of the child, desire that the child should remain without ability or will-power because we deprive him of that adult superintendence. On the contrary, we do not understand the idea so simply; our education is not negative, it takes away nothing, but it changes, it intensifies, it refines.

One ought to teach everything, one ought to connect everything with life, but there ought not to be suppressed, by directing them ourselves one by one, the actions which the children have learnt to carry out and to place in practical life. This assigning of their proper places to actions is one of the most important things which the child has to do. He has not only learnt to be silent, but he has learnt where he ought to be silent; he will be

9

silent in church. He has learnt not only how to bend the knee, but also where to do it—before the altar. He has learnt not only every kind of greeting, but has also learnt how to allocate them according as to who is presented to him—another child, a relative, a stranger or a venerable personage. That means that the various things which he has learnt perfectly must be used and given their right place in the different times and circumstances of life. It is he who decides; this application is the work of his understanding, the exercise of his own responsibility. In this way he is set free from the greatest of dangers, that of placing upon the adult the responsibility for his doings, thus condemning his own intelligence to the inertia of sleep.

The new education consists not only in supplying the means of development for separate actions but in leaving the child at liberty to make use of them.

It is this which transforms the child into the thoughtful and diligent little man who makes, in the secrecy of his heart, decisions and selections very different from what we would have expected, or who, with the rapidity of a generous impulse or with delicate affection, does things which are prompted suddenly by his inward thought. In this also, more than in anything else, does he exercise himself; and so he travels onwards with surprising confidence along the ways chosen by his own intelligence.

The inner work of the child is marked by a kind of modest sensibility and is expressed only when the adult refrains from interfering with his directive doings, his inspections, advice and exhortations. Let us leave the child free to make use of his powers and he will show himself capable of successes greater than those which he is making. He will act with scrupulous diligence in assigning to every activity its proper place, just as the younger child (that is, two years old) takes pride in being able to put every object in its place.

When he greets a person of rank who is visiting the school, he feels that he not only knows how to salute, but how to choose that form of salutation which is fitting. When he sits down in school, or kneels in church, it is he who places in the right order the actions learnt and perfected. In this there is a knowledge as well as a power which raises the understanding. The child who has finished his first plate of soup will not ask for more if he has learnt that he ought not to do it, that his natural desire is forbidden at this time. He will wait patiently till the waiter, anxious like himself to do the right and to practise at the right time everything learnt, begins his second round, inviting all who have finished to have their plates refilled.

As guest or waiter, artist or student, the inward satisfaction of the child consists in doing the right knowingly, according to high principles.

GYMNASTICS AND GAMES

What opinion ought we to have about games in the open air? It is a way of expending an overflow of energy, that is the residue of energy. They ought to be the gay, unfettered employment of a strength which the demands of daily work have not used up. This is a very different thing from considering games and gymnastics as being in themselves the sole means of physical exercise—almost as a reaction which saves us from the dangers of inertia.

Nowadays we talk about the great moral influence of sport, not only because it uses up with definite purpose energy abnormally penned up and constituting a danger to the equilibrium which the will has to preserve in man's actions, but—and this is one of the most important points—because organized games demand the exact use of apparatus, and therefore the exact co-ordination of movements as well as disciplined attention. Exactitude is the basis of perfection in movements and the point which requires the co-operation of the attention. It follows that games foster the spirit of co-operation and maximum effort. This, by comparison with aimless play, represents moral progress.

Now everyday tasks include part of these advantages, as for example, accuracy in the use of objects, the discipline of attention, and the final perfection which is arrived at by movements. The moral and social aim, however, is different, because the exercises do not claim such a conscious social co-operation, but are prompted by the individual love of the children for their surroundings. Through games of this character there is, therefore, developed a true ' social sense,' because the children are working in the surroundings in which they live as a community, without troubling themselves as to whether they are working for themselves or for the common advantage. In fact, they correct all mistakes with the same readiness and the same enthusiasm—their own and those of others—without stopping to find out the culprit in order to make him put the matter right.

Everybody, not only children, ought to exercise his muscles in work and make *a first choice* of this very human and superior way of expending his energy. This is not merely to establish individuality as an entity, but to unify it also with social needs, to which the work of man is directed. Up till now no man of government rank has been able to boast that he has obtained from games or sport help *as* great as that which working on the soil gave to Cincinnatus; and no young sportsman will have gained from his exertions the moral advantages which daily work gives to the young monk, who works out his noviciate that he may obtain peace.

GYMNASIUM FOR LITTLE CHILDREN

If by gymnastics we mean exercises done with the help of special instruments like those used in a gymnasium, I was the first to start them with children from three years of age. The first edition of this book spoke extensively about them. I had observed that the smallest children, of about three years of age, spontaneously did some exercises on the railings round the flower beds in the courtyard. These railings were made of iron bars running parallel and supported by wooden sticks. The children held the upper bars and put their feet on the lower ones. The distance between the two corresponded by chance to their height. Thus they moved sideways along them.

I then had a similar apparatus made which was the first gymnastic instrument for tiny children.

Afterwards I had a special kind of swing made. It was like a small chair, raised above the ground with a long seat so that their feet also could rest upon it. This swing moved towards a vertical wall. The child, after an initial push, could keep the swing moving by pushing with its feet against the wall every time it came near it. This was a gymnastic exercise to strengthen the knees without the effort of walking.

Other simple instruments were also prepared, e.g. the " round stairs " with lines painted upon them to learn to come down the stairs in a correct manner, keeping to the same direction without swerving either to the left or the right.

Finally there were various contraptions for jumping from different heights.

I was then severely criticized for giving a gymnasium to children of only three years of age! Afterwards, however, the idea made headway and was perfected in every country. Also in our own schools greater perfection was achieved and new applications were found.

Children of about 5-6 years of age love to climb the branches of trees, and this is a very good practical exercise for them. I therefore had some instruments built that were similar to empty prisms with boards fixed at regular distances. These were used as stairs or ladders to reach the trees. In California we also had small huts built with balconies resting on the branches of trees. They gave an opportunity to the children to stay up there and even to work there.

As a last example I wish to mention the " pagoda ". This is an application of those contraptions that are everywhere in use on which children go up a ladder on one side and then slide down on the other. Instead of the small platform at the top, serving merely to pass from the ladder to the slide, I had a much larger platform laid out, so that they could also bring their chairs there and sit down. It is reached on one side by either a ladder or by simple transversal bars along which they climb whilst they can slide down on the other side. This "pagoda" was built specially in those places where some kind of tennis-court existed. This court was very useful; small children pushed small handcarts there, sometimes with another small child in them, or they used it for cycling. Children of three years of age can very well use bicycles (built according to their size) and those of four become real cyclists. In Holland, where there are special cycle-paths, many children come to school on cycles instead of by tram.

Also swimming pools were built in many of our schools; the first having been built in Vienna. There they had a pool in the shape of the figure eight with various depths for smaller and bigger children.

We thus had an opportunity to observe that children of four years of age can learn how to swim (as for that matter we can see the children of Italian fishermen doing, even without any formal teaching, at that same age).

All these possibilities are like games, very amusing but not necessary. That is why later on we did not speak about them any more and we substituted for them *practical work* and permanent abilities (like cycling and swimming). Another reason why in later years we did not stress them was that these applications are not easily realized in schools for the poor.

SILENCE: THE INHIBITION OF MOVEMENTS

In the common schools, for long, it has been thought that silence could be obtained by a command.

The meaning of the word has not been studied. It has not been realized that it demands immobility, almost the suspension of life for that particular instant during which silence is maintained. Silence means the suspension of every movement; it is not, as is generally considered in schools, in a rough and ready way, the secession of noises greater than the normal noises tolerated in the place.

Silence in the ordinary schools means stopping talking, quelling a disturbance, the opposite of noise and disorder.

On the other hand, silence may have a positive meaning, indicate a state of things on a higher level than that of normal conditions. It may be like an instantaneous inhibition which costs an effort, a dictate of the will, something which detaches us from the noises of common life, almost isolating the mind from outside voices.

This is the silence which we have attained in our schools—profound silence, although it is produced in a class of more than forty little children between the ages of three and six.

A command could never have secured the marvellous victory of wills united in preventing all action, during that period of life in which movement seems to be the irresistible, ever-present characteristic of life.

This collective work is done by children who are accustomed to act independently in satisfying their own desires.

It is necessary to teach the children silence. To accomplish this we get them to perform various silence exercises which contribute in a noteworthy way to the surprising capacity for discipline displayed by our children.

The exercises of silence and afterwards the " silence lesson," one of the most characteristic peculiarities of our schools, had their origin in a casual episode.

During a visit paid to a Children's House, I met in the courtyard a mother who was holding in her arms her four-months' old baby, swaddled as was still the custom among the people of Rome. Tiny infants were so tightly swathed in the bands moulded round their little bodies having no other coverings, that they are known as pupi (puppets). This little one, fat and tranquil, looked the incarnation of peace.

I took her in my arms where she lay quiet and good. I went inside with her in my arms, to be met by the children of the House who rushed out to meet me, as they usually do, all trying to embrace my knees in such a tumultuous fashion that they almost upset me. I smiled at them, showing them the ' cocoon '. They understood and danced round me but without touching me out of regard for the little creature in my arms. So I entered the room with the children walking all round me. We sat down, I in front of them on a high chair, not on one of the small chairs which I generally used. That is to say, I seated myself with some solemnity. They gazed on my little one with a mixture of tenderness and joy; we had not yet pronounced a single word. I said: " I have brought you a little teacher." They were surprised; they laughed. " A little teacher, for no one can keep as still as she does." Every little figure stiffened itself in its place. " No one keeps his legs as still as she does." They all carefully adjusted their legs so as to keep them still. I looked at them smiling: " Yes, but they will never be as motionless as hers; you will move them a little, she will not; no one can be like her." The children were serious; they seem to have realized the superiority of the small teacher; some of them smiled, and seemed to say with their eyes that the bandages deserve the credit. " No one can keep as quiet as she does." General silence. " It is not possible to keep silent like her; you hear how delicate her breathing is. Come close up on tip-toe." Some of them rose up and crept up to me very, very slowly, on the tips of their toes, stretching out their heads and turning their ears towards the little one. Deep silence. " No one can breathe as silently as she does." The children gazed in astonishment; they had never thought that even when they keep still they were making noises, and that the silence of the little ones were deeper than that of the big ones. They almost tried to stop breathing. I got up. " I am going away very, very quietly " (I walked on the tips of my toes without making any noise), " yet you hear that I make some noise, however quietly I go; but *she* walks with me in silence, she goes away in silence." The children smiled but they were moved, for they understood the truth and the joking in my words. I restored the ' cocoon ' to the mother through a window.

Behind the little one there seems to remain a fascination which takes possession of every mind; nothing in nature is sweeter than

the silent breathing of the newly born. Human life renewed, resting in silence, what majesty! Compared with that how colourless are the words of Wordsworth about the silent peace of Nature—
" How calm, how quiet! One single sound, the drip from the suspended oar."

Even the children feel the poetry of the silence of the tranquil, new-born human life.

THE SILENCE LESSON IS ESTABLISHED

After this surprising experience I felt a desire to repeat it, but how to achieve this? One day I decided in favour of simplicity and asked the children: " Shall we make silence?" To my astonishment all the children seemed happy at the prospect and answered:
" Yes, yes! "

I then began my attempt. " In order to obtain silence nobody should move. . . ." " Even a foot that moves, makes a noise. . . ." " Also loud breathing may make a noise. . . ." All tried to keep still and so did I with them.

During these attempts the children remained enchanted, all of them competed in the effort to avoid even the slightest movement. Thus the attention of the children was drawn to every part of their body.

Whilst these doings are going on, and my short, excited speeches are being interrupted by intervals of immobility and silence, the children listen and watch with great delight. Very many of them are interested by the fact which they had never noticed that they make many noises of which they are not aware, and also that there are many degrees of silence. There is an absolute silence, in which nothing, absolutely nothing, moves. They look at me in astonishment when I stop right in the middle of the room; it is really as if I were not there. Then they all set themselves to imitate me and try to do the same. I point out that here and there a foot is moving about almost inadvertently. The attention of the children is fixed on every part of their bodies, in an anxious desire to attain immobility. Whilst they are doing this, there is truly created a silence which is different from that thoughtlessly called silence. It seems that life gradually vanishes, that the room by degrees becomes empty, as if there were no longer anybody in it. Then there is heard the tik-tak of the clock on the wall; and this tik-tak seems to grow in intensity little by little as the silence becomes absolute. From the outside, from the courtyard which had seemed silent, there come various noises—a bird chirping, a child passing. The children are fascinated by this silence, as by a real conquest of their own. " See," I said, " it is now quite as quiet as if there were no longer any one here."

This stage reached, I darkened the windows and said to the children, " Now listen for a gentle voice to call you by name."

Then from an adjacent room, situated behind the children, through a wide-open door, I called in a muted voice but lengthening out the syllables as one would in calling to someone across the mountains, and this half-hidden voice seemed to reach the hearts of the children and to call upon their souls. Every one I called rose up silently trying not to move the chair, and walking on the tips of the toes so silently that one scarcely knew they were walking; nevertheless the step resounded in the absolute silence which was never broken whilst all the others remained motionless. The one called gained the door with a countenance full of joy, making a little leap into the next room, stifling little outbursts of laughter; or he laid hold of my dress leaning against me; or he set himself to watch the companions who were still waiting in silent expectation. He felt almost as if he had received a privilege, a gift, a reward, yet he knew that all would be called, beginning with the most absolutely silent one who was left in the room. In this way each one tried to deserve by waiting in perfect silence the call which was sure to come. I once saw a little one of three trying to check a sneeze and managing to do it; she held back the breath in her heaving little chest, and resisted, to emerge triumphant.

Such a game fascinates the little ones; their intent faces, their patient immobility, show that they are eager to get the pleasure it affords. At first, when I was still ignorant of the child's mind, I used to show them little sweets and toys, promising to give them to whoever was called out, imagining that presents were necessary to stimulate such efforts in childhood. But very quickly I had to acknowledge that they were useless.

The children arrived like ships in port, after having experienced the efforts, the emotions and the delights of silence; they were happy, because they had felt something new and had gained a victory. This was their reward. They forgot the promised sweets, and did not trouble to take the toys which I had supposed would attract them. So I abandoned this useless method, and was amazed to find that after the game had been repeated again and again, even children three years old could keep silent during the whole of the period necessary for calling out of the room some forty other children. It was then that I learnt that within the mind of the child dwell its own reward and its own spiritual pleasures. After such exercises it seemed to me that their love for me was greater; they certainly became more obedient, sweeter and gentler. We had really isolated ourselves from the world and had passed a few moments of intimacy among ourselves—I in desiring them and calling for them, they in hearing in the deepest silence [1] the voice directed to each one of them personally, adjudging him at that moment to be the best of all!

FREEDOM OF CHOICE

We now arrive at practical work; we are at school. The materials for the training of the senses, decided upon after experimental research, form part of the environment.

[1] Silence, which has become one of the best-known characters of the Montessori method, has been adopted in many ordinary schools, and so to some extent the Montessori spirit has penetrated into these schools. It was this influence which caused to penetrate into the public manifestations of social and political order the silence of immobility, and it was also used for religious education.

Little by little, following the directions arrived at after long experience, the teacher presents now one part, now another of the material, in accordance with the age of the child and the systematic gradation of the objects.

But such a presentation is only a preliminary which acts as an introduction and nothing more. It is afterwards that the important doings begin. Influenced by the various attractions, the child will choose, as it pleases him, any one of the objects with which he has made acquaintance and which have already been presented to him.

The material is set out for him; he has only to stretch out his hand to get it. He may carry what he has chosen anywhere he pleases—to a table, near a window, into a dark corner, or to a nice little mat spread out on the ground; he may use it over and over again as often as he chooses.

What influences him in the choice of one subject rather than another? Not immediate imitation, for there is only a solitary specimen of every object, and if one child is using it, that is the very time when no other child can use it.

So it is not imitation. The way also in which the child will use the material shows this, for he becomes absorbed in his doings with such intense fervour that he becomes oblivious to everything around him and continues his work, repeating his actions consecutively dozens of times. This is that phenomenon of concentration and repetition of an exercise with which is bound up the inner development. No one can concentrate by imitation. Imitation, in fact, binds us to the outside world. Here we are dealing with a diametrically opposite phenomenon, that is, abstraction from the external world and the closest union with the intimate and secret world which operates within the child. No influence is exerted here by an interest in learning or by an external objective nothing of that sort can be connected with this moving and displacing of objects which are invariably put back into their original positions. It is thus quite a personal fact, connected with the needs which exist then in the child, and therefore with th conditions characteristic of his age. Indeed an adult would never maintain an interest in such things to such an extent as to repeat their displacement dozens of times and find pleasure in doing it; still less would it be possible for the inner faculties of an adult to concentrate on these doings in such a way to make him insensible to external events. The teacher therefore exists on quite a different psychical plane compared with the child and could not in the smallest degree influence such a phenomenon. We are face to face then with a veritable revelation of the inner world. External stimuli like a great calamity call forth some manifestations belonging to the depths of the soul. Here we find ourselves in front of a phenomenon of development, pure and simple.

The fact is very clearly evident when we observe the behaviour of very young children. They sometimes show a similar symptom, though only in the motor field; it consists in carrying similar objects one by one from one place to another. Only at a later age does the child love to transport things actuated by an external purpose to be attained, like laying a table, replacing things in a cupboard, etc. There exists then a formative period in which actions are apparently aimless, have no external application. Analogous facts are met with in the course of the development of speech, when the child for a long time repeats sounds, syllables and words without yet using language, far less applying it to external objects.

This phenomenon, so general in all manifestation of the development of mental life, therefore possesses the highest interest.

It necessitates that the child should be allowed free choice of objects. It will develop the more readily in proportion as there can be eliminated any obstacle which may interfere between the child and the objective to which his mind is unconsciously aspiring.

Every external thing, in particular every external activity, will be an obstacle hindering that frail and mysterious vital impulse, which acts as a guide though still unconsciously. The teacher may therefore become the principal obstacle, because here is a more energetic and intelligent activity than that of the child. In that environment in which the sense stimuli are set out for the free choice of the child, the teacher (after she has in the first instance shown them and pointed out the use of them) should try to eliminate herself.

The activity of the child is spurred on by his own mind and certainly not by that of the teacher.

THE MATERIAL FOR DEVELOPMENT

OUR material for the development of the senses has a history of its own. It represents a selection, based upon careful psychological experiments; from material used by Itard and Seguin in their attempts to educate deficient and mentally defective children; from objects used as tests in experimental psychology; and from a series of material which I designed in the first period to my own experimental work. The way in which these different means were used by the children, the reactions they provoked in them, the frequency with which they used these objects, and above all the development they rendered possible, furnished us gradually with reliable criteria for the elimination, the modification or the acceptance of these means in our apparatus. Colour, size, shape, all their qualities in brief were experimentally established. As in this book we do not deal with this phase of our work, it is worth while to mention this fact.

To avoid misunderstanding and refute criticism expressed after our Method became known all over the world, it may be equally useful to state the aim of our sense training. There is the obvious value of the training and refinement of the senses which, by widening the field of perception, furnish an ever more solid and richer basis to the development of the intelligence. It is through contact with and exploration of the environment that the intelligence builds up its store of operational ideas without which its abstract functioning lacks both foundation and precision, exactitude and inspiration. This contact is established by means of the senses and of movement. If it is at all possible to train and refine the senses, even if this be only a temporary achievement in the life of those individuals who later on do not use them to such an extent and with such constancy as in certain specifically practical and sensorial professions, its value stands undiminished, because it is in this period of development that the fundamental ideas and habits of the intelligence are formed.

There is, however, another side to the importance of sense training. The child of two and a half or three who comes to our Children's Houses, has, during the previous very active and mentally alert years of his existence, accumulated and absorbed a host of impressions. This remarkable achievement, the extent of which can hardly be exaggerated, was, however, made without any outside help and guidance. Essential and accidental impressions are all heaped together, creating a confused but considerable wealth in his subconscious mind. With the gradual assertion of consciousness and will, the need to create order and clarity, to distinguish between the essential and the accidental becomes imperative. The child is ripe for a re-discovery of his environment and of his inner wealth of impressions of it. In order to realize this need he requires an exact and scientific guide, such as that given by our apparatus and exercises. He may be compared to an heir unconscious of the great treasure he possesses, eager to appreciate them with the knowledge of a professional connoisseur and to catalogue and classify them so as to have them at his full and immediate disposal.

If doubt as to the permanence of increased and refined sensorial activity in certain walks of life seems possible, this last achievement certainly seems to be an acquisition of the greatest permanence. Generally the first aim of sense training has been taken as the reason of the importance given to it in our Method, while the second to us is not less, but actually its prime motive. Our experience and that of our followers has only served to strengthen our idea.

We may, in conclusion, mention the great service rendered by our sensorial apparatus and the exercises done with it, for the detection of defects in the functions of the senses at a period when much can yet be done towards remedying them.

GENERAL REFERENCE TO THE MATERIAL FOR THE EDUCATION OF THE SENSES

Material for training the senses comprises a system of objects which are grouped together according to some definite quality which they possess, such as colour, shape, dimension, sound, surface texture, weight, temperature, etc. Examples of these are: A set of bells which reproduce musical tones; a collection of tablets which present different colours in a graduated scale; a group of solids which have the same shape but graduated dimensions and others which differ among themselves in geometrical form; things of different weight but of the same size, etc., etc.

Objects of every single group represent the same quality but in different degree; it is then a question of gradation in which the difference between object and object varies regularly, and is when possible fixed mathematically.

Such general rules are, however, subject to a practical consideration which depends on the mentality of the child; and as being suitable for education there will be chosen, as the result of experience, only material which effectively interests the little child and attracts him into doing voluntarily and repeatedly an exercise chosen by himself.

Every group of objects (material for sounds, material for colours, etc.) which presents a gradation has therefore its extremes, the maximum and minimum of the series, which determine the limits of it and which, more correctly, are fixed by the use which

10

the child makes of it. These two extremes, when brought together, demonstrate the most striking difference which exists in the series, and thus establish the most outstanding contrast which the material renders possible. The contrast, being a striking one, makes the difference very evident and even before he has used the things the child is interested in them.

ISOLATION OF A SINGLE QUALITY IN THE MATERIAL

Whatever object we wish to use for the education of the senses, it, of necessity, presents many diverse qualities like weight, roughness, colour, form, size, etc. How then ought we to proceed so that the series will bring one quality only into prominence? We must isolate, from among the many, one single quality. This difficulty is overcome by the series itself and its gradations; we must prepare objects identical among themselves in all respects except the variable quality.

If we want objects suitable for teaching colour differences, we must have them made of the same substance, form and size and differing in colour only. Or, if we want to prepare objects with a view to teaching the various tones of the musical scale, it is necessary that they be perfectly alike in appearance, as are the bells which we use in our system; these are of the same shape and size and are mounted on identical supports, but when struck with a small mallet, they give out different sounds and these sounds constitute the only difference, perceptible to the senses.

For this reason the little instruments which are put into the hands of children as musical toys, which have longer or shorter rods or tubes of different heights arranged like organ pipes, do not lend themselves to a real exercise in musical sense, tending to differentiate sounds; for the eye is able to help in distinguishing them, being guided by the different dimensions, whereas the ear ought to be the sole receiver and the sole judge.

This method is successful in differentiating between things very clearly; it is evident that clearness constitutes the principal factor for raising interest in making distinctions.

On the psychological side, it is known that to enhance any single quality, it is necessary to isolate the senses as far as possible. A tactile impression is clearer if it is confined to an object which does not conduct heat, that is, which does not at the same time give rise to sensations of temperature, and if the subject stands in a dark, silent place, free from ocular or auditory impressions which disturb the tactile impressions, the process may be doubled—in the subject isolated from all other impressions arising in the surroundings; in the material with its system graduated in respect of one quality only.

This precision, which serves as the standard of perfection at which we must aim, renders possible a work of internal and external analysis fitted to bring order into the mind of the child.

The little child, who is by nature an eager explorer of his surroundings because he has not yet had time or means for getting to know them intimately, willingly ' closes his eyes ' or is blindfolded in order to shut out the light when he is exploring shapes with his hands, or willingly accepts darkness in order to listen to slight noises.

FUNDAMENTAL QUALITIES COMMON TO EVERYTHING IN THE EDUCATIONAL ENVIRONMENT OF THE CHILD

To the above-mentioned characters, others have to be added; these, however, do not refer exclusively to sense-objects, but must be made to include everything which surrounds the child. They are as follows:

1. *The Control of Error.* In several cases the materials offered to the child involve in themselves the ' control of error,' as is instanced by the solid insets; these have wooden bases which are provided with holes into which are fitted cylinders of graduated dimensions, ranging from narrow to wide, or from tall to short, or from small to large. As the hollows correspond exactly to the cylinders to be deposited in them, it is not possible to place them wrongly, since at the end there would remain one without a place; this indicates that an error has been made.

In the same way, when buttoning is being done, if the procedure is bungled or one button is forgotten, the fact is revealed at the end by an empty button-hole. In other materials, as in the three series of blocks, the colour, size, etc. of the objects and the fact that the child has already accustomed himself to recognizing errors, bring mistakes into evidence.

The material control of error leads the child to apply to his doings his reasoning power, his critical faculty, an attention which grows more and more interested in exactitude and an intelligence growing more alert to distinguish small differences. In this way the mind of the child is prepared to control errors, even when these are not material and apparent to the senses.

Not only the objects are set apart for the education of the senses and for general culture, but the whole environment is prepared in such a way as to make the control of mistake an easy matter. All objects, from the furniture to the special material for development, are informers whose warning voices cannot be ignored.

Bright colours and shining surfaces denounce spots; the lightness of the furniture tells of movement which is still imperfect and clumsy by noisy falls and scrapings on the floor. Thus the whole environment forms a stern educator, a sentinel always on the alert, and each child hears its warnings as if it stood alone in front of this inanimate teacher.

2. *Æsthetics.* Another character of the objects is that they are attractive. Colour, brightness and harmony of form are sought after in everything which surrounds the child. Not only the sensorial material, but also the environment is so prepared that it will attract him, as in Nature brilliant petals attract insects to drink the nectar which they conceal.

" Use me carefully," say the clean, polished tables; " Do not leave me idle," say the little brooms with their handles painted with tiny flowers; " Dip your little hands in here," say the washbasins, so clean and ready with their soap and brushes.

The pieces of cloth for fastening up having silver buttons placed on green material, the beautiful pink cubes, the tablets of sixty-three graded colours, the beautiful coloured letters of the alphabet lying in their compartments—all these are invitations given by things.

The child obeys any object which at that moment corresponds with his most acute need for action. In the same way in a field, the petals of all the flowers are calling to other living things with their perfumes and their colours, but the insects chooses the flower which is made for him.

3. *Activity*. Another character of the material of development is that it must lend itself to the activity of the child. The possibility of rousing the interest and attention of the child does not depend so much on the quality of things as on the opportunities which they offer for doing something with them.

That is, in order to make a thing interesting, it is not enough that it should be interesting in itself, but it must lend itself to the motor activity of the child. There must be, for instance, small objects which can be moved from their places; it is then the movements of the hand which pleases the child as he busily makes and unmakes something, displaces and replaces things many times in succession, thus making prolonged occupation possible. A very beautiful toy, an attractive picture, a wonderful story, may doubtless rouse the interest of the child, but if the child may only look and listen and touch an object which remains in its place, his interest will be superficial and will pass from one object to another. Hence the environment is all so planned that it lends itself to the child's love of being active; it is beautiful, but that would interest the child for only a single day, whilst the fact that every object may be removed, used and put back in its place makes the attractions of the surroundings inexhaustible.

4. *The Limits*. Finally another principle common to all the material means provided for education is the following, up till now very little understood and yet of the very highest pedagogic interest: the material must be limited in quantity. This fact, once stated, is logically clear to our understanding; the normal child does not need stimuli to wake him up, to put him in connection

with the material world. He is awake and his connections with the outside world are innumerable and unbroken. His need, instead, is to bring order into the chaos which is created in his mind by the multitude of sensations which the world has given him. He is not asleep in life like the deficient child; he is an ardent explorer in a world which is new to him, and like an explorer, what he needs is a *road* (that is, something limited and direct) which may lead him to his objective and save him from the wearying deviations which hinder his progress. Then he is passionately attached to those things, limited and direct in their scope, which bring order into the chaos accumulated within him. They set up conditions of clarity in his exploring mind and furnish him with a guide in his exploring operations. The explorer, at first abandoned to himself, becomes then an enlightened man, who at every step, makes new discoveries and advances with the strength which is given by inward satisfaction.

How this experience ought to modify the conception still held by many that the child is helped in proportion to the quantity of educational objects which can be placed at his disposal! We all believe wrongly that the child who has the most toys, who gets the most help, ought to be the best developed. Instead of that, the confused multitude of things raises new chaos in his mind, and oppresses him with discouragement.

The limits to the aids which enable the child to reduce his mind to order, and to make it easy for him to understand the infinite number of things which surround him, are represented by the maximum necessity for economizing his energy and for enabling him to advance along the difficult way of development.

THE EXERCISES

HOW THE TEACHER OUGHT TO GIVE LESSON

Comparison with the Old Systems

THE lessons to initiate the children in the education of the senses, are *individual* lessons. The mistress makes an almost timid attempt at *approaching* a child, whom she presumes to be ready to receive it. She sits down at his side and brings an object which she deems capable of interesting him.

In this lies the preparation of the mistress. She should have been trained in attempting experiments only; the response she expects from the child is that an activity is aroused in him which urges him to use the material that has been presented.

The lesson constitutes a call for attention. The object, if it meets the inner requirements of the child and represents something which will satisfy them, incites the child to prolonged activity, for he makes himself master of it and uses it again and again.

Words are not always necessary; very often showing how to use the object is all that is needed as a lesson. But when it is necessary to speak and to initiate the child into the use of the material of development and culture, the characteristic of such a lesson must be its brevity; perfection is achieved in speaking the necessary and sufficient minimum. Dante is teaching these mistresses when he says, " See that thy words be counted ".

A lesson will approach closer to perfection in proportion to the number of words which we contrive to leave out. Special care must be devoted in the preparation of a lesson to counting and choosing the words which will have to be spoken.

Another quality characteristic of the lesson is its simplicity; it ought to be shorn of everything but the absolute truth. That the mistress should not lose herself in empty words is included in the first quality; this second thought is therefore a character of the first, that is, the counted words ought to be of the simplest kind and should represent the exact truth.

The third quality of the lesson is its objectivity, which means that the personality of the teacher disappears, and there remains in evidence only the object on which it is desired that the attention of the child should be focussed. The short and simple lesson is for the most part an explanation of the object and of the use which the child can make of it.

The teacher will take note as to whether or not the child is interested in the object, in what manner he shows his interest, for how long, etc. and she will take care never to force the child into following her when he does not seem to be interested in what she is offering. If then the lesson, prepared with due regard to brevity, simplicity and verity is not understood by the child as an explanation of the object, the mistress must be given two warnings: first, not to insist on repeating the lesson; second, to refrain from making the child understand that he has made a mistake, or that he has not understood, because that might arrest for a long time the impulse to act, which forms the whole foundation of progress.

Let us suppose, for example, that the teacher wishes to teach a child the two colours, red and blue. She wishes to attract the child's attention to the object; so she says to him: " Look, pay attention." If she aims at teaching him the names of the colours, she says, showing the red one, " This is red," raising her voice and pronouncing the word ' red ' very slowly. Then she shows the other colour with " This is blue." In order to test whether or not the child has understood, she says to him, " Give me the red, give me the blue." Suppose the child makes a mistake; the mistress neither repeats nor insists; she smiles and puts away the colours.

Ordinary teachers are amazed at such simplicity; they usually say, " Everyone can do this." Really we have here again something like the story of the egg of Christopher Columbus, but the fact is that they cannot all do it. In practice estimating one's own actions is very difficult; all the more so in the case of ordinary teachers trained according to the old methods. They overwhelm the child with a deluge of useless words and misstatements.

For instance, in dealing with the example just given, an ordinary teacher would have had recourse to collective teaching, attaching excessive importance to the simple thing which she had to teach and compelling all the children to follow her, when perhaps not all of them were inclined to do so. Possibly she would begin her lesson in this way: " Children, can you guess what I have in my hand?" She knows that the children cannot guess and she thus claims their attention with a falsehood. Then she probably would say: " Children, do you ever take a little look at the sky? Have you ever seen it? Have you ever gazed at it at night when it is glittering with stars? No? Look at my apron, do you know what colour it is? Does it seem to you to be of the same colour as the sky? Well, look at the colour which I have here; it is the same as the sky and my apron, it is *blue*. Look all round about; do you see any other things which are blue? And do you know what colour cherries are? And burning coals? " etc., etc.

In this way the child's mind, after the bewilderment of guessing, is overcome by a mass of ideas—the sky, aprons, cherries, etc.; from this confusion it is difficult for him to perform the task of extracting the subject, the aim of the lesson, which is to recognize the two colours, blue and red. Further such a feat of selection is impossible for the mind of a child, especially considering that he is not able to follow a long speech.

I remember being present at an arithmetic lesson in which children were being taught that two and three make five. For this purpose was used a checkered board set up so that balls could be fixed into corresponding holes. For example, two balls were placed at a higher level, three lower down and finally five of them. I do not remember exactly the proceedings adopted in this lesson; I know, however, that the teacher had to place beside the two upper balls a paper dancer wearing a blue tunic, which was christened there and then with the name of a child in the class —" This is Mariettina." Then beside the three balls was placed another dancer, differently dressed, who was " Gigina ". I do not know precisely how the teacher arrived at a demonstration of the sum, but she certainly talked for a long time with these dancers, moved them about and so on. If *I* remember the dancers better than the working out of the sum, what would it have meant for the children? If by such means they have not learnt that two and three make five, they must at least have made a great mental effort, and the mistress must have talked with the dancers for many hours!

In another lesson the mistress wished to show the difference between noise and sound. She began by telling a rather long story to the children; suddenly someone working in agreement with her knocked noisily at the door. The mistress broke off her story to cry: " What is it? What has happened? What have they done? What is it, children? Oh, I have lost the thread of my ideas; I cannot go on with the story; I can remember nothing; I must let it go. Do you know what is the matter? Have you heard? Have you understood? It is a *noise*! *That* is a noise. Oh, I would rather nurse this baby." (She takes up a mandoline wrapped up in a cover.) " Dear baby, I prefer to play with you. Do you see it? Do you see this baby which I am holding in my arms? " Some of the children call out, " It is not a baby "; others, " It is a mandoline." The teacher says: " No, no, it is a baby, a real baby; I am very fond of it, it is really a baby. Do you want a proof of it? Oh, do be quiet; it seems to me that it is weeping, that it is crying out. Oh, will it perhaps say 'papa' and 'mama'?" She touches the strings underneath the covering. "Ah, did you hear? Did you hear what it did? Did it weep, did it call out?" Some of the children say: "It is the mandoline, it is the strings, you have touched them." The mistress answers, "Quiet, children, listen carefully to what I do." She uncovers the mandoline, and touches the strings lightly, "That is a *sound!*"

To expect the child as the result of such a lesson to understand the intention of the teacher, that she wanted to show the difference between noise and sound, is impossible. The child will have understood that the teacher wanted to make a joke. It will think that she is rather silly to lose the thread of her discourse because of a mere noise and that she confuses a mandoline with a baby. Certainly the figure of the mistress will be well fixed in the child's mind, but not the object of the lesson.

To get a simple lesson from a teacher trained according to the usual methods is a most laborious business. I remember that, after many explanations on the subject, I asked one of my teachers to teach by the use of the insets (vide later) the difference between a square and a triangle. She had merely to get a square and a triangle of wood fitted into empty spaces which suited them, make the child trace with its finger the outlines of the inset pieces and of the frame and say: "This a square," "This is a triangle." The mistress, making them touch the outlines, began by saying: "This is one line, another, another, another; there are four; just count with your finger how many there are. And the corners? Count the corners, feel them with your finger, press on them; there are four of them also. Look at it carefully; it is a square!" I corrected the teacher, pointing out to her that she was not teaching them to recognize a shape, but was giving them ideas about sides, angles, numbers—a very different thing from what she had to teach. But she defended herself saying, "It is the same thing." It is not the same thing, it is the geometrical and mathematical analysis of the thing. One could have grasped the idea of a square form without knowing how to count up to four, and therefore without finding out the number of sides and angles. Sides and angles are abstractions which do not exist of themselves; what does exist is a piece of wood of a definite shape. Again, the lengthy explanations of the teacher not only confused the child's mind, but crossed that abyss which separates the concrete from the abstract, the shape of an object from mathematics.

Suppose, I said to the teacher, that an architect was showing you a cupola, the form of which interested you. He might give you two illustrations. He might point out to you the beauty of the surroundings, the harmony of the parts; might make you ascend and climb round the dome itself in order to appreciate the relative proportions of its parts, so that the appearance of the whole should be realized, and then recognized and believed in. Or he might make you count the windows, the wide and the narrow cornices and finally make a drawing of the structure, to illustrate the laws of stability and to teach you the algebraic formulæ necessary to be resolved for the calculations relative to these laws. In the first case you would visualize the form of the cupola; in the second, you would understand nothing and instead of an impression of the cupola you would get one of this architect who imagined that he was talking to engineering colleagues instead of to a lady who was travelling for amusement. The case is just the same. Instead of saying to the child, " This is a square," and simply make him touch it and ascertain its material outlines, we proceed to the geometrical analysis of it. We believe that it is premature to teach plane geometrical forms to the child, just because we associate them with the mathematical concept. But the child is not incapable of appreciating simple form; in fact, he can see square windows and tables without making any effort; his eye rests on all the forms round about him. To direct his attention to one particular form is to make it stand out clearly and to fix an idea of it. In the same way, we ourselves may be standing on the margin of a lake, looking at its shores without taking much notice, when suddenly an artist comes up and exclaims: "How exquisite is the bend which the bank makes under the shadow of that cliff!" We at once feel the hitherto life-less scene come to life within our consciousness as if illumined by a ray of sunshine and we experience the joy of having realized to the full what we had felt before only imperfectly.

This is our mission: to cast a ray of light and pass on.

I compare the effects of these first lessons with the impressions of a solitary wanderer who is walking, serene and happy, in a shady grove, meditating; that is, leaving his inner thought free to wander. Suddenly a church bell pealing out nearby recalls him to himself; then he feels more keenly that peaceful bliss which had already been born, though dormant, within him.

To stimulate life, leaving it free, however, to unfold itself, that is the first duty of the educator.

For such a delicate mission great art is required to suggest the right moment and to limit intervention, lest one should disturb or lead astray rather than help the soul which is coming to life and which will live by virtue of its own efforts.

This art must accompany the scientific method, because the simplicity of our lessons bears a great resemblance to experiments in experimental psychology.

As soon as the teacher has touched the hearts of her pupils, one by one, awakening and reviving life in them as if by the touch of an invisible fairy, she will possess these hearts; and a sign, a word will be sufficient, because each of them is keenly aware of her, acknowledges her and listens to her.

There will come a day when the mistress, to her great astonishment, will realize that all the children obey her like gentle baby lambs, not only ready for her signal but watching for it. They regard her as one who gives them life, and they hope insatiably to receive new life from her.

Experience has revealed this to us and what constitutes the greatest marvel for those who visit the Children's Houses is that collective discipline is obtained as if by some magic power. Fifty or sixty children from two and a half to six years of age, all together, at a single sign, keep silent so perfectly that the absolute silence is like the solemn stillness of a desert; and if a gentle order, expressed in a low voice, tells the babies: " Stand up, walk about for a moment on the tips of your toes and then go back to your places in silence," they all together, like a single person, rise and execute the movements with the minimum of noise. The teacher, by her one voice, has spoken to each one and every one hopes to get from her intervention some light, some inner joy and goes onward, intent and obedient, like an earnest explorer who is following a way of his own.

Here again is something like the egg of Christopher Columbus. A concert conductor must train the members of his orchestra one by one if he is to secure from their collective efforts a noble harmony; and each artist must make himself perfect before he is fitted to obey the silent guidance of the conductor's baton. We, on the contrary, in the ordinary school, instal as a conductor one who teaches, at one and the same time, to instruments and voices of the most diverse characters, the same monotonous and even discordant melody.

So it is in society that the most highly disciplined are the most perfected men; but perfection of behaviour, for instance among English citizens, is not of the heavy, brutal, military type.

We are full of prejudices rather than of wisdom as regards child psychology. Up till now, we wanted to dominate the children from the outside with the rod, instead of trying to subdue them internally by guiding them like human beings. Thus it is that they have passed close by us without our getting to know them.

But when we throw aside the artificiality in which we tried to wrap them and the violence which we deceived ourselves into thinking meant disciplining them, then they reveal themselves to us under a new aspect.

Their gentleness is sweet and absolute, and their love of knowledge is such that it enables them to overcome obstacles by which one might have imagined their desires would be obstructed.

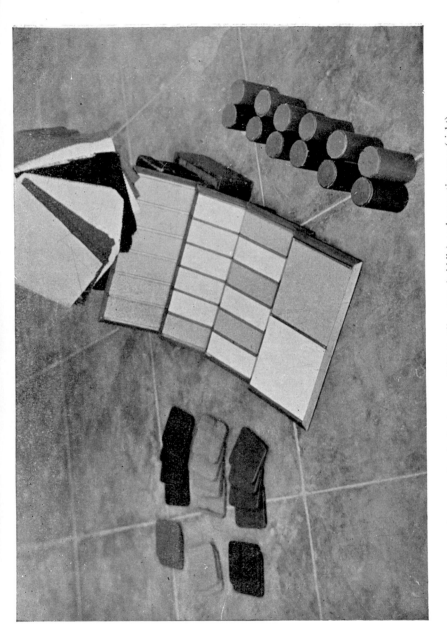

Apparatus for the baric sense (left), tactile sense (middle) and acoustic sense (right).

How to Initiate the Child into the Exercises
With the Sense Material, Contrasts, Identities, Gradations

One ought to begin with very few contrasting stimuli, for which purpose is collected a number of objects similar in kind but showing gradation, growing finer and less perceptible. For example, when it is a matter of recognizing tactile differences, we begin with only two surfaces, one perfectly smooth and the other very rough; if we are experimenting with the weight of things, first will be presented tablets which are the lightest of the series and afterwards the heaviest; for sounds, the two extremes of the graduated series are offered; for colours, the brightest and most highly contrasting tints like red and yellow are chosen; for shapes, a circle and a triangle, and so on.

In order to make the differences still clearer, it is well to mix together with the greatest contrasts the identities (in contrast to the great differences), offering a double series of objects; in a mixture of pairs, in which all are mixed in confusion, would be sought similar things two by two—two sounds equally loud and two equally faint, two things having the same yellow colour and two of an identical red. The exercise of searching for similarities among contrasts marks the differences strongly, by making them prominent.

The final exercise, that of gradation, consists in placing in graded order a system of similar objects mixed up confusedly; for example, a series of cubes of the same colour but of different dimensions, the difference being systematically graduated (for example, having a difference of 1 cm. in the length of the sides). Of a similar character will be the presentation of a series of yellow objects, the shades of which will grow gradually paler, from dark to light; or a series of rectangles having one pair of equal sides fixed, and the other decreasing systematically. Such objects must be arranged side by side in the positions which they should occupy in a graduated series.

Technique for Beginning Tactile Exercises

Although the tactile sense is distributed over the whole skin, the exercises with which the children begin are limited to the tips of the fingers and in particular to those of the right hand.

Such a limitation is rendered necessary in practice and is also an educational necessity, inasmuch as it prepares for daily life, when man exercises and utilizes the tactile sense with these very areas.

The exercise is specially useful for our educational aims, for as we shall see, the various exercises of the hand form an indirect and remote preparation for writing.

I make the children wash their hands well with soap in a hand-basin; then in a nearby basin they have to give them a short bath of tepid water. Then I make them dry them and a slight massage completes the preparatory work of the bath. Then I teach the child to ' touch,' that is, the way to touch the surface, for it is necessary to take the child's fingers and guide them so that they stroke the surface very lightly. Another detail of the method is to teach the child to keep his eyes closed whilst he is touching, encouraging him by saying that he will feel better and that he will recognize, without seeing them, changes in the surface. The child learns at once and shows his great pleasure in the proceedings. So true is this that, on occasions after the exercises have been practised for some time, when we enter the Children's House, it often happens that the children run forward to meet us, close their eyes and with the very lightest of touches feel the palms of our hands, trying to find the places where the skin is smoothest; or they stroke our clothes, especially silk or velvet trimmings. They are really exercising the tactile sense, for they never seem to tire of touching smooth surfaces like satin. They become very skilful in discerning the differences between polished cards.

The material for first use consists of:

(*a*) A very long rectangular wooden board, which is divided into two equal rectangles, one covered with extremely smooth paper, the other with rough paper.

(*b*) A board resembling (*a*), but covered with alternating strips of smooth and rough paper.

(*c*) A similar board having strips graduated from roughness in decreasing stages towards smoothness.

(*d*) A board on which are placed papers uniform in size and varying in smoothness from parchment to the smooth cardboard of the first board.

These boards, which keep immovable the different objects to be touched, serve to prepare the hand for touching things lightly, in addition to giving lessons in identifying differences in a systematic manner.

The child, with his eyes closed, strokes the different areas of the board and thus begins to measure distances by the movement of his arm.

As in many of the exercises which are called sensorial, the sensitive stimulus is a means of leading to the determination of movements.

To follow this first series, I have prepared movable material, each part constituting a group by itself and therefore determining a separate exercise.

The collections comprise:

(*a*) Smooth cards of varying grade,

(*b*) Graduated sandpaper cards,

(*c*) *Fabrics* of different kinds.

This material is used in the usual way, that is, by mixing up the objects of a series, proceeding sometimes in pairs, sometimes in graduated order.

The fabrics are duplicated in pairs and are kept in a special little cupboard which contains velvet, silk, wool, cotton, linen, net, etc. The children are able to learn the names of these materials.

All the above-mentioned exercises are carried out with the eyes bandaged.

IMPRESSIONS OF TEMPERATURE

I utilize for this exercise various small metal receptacles, of ovoid shape and hermetically closed. Using warm water at a

11

constant temperature (75°C), I place some of it in gradually differing quantity into every vessel and then fill up the rest with cold
water at 15°C.   Or I prepare receptacles in equal pairs.   Although
the temperatures change quickly during the operation, the exercise
nevertheless serves to give a certain amount of exactness.

A series of substances which differ in their heat-conducting
properties, like wood, felt, glass, marble, iron, is used for more
delicate exercises.

IMPRESSIONS OF WEIGHT

For the education of the baric sense rectangular tablets 6 cms.
by 8 cms. in area and ½ cm. thick, made of three different
qualities of wood—wistaria, walnut and fir—are used; they weigh
respectively, gr. 24, 18, 12; that is, they differ by gr. 6.   They ought
to be very smooth and brightly polished, so that all roughness is
removed; the natural colour of the wood remains.   The child,
whilst observing the colour, knows that they have different weights,
which gives him a check for his exercise.   He takes two tablets
into his hand, places them on the palm with the fingers extended,
and executes an up-and-down movement in order to gauge the
weight; such a movement should, little by little, be made unnoticeable.   The child is advised to proceed to make comparisons with
his eyes closed; so he grows accustomed to acting by himself with
great interest, in order to see if he guesses.

The above-mentioned methods refer to a technique which is
necessary for reaching sufficient exactitude in the estimation of
weights.   It is absolutely necessary to place the object lightly on
the skin, avoiding any feeling of temperature (hence the wood),
in order to obtain a true and exact idea of the weight of the particular object.   Moving the hand up and down alters the weight by
altering the atmospheric pressure which is bearing down on it and
by making the weight more appreciable.   This method of ' sub-
weighing ' is instinctive, but in order to secure a more exact
valuation of the weight of the object it is necessary to make these
movements as small as possible.

Here we see the concentrated balancing of the baric tablets with closed eyes. The expression of the face betrays the intelligent inner activity. Below: Two sound-boxes are compared in order to find a pair of identical noises among the slightly graded contrasts. Photo by Mrs. V. A. Baker in an English Montessori School.

The above method of procedure reaches a pitch of exactitude which in itself is very interesting.

IMPRESSION OF FORM THROUGH TOUCH ALONE
(EDUCATION OF THE STEREOGNOSTIC SENSE)

To recognize the form of an object by feeling it all over, or rather touching it with the finger-tips (as the blind do) means something more than exercising the tactile sense.

The fact is that through touch one perceives only the superficial qualities of smoothness and roughness. But, whilst the hand (and the arm) is moving all round the object, there is added to the tactile impression that of the movement carried out. Such an impression is attributed to a special sense (a sixth sense) which is called the muscular sense, and which permits many impressions to be stored up in a 'muscular memory,' or a memory of movements accomplished.

It is possible for us to move without touching anything and to be able to reproduce and remember the movement made, with regard to its direction, the limits of extension, etc. (a pure consequence of muscular sensations). But when we touch something as we move, two sensations are mixed up together—tactile and muscular—giving rise to that sense which the psychologists call the " stereognostic sense ". In this case, there is acquired not only an impression of movement accomplished, but knowledge of an external object. This knowledge may be integrated with that gained through vision, thus giving a more concrete exactness to the perception of the object. This is very noticeable in little children who seem to be possessed of greater certainty in recognizing things, and above all greater facility in remembering them when they handle them than when they only see them. This fact is made evident by the very nature of the children in their early years. They touch everything they see, obtaining the double image (visual and muscular) of the innumerable different things with which they come in contact in their environment.

But this ' touching everything,' besides being a verification of vision, is, according to our experience, the visible expression of a very acute muscular sensibility which exists in the small child during that period of its life when are fixed the fundamental co-ordinations of movement.

It is not then a question only of verifying vision, but of performing the movement itself, and of building up that physiological edifice which is the co-ordination of movements necessary for preparing the organs of expression.

Furthermore, the fact that nearly all the sensorial exercises are accompanied by movements shows how the muscular sensibility may possess, in early years, a pre-eminent function. For this reason we have used extensively in our method the stereognostic sense, for the furthering of education itself, in the matters of its expressive manifestations (drawing, writing, etc.), and to attain this end, which for us implies special value in these sensations, we have paid particular attention to the development of it in the formative period of early childhood.

On this subject we have conducted wonderful experiments with educational success, which deserve to be described that they may offer help to the teacher.

The first material used consisted of Froebel's cubes and bricks. Having called the attention of the child to the shapes of the two solids, we made him feel them over carefully with his eyes open, whilst we repeated some sentences with which to keep his attention fixed on the details. After that the child was told to put the cubes on the right hand and the bricks on the left, fingering them all the time without looking at them. Finally the exercise was repeated by the child blindfolded. Almost all the children succeeded in doing the exercise and after a few repetitions every error was eliminated. The bricks and cubes were twenty-four in number; therefore the attention could be kept fixed for a long time on this kind of game. But without a doubt its maintenance is assisted by the child's knowledge that he is being watched by curious companions ready to laugh at his mistakes and also by his own pride in guessing. On one occasion one of the teachers presented to me a little girl of three, that is, one of the smallest, who had been in the habit of repeating the exercise perfectly. We placed the little one comfortably in her armchair close to the table; we put the twenty-four objects on the table, mixing them together; and after having called her attention to their shape, we asked her to place the cubes on the right and the bricks on the left. Having been blindfolded, she began the exercise as we teach it, that is, taking up by chance two objects with the two hands at the same time, feeling them all over and putting them into their places. Sometimes she picked up two cubes, sometimes two bricks, or a brick in the right hand and a cube in the left. The child had to recognize the form and remember throughout the exercise the position assigned to the different objects. That seemed to me very difficult for a child three years of age.

But as I watched her I noticed that she not only carried out the exercise very easily, but also that she did not require to explore the objects by feeling them. In fact, directly she took up the two objects, handling them with a very light touch because she was a child rather graceful and elegant in her actions, if it happened that the brick was in her right hand and the cube in her left, she *immediately* exchanged them, *then* began the laborious stroking with the hand as she had been taught, which she regarded as a duty; but the objects had already been recognized by her solely by touching them lightly, that is, the recognition took place directly she took them up. Studying the subject afterwards, I realized that the child possessed functional ambidextry, which is very common among children of three or four years old, but which disappears later. I then had the exercise repeated by more children and found that they recognized the objects before feeling them over, and that this happened often among the smaller children. Our educational methods therefore constituted wonderful practice in association, and were admirably adapted to the age of childhood.

These exercises in the stereognostic sense may be extended a great deal and amuse the children greatly, because they are not concerned with the perception of merely one stimulus, such as that of heat, but reconstruct a whole, well-known object. They can stroke the toy soldiers, the balls and above all the money. They gain the power ultimately to discriminate between things which are small and closely related, like bird-seeds and rice.

They are proud of seeing without eyes; they shout, holding out their hands: " Here are my eyes, I see with my hands, I do not need eyes." And I always reply to these gay cries: " Ah, well! let us all get rid of our eyes; what more shall we do?" And they break out into laughter and cheers.

Truly our little ones, walking in ways beyond our vision, make us wonder at their unforeseen, unexpected progress; and, whilst they seem sometimes to be little creatures mad with joy, we are left in profound meditation.

Later on, the children showed an inspiration which has been adopted and which today forms part of the most interesting exercises in the Children's Houses. They have begun to use over again systematically all the material which lends itself to being recognized by the feel of it—the solid insets, the geometrical insets and the three series of blocks. Children who have forsaken them some time before to pass on to more advanced work return to take up the three stands of solid insets, and, blindfold, set about feeling the cylinders and the corresponding holes, often taking all the three stands and mixing up the cylinders of the three series. Or, going back to the geometrical insets, with closed eyes, they follow their outlines accurately and almost thoughtfully, seeking the corresponding space in the frame. Very often the children place themselves on the ground on rugs and repeatedly stroke the long rods, running their fingers down them from top to bottom, as if to determine the extent of the movement made by the arm; or seated, they gather round them the cubes of the pink tower and build it up with their eyes closed.

Muscular exercise, therefore, does over again all the education which, through sight (as will be described later) leads to the exact appreciation of differences in the shapes and dimensions of objects.

SELF-EDUCATION IN TASTE AND SMELL

The exercises relative to these senses are not very easily rendered attractive. I can only say that exercises like those commonly adopted in psychometry do not seem to me suitable and practicable at least for little children.

So our second experiment was to organize 'games of the senses,' which the children could repeat among themselves. We made the child smell fresh scented violets and jasmine; or in late May, we used the roses gathered for the flower vases. Then we blindfolded a child, saying to him, " Now we are going to give you some presents; we will present you with some flowers." A companion brings close to his nose perhaps a bunch of violets, which the child is expected to recognize. Then, as a test in intensity, he is presented a single flower, or a quantity of flowers.

Then we adopted the simpler idea of letting the environment do a great part of the educational work. Really, the odours for exercising the senses must first of all be available and as they are not necessarily in existence around us, like light and like the sound which results from every movement, we got the idea of dispersing perfumes systematically in the surroundings, arranging to make them more and more delicate.

Some sachets decorated in Chinese fashion were hung up as ornaments, attached to the walls. Flowers and garden herbs, soaps scented with natural perfumes such as almond and lavender were prepared and placed round the children.

Only later, having made little plots of sweet herbs, forming almost a green alley, in order that colour should not claim attention as happens with pretty flowers, we found that the greatest interest in finding different odours existed in children about three years of age. To our astonishment, we saw little ones bringing to us small herbs which we had not cultivated and which we did not know to have scent; but when the children insisted and we smelt them, we discovered that they really possessed a delicate perfume.

The ground thus cultivated, in which uniformity of colour and only slight differences in shape combine to isolate, up to a certain point, the olfactory sensations, is a place of 'research' and therefore of exercise for the olfactory sense.

When the attention is directed methodically into activity through various sensorial stimuli, even smell is more intelligently exercised and becomes an organ for exploring the surroundings.

But that smell acts naturally in conjunction with taste in the act of feeding was more clearly shown to us even in the smallest children through their ability to choose or to reject foods. This part of education is mixed up with nutritional life, but is so delicate that it deserves special treatment. Remembering that taste identifies only the four fundamental tastes, one understands how it is that the most natural place to exercise the olfactory sense is that of the meal.

Getting children to distinguish sensations due solely to taste, to know the four fundamental tastes, excites undoubted interest. Whilst sweet and saline are both pleasing tastes, even bitter is tried as an experiment, and acid, especially in various fruits, is distinguished in its different degrees.

Once interest has been roused in tastes and the very distinct limitation of them, the world of odours is distinguished more clearly in the vast variety of those mixed sensations of smell and taste which is met with in nutrition—as in milk, fresh and dry bread, soup, fruit, etc. And the tactile sensations of the tongue, such as those of sticky, oily substances, are distinguished from those of taste and smell through an effort of the intelligence which is a real and proper exploration of oneself and of the environment.

The method of touching the tongue with a specific solution— bitter, acid, sweet or salt—such as is used in estesiometry,[1] was

[1] Measurement of sensibility.

applied to children of five years, who lent themselves to such research as to a game, amusing themselves by rinsing out their mouths, without suspecting that they were being subjected to experiments clothed by the adult with the solemn mantle of science. In the meantime the little things had reserved the serious sides of their minds to search for those perfumes which Nature has bestowed on the small herbs of the field.

VISUAL AND AUDITORY DISTINCTIONS

Material: Solid insets and blocks. Recognition of Dimensions by Visual Means only.

The various series demonstrate differences in dimensions. In one series, the differences are concerned with one dimension only (height); in another, there is a graduated difference in two dimensions (area); in another, there is a graduated difference in all three dimensions increasing harmoniously; in another, the difference also concerns the three dimensions, but in the inverse sense.

SOLID INSETS

There are four strong blocks of natural coloured wood, brightly polished; all four have the same shape and dimensions (55 cms. long, 5 cms. high, 8 cms. wide). Each of one of these contains ten insets, which are cylindrical in shape, smooth and slippery and which are handled by means of a knob placed on the top. They can be taken out of, and replaced easily, in holes which, hollowed out in the stand, correspond perfectly and exclusively to each cylinder.

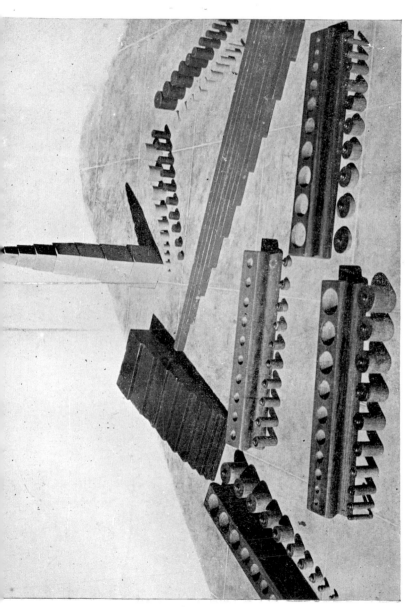

Cylinder Blocks, Pink Tower, Broad Stairs, Long Stairs and Knobless Cylinder Material for the training of visual discrimination of variations in dimension.

The stand together with the cylinders belonging to it, looks rather like the ordinary receptacle for weights belonging to a balance.

Within the cylinders embedded in their supports there exists a regularly graduated difference:

1. In the first stand, the cylinders are all of the same diameter, but differ in height. The shortest is ½ cm. high, and others increase each by half a centimetre, up to the tenth, which is 5 cms. high.

2. In the second stand, the cylinders are all of equal height, but the circular section decreases regularly. Whilst the diameter of the section of the smallest cylinder is ½ cm., the diameters of the other sections increase by half a centimetre up to a diameter of 5 cms.

3. In the third stand, the cylinders diminish in all three dimensions, combining the differences met with in the two other sets.

4. Finally, in the fourth stand, the cylinders differ in three dimensions, but height and section in opposite directions.

At first, the children take only one of the stands, hence four children can find occupation with them at the same time. The exercise is the same with all four insets. After being placed on the table, they are used by removing all the pieces, mixing them up and then replacing them, fitting each piece into its appropriate hole. In this exact correspondence between the cylinder and the hole in the stand there exists the ‘ control of error ’.

If, for example, in the case of the first inset the child makes a mistake in putting it back, one cylinder will disappear within a hole which is too deep, and another will project because one is not deep enough. The irregularity which results, apparent to sight and touch, affords an absolute, material control of the mistake made. It follows that the objects must be put back into their places with care, that the replacement of them must be repeatedly tested, so that all may be in place at the same level in the stand.

Still plainer is the error in another inset apparently the same as the one described; that, however, when carefully noticed, differs from it to some extent. The cylinders are all of the same height, but the circular sections differ gradually from the first to the last; from the smallest to that of largest section. That is, there are narrower and wider cylinders instead of shorter and longer, as were those of the first set. If, handled by the knob which is used to replace them, a cylinder is replaced in a hole too wide for it, the error may for the first moment pass unnoticed and by continuing to inset cylinders narrower than the space needed, there may persist for a long time the illusion that all is going well. But, in the end, there will be left one cylinder for which no place is big enough, one object out of all left outside the stand.

Here the mistake is so glaring that it at once destroys the illusion so long cherished. Attention is directed to an evident problem. All the wrongly placed cylinders must be taken out again and each one put back into its own hole.

We come to another inset of the same kind. Here, the cylinders are graduated according to all the dimensions. Not only are the circular sections diminished gradually as in the second insets, but the heights also decrease from the tallest cylinder to the shortest; the cylinders are thus larger and smaller, keeping the same form with different dimensions. With this inset also, which presents the material control of error, there is repeated a similar exercise.

The four insets, at first sight indistinguishable one from the other, present to the child who uses them their minute differences, and all four by degrees rouse more and more interest, as use reveals them. There follows as a consequence repetition of the exercise, which increases the power of the eye for distinguishing things, makes more acute the faculty of observation, regulates and guides the attention thus trained systematically, stimulates the reasoning power by applying itself to error and its correction, and if one may say so, by laying hold of the mental personality of the child through the senses, furnishes him with constant and far-reaching exercise.

Two examples of the exercises with the apparatus for visual discrimination of dimensional gradations. Note the intentional movement of the hands and the attitude revealing total concentration of mind and body. The careful scrutiny is a clear manifestation of the child's desire for perfection. Top: Montessori School, Adyar, Madras, India. Photo by C. T. Nachiappan. Bottom: Photo taken in an English Montessori School by Mrs. V. A. Baker.

THE BLOCKS

Quite different in external appearance, three sets of blocks repeat the graduation in one, two and three dimensions.

We have here large pieces of wood painted in bright colours, in three systems which we call—the system of rods and lengths, the system of prisms, the system of cubes.

The rods, having the same square section of 2 cms. sides, are painted red, differ from each other by 10 cms. the longest of the series being a metre long; from that the rods decrease by one decimetre at a time.

The manipulation of such long, cumbrous objects demands from the child movement of the whole body. He has to go back and forth to transport these rods and then he has to place them side by side in the order of length, giving to the whole the appearance of organ pipes.

The place for their disposal is the floor, on which, however, the child has previously spread a mat sufficiently large to accommodate himself and the working material, having built up his organ pipes, he pulls them apart, mixes them up and starts afresh, repeating this just as often as he gets pleasure from it.

A similar exercise carried out on mats is that of putting together a series of prisms of chestnut colour, all of the same length (20 cms.), but having different square sections, ranging from 10 cms. sides in the largest square, down to 1 cm. in the smallest. The prisms, from the thickest to the thinnest, are placed one beside the other in graduated order, in a manner which suggests a staircase.

Finally, a series of cubes, the square end of which decreases from 10 cms. to 1 cm., coloured bright pink, presents objects differing in the three dimensions, from the largest to the smallest. The largest cube is placed first on the carpet, then all the rest, one above the other, thus building up a kind of tower. This is demolished, then re-built.

FORCE AND MUSCULAR MEMORY

The children take up the blocks with one hand only. The hand of a child three and a half years old finds it difficult to grasp blocks 10 cms. wide. Besides these and above all, the prisms two decimetres long are heavy for the child. He has, then, to make efforts with his little hand, which stretches and grows stronger. Taking up in repeated exercises all the brown blocks, the hand finally adopts automatically the precise position which is necessary for covering the space of 10 cms. of 9, of 8, of 7, of 6, of 5, of 4, of 3, of 2, of 1; that is, the muscular memory is fixed in agreement with the exact gradation of space. This is repeated with the pink block. Here there is another means of improvement; the cube smaller than that preceding it must be placed in the centre (a strip $\frac{1}{2}$ cm. wide remains all round); the arm and hand must therefore respond to this definite intention; thus they execute precise, purposive movement. Of these, the most difficult belongs to the cube of the least weight, namely the small cube of 1 cm. side. The arm has to be very certain if it is to place this little object in the centre and this is apparent in the intense concentration of the child and his evident efforts.

Without a doubt it is the visual sense which benefits most in the exercises with the solid insets and the blocks. By degrees, the eye begins to distinguish differences which previously were beyond them.

When the four sets of insets are in use together (the children make a triangle of them and deposit in confusion in the space so marked off the cylinders of the four series), it forms an exercise in reasoning and memorizing which is set up, because the comparisons made among the cylinders are most complicated and the recollection of the series to which they belong, and therefore of the stand which will accommodate them, comes into action. The fascination inherent in the exercises is this—that the small intelligence finds it a great piece of work and devotes to it the greatest natural and agreeable effort of which it is capable.

In the case of the blocks also, it is above all the eye which acts in recognizing gradations and therefore in revealing chance errors. Misplaced organ pipes, a staircase which looks as if it had irregular steps, a tower which bulges because a large cube has been placed

Material for the chromatic sense showing pairs of the three fundamental colours, those of the eleven colours and the gradation series

between two others of smaller size—all strike the eye, which is also drawn to them by the bright colours. And this striking whole calls upon the eye to recognize the error and the hand to remedy it by rearrangement.

A fact which accompanies the eye exercise is motor activity, sometimes as the manipulation of the small objects to be moved about (the cylinders of the solid insets), sometimes as carrying and placing heavy blocks of wood. The work of the senses is then carried out by movements which are co-ordinated round some intelligent purpose to be achieved.

By observations made, it is seen that this movement helps to concentrate the attention with constant fixity on a repetitive exercise.

If we consider the relative differences present in the three series of blocks, we find them to be of mathematical proportions.

The ten rods are, individually, in agreement with the numbers —1, 2, 3, 4, 5, 6, 7, 8, 9, 10.

The ten prisms of the same length which, however, vary in cross section, correspond with the squares of the numbers—

$$1^2, 2^2, 3^2, 4^2, 5^2, 6^2, 7^2, 8^2, 9^2, 10^2.$$

Finally, the ten cubes, having three varying dimensions, stand in relationship to the cubes of the numbers—

$$1^3, 2^3, 3^3, 4^3, 5^3, 6^3, 7^3, 8^3, 9^3, 10^3.$$

It is true that these proportions appeal to the child only through the senses, but the mind is working on exact foundations fitted to prepare it for mathematical operations.

The child finds easiest of all the exercises those with the cubes (maximum differences) and most difficult those with the rods (minimum differences).

When, however, in the elementary classes he begins to be interested in arithmetic and geometry, he takes up again the cubes of his early childhood and studies them over again in their relative proportions, applying the science of numbers.

Materials for Colour

The material on which is based the recognition of colours (education of the chromatic sense) is the following, which I have decided upon after a long series of trials with normal children. (In institutions for defectives, I have used insets of wood consisting of many series of round, coloured plaques.) The prescribed material consists of tablets round which are wound threads of vividly coloured silk. The tablets are furnished at their two extremities with double rim, so that the colours will not spread out on the table, and also to make it easier to handle the object without ever touching the coloured thread. In this way, the colour remains unimpaired for a long time.

I have chosen nine colours, and to each of them there correspond seven shades varying in intensity. There are thus 63 colour tablets. The colours are grey (from black to white), red, orange, yellow, green, blue, violet, chestnut (maroon), pink.

Exercises. There are chosen three of the most sharply contrasting colours (e.g. red, blue and yellow), a double set of them, and they are placed on the table in front of the child. Being shown one colour, he is invited to find its match in the mixture. The tablets are arranged in a double column, that is, in pairs of identical colour. Afterwards a gradual increase is made in the number of coloured tablets employed until all nine colours are presented, that is, eighteen tablets.

Finally, two or three tablets of the same colour but of different shades are presented choosing, for example, the lightest, the medium and the darkest of the shades and having them arranged in graded order, until at last all the nine shades are in use.

Successively before the child are placed the given shades of two different colours, mixed up together (e.g., red and blue). The groups have to be separated and each one arranged in graded series. The next stage is to offer, mixed up, colours nearer to each other (e.g. blue and violet, yellow and orange, etc.).

With infinite care the 11 fundamental colours are matched on top. Below a girl arranges the 7 shades of each of the 9 colours from dark to light. Top: Amsterdamsche Montessori School, Holland. Bottom: Photo by Mrs. V. A. Baker in an English Montessori School.

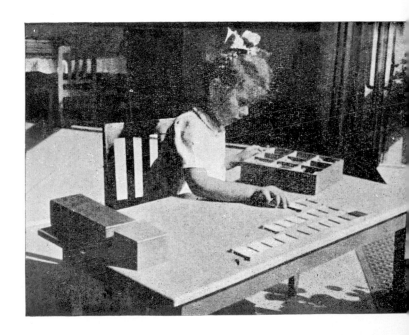

In one Children's House I have watched the following game being carried on, with great and increasing interest and surprising speed. The mistress places on the table round which some children are seated as many grading groups as there are children, e.g., three. She makes every child notice the particular colour which belongs to him and is to be chosen by him. Then she mixes all the groups together on the table. Every child then selects from the complicated heap all the shades of his own colour, makes a pile of them and then proceeds to arrange the shades in a graduated series which resembles a ribbon in which the shades fade away.

In another House I have seen the children take the whole box of sixty-three colours, turn them out on the table, spend a long time mixing up the tablets, then re-form the groups and arrange them in gradation, making up a kind of little mat, beautifully coloured and shaded, spread out on the table.

The children quickly acquire a skill which astonishes us. Children three years old succeed in putting all the shades in graduated order.

One can test the memory for colours by showing a child a certain colour and inviting him to go to a distant table where all the colours are laid out and choose the identical colour. Children succeed in the exercise, making few mistakes. There are children of five years of age who amuse themselves with this last exercise. They are very fond of comparing two shades and making a decision about their identity.

SENSE KNOWLEDGE OF GEOMETRY

PLANE INSETS AND GEOMETRICAL SHAPES

Material:—Flat insets of wood—history. In the school for defectives I had provided insets of the same shapes as those used by my illustrious predecessors, that is, I placed, one above the other, two frames, the lower having a uniform surface, the upper hollowed out into various shapes. To fit within the sockets

12

thus formed corresponding figures of wood, provided with a brass knob so that the handling of them might be easier, were made.

Seguin used a star, a rectangle, a square, a triangle and a circle, differently coloured, so that colour and form were combined; the sockets were all in the same wooden frame.

In my school for defectives I increased the number of examples, separating those to be used for colours from those to be used for shapes. The insets used for colours were all circular plates, whereas those for form were all of the same colour (blue). I provided a large number of frames with many colours, graded, always grouping more figures into the same rigid frame which kept them together.

But in my new experiments with normal children, I completely excluded flat insets for colours, because such material affords no control over error, the child having to cover up the colour needed for comparison.

DEFINITE MATERIAL

I retained the flat insets illustrating form, but I modified the material, separating one figure from another, so as to give to every object to be inset a simple border, one with the piece, almost like what carpenters make in exact joined constructions, which form the first test of the workman's skill.

Every one of the various shapes (squares, rectangles, circles, triangles, trapeziums, ovals, etc.) was painted a bright blue colour, whilst the various borders belonging to each piece were square in shape, all of the same dimensions and yellow in colour. Thus the pieces when separated could be arranged in different combinations for increasing the number of groupings, it being an easy matter to place the square frames side by side.

In order to keep the groups together, I used wooden containers, or frames, large enough to take six squares, and therefore to hold six figures in two rows of three each. The blue background of these containers being indentical in form and colour with the insets themselves comes into view when the framed shapes are deposited there and the insets are taken away.

For the first exercise I used a frame having a rectangular area of the same dimensions (inside the rim) as the frames described; the dark blue interior is surrounded by a raised border about 6 mms. deep and 2 cms. wide. On this frame is hinged a frame-cover made from strips about two centimetres thick, crossed in such a way that they form a rim which fits exactly over the lower structure, and is divided into six equal squares by one transverse and two longitudinal bars. This lattice-work cover turns on a small hinge and is fixed in front with a small stud.

Into the blue background can be fitted exactly six square frames of 10 cms. sides and 6 mms. thick, which are kept in position by the cover when it is closed, because every spar forming the grating is superposed on the extreme sides of the adjacent plaques; the latter thus remain securely in place and the whole can be handled as a single piece.

In addition to the advantage offered by the other pieces described, this frame makes it feasible to have all the combinations possible with the geometrical figures by changing the plaques, as well as that of keeping the individual frames in place.

The border and the external and internal outlines of the frame are enamelled yellow; the pieces to be imbedded (the flat geometrical figures) are blue like the bottom of the frame.

I had provided also four flat plaques of the same yellow colour, because by employing these one can adapt the frame to take only one, two, three, four or five geometrical figures instead of six. It is more helpful, in the first lessons, to work with only two or three contrasting figures, or which at least differ a great deal in shape (e.g., a circle and a square; or a circle, a square and an equilateral triangle).

In such ways we may multiply the possible combinations. A cabinet with six drawers is also provided; it may be of cardboard or of wood. It consists essentially of a box; the six trays or drawers, resting on small side supports, will each hold six plaques. In the first tray are placed six triangles; in the second, a square and five rectangles of the same height and decreasing in breadth; in the third, six polygons from the pentagon to the decagon; in the fourth, six circles decreasing in diameter; in the fifth, two plain plaques, and a rhombus, a rhomboid, a trapezium and a trapezoid; in the sixth, various curved figures such as the ellipse, the oval, a floral design (four crossed arches) and a curved triangle and two plain plaques.

THE THREE SERIES OF CARDS

To this material are added several white square cards of 14 cms. side. On one series of these is printed a geometrical figure of the same blue colour as the inset pieces, embracing in dimensions and shape all the geometrical figures of the collection. On a second series of similar cards are printed, in outline, also in blue, the same geometrical figures, the outline being 1 cm. thick. On a third series of similar cards, is printed with a thin blue line the outlines reproducing the same figures in dimensions and shape. This idea is to be found in Seguin. The material comprises the frame, the collection of plane figures and the three sets of form cards.

Exercise with the insets. This consists in presenting to the child the frame with various figures, taking out the pieces, spreading them out, mixing them up on the table and inviting the child to restore them to their places.

This game is suitable for children even below the age of three, and keeps the child's attention for a long time, though not for so long as the solid insets. I have never seen the exercise repeated here more than five or six times in succession.

The child devotes a great deal of energy to this exercise. He has to recognize the shape and give it a lengthy examination. At first many succeed only after repeated attempts to embed the

Geometrical insets and cards and the constructive triangles forming various regular quadrangles and hexagons

pieces, trying for example, to fit a triangle into a trapezium, into a rectangle, etc. Or, when they take up a rectangle and recognize the place where it ought to be put, they arrange it with the long side across the short side of the place, and only after many trials do they succeed in putting it into its right place. After three or four successive attempts, the child recognizes the geometrical figures with extreme facility and replaces the insets with a confidence which carries with it an expression of indifference, of disparagement for it as being an easy bit of work.

This is the moment at which the child may advance to a methodical examination of the shapes, changing the insets on the desk at his convenience and passing from contrasts to similarities. Then the exercise becomes easy for the child, who gets accustomed to recognizing the figures, and to putting them back in their respective places without effort or mistake.

At the first stage of attempts when to the child figures of contrasted form are presented recognition is helped a great deal when tactile-muscular sensations are associated with visual sensations. I make the child trace with the forefinger of the right hand the outlines of the pieces as well as the inner edge of the socket which reproduces the shape of the piece itself. I get this to become a habit with the child. It is an easy habit to acquire in practice, because little children love above everything to touch things. Some children who do not yet recognize a shape when they see it, do so when they touch it, when they execute the movements needed to trace the outlines of it. Turning round and round in all directions a piece which they vainly try to fit into its place, they get worried; but directly they trace the outlines of the piece and of the socket, they succeed in the attempt. Undoubtedly the association of the tactile-muscular sense with the visual, helps in a marked degree in the perception of shapes and fixes the memory of them.

In such exercises the control is absolute as with the solid insets; the figure can be put in nowhere except into its own socket; the child therefore must exercise itself alone and carry out real self-education of the senses, as far as it concerns the recognition of shapes.

EXERCISES WITH THE THREE SERIES OF CARDS

1st series. The child is given the cards in solid colour and the inset pieces (that is, the central figures without the surrounding frame) corresponding to the figures. They are mixed up together. The child must put the cards in a row on the table (which amuses him greatly), and then place the pieces over them. In this the control is exercised by the eye; the child must recognize the figure and fit it perfectly over the shape on the card so that it covers and hides it. The child's eye here takes the place of the rim which, in the first instance, materially led to the fitting together of the two pieces. In addition to this the child must get accustomed to touching the outlines of the solid-coloured figures, as a simple exercise (and the child is always willing to make movements); after he has covered the printed shape he again traces it all round almost as if he were adjusting the superposition with his finger in order to make it perfect.

2nd series. A pile of cards is given to the child together with the group of inset pieces which correspond to the figures outlined in thick blue lines.

3rd series. The child is given the cards on which the figures are thinly outlined in black, and the pieces as directed above.

The child is thus prepared to interpret with the eye the outlines of the drawn figures, and also the hand is prepared for drawing these objects through the movements which are made.

EXERCISES FOR DISTINGUISHING SOUNDS

Education in hearing carries us in a special way to the relationship between the individual and the movement in his environment by which alone sounds and noises can be produced, for, when all is at rest, there exists absolute silence. Hearing is therefore a

On top we see a girl placing the geometrical figures with careful, intentional movements on their bi-dimensional reproduction. Below a boy uses the "constructive triangles" to compose quadrangles known to him through the geometrical figures. Top: Photo by Mrs. V. A. Baker in an English Montessori School. Bottom: Montessori School, Adyar, Madras, India. Photo by C. T. Nachiappan.

sense which can receive impressions only from movement which takes place round the hearer.

An education in hearing, if it starts from immobility to proceed to the perception of noises and sounds caused by movement, begins from silence.

We have already explained the importance (many-sided) which our method attaches to silence, which becomes the controlling factor in the voluntary inhibition of the movements from which it is derived.

Silence leads also to training in collective effort, for, in order to obtain silence in a certain place it is essential that all objects (or people) within it should be completely motionless.

There is no doubt that trying to establish complete silence ought to awaken keen interest, as indeed happens among the children, who obtain satisfaction from this research in itself. (Analyses of independent factors.)

The sense of hearing also gives us a clear idea of what the first fundamental education of the senses consists in. It consists, in fact, in being able to hear more.

We hear more (acquire greater acuteness of hearing) when we can hear slighter noises than before. Education of the senses leads then to an appreciation of the smallest stimuli, and the smaller that which is perceived the greater is the sensorial capacity.

The education of the senses strengthens in an essential manner the minimal appreciation of external stimuli.

For example, a half-deaf person (as Itard has shown so conclusively) can be educated to perceive slighter noises than those which, if he had been left to himself without any education, generally he could hear before, until by stages, he is led to hear the ordinary noises which the normal man hears without any education in hearing.

And basing his proceedings on this idea, Itard, using a succession of stimuli which were graded from the strongest to the lightest, trained many deaf-mutes till they could hear the speaking voice and after that till they could speak—thus curing a large number of mutes.

Another principle of sensorial education is that of distinguishing differences between stimuli.

That includes as teaching preparation a classification of the different groups of sensations, and then the grading of every group which lends itself to it practically.

We can first of all distinguish between noises and sounds, beginning with strongly contrasting differences and passing on to almost imperceptible differences. Then we proceed to the different qualities of sound which have different origin, e.g., the human voice and instruments; and finally we deal with the scale of musical sounds.

To sum up and emphasize the fundamental groupings, we will indicate the four classes of auditory sensations—silence, the speaking human voice, noises, music.

The lesson on silence are separate, independent exercises which have an important practical effect on discipline.

The analysis of sounds relative to speech are exercises connected with the learning of the alphabet.

For studying noises, there is in our present system illustrative material of quite simple and primitive character consisting of a set of wooden (or cardboard) boxes, made in identical pairs, and prepared in such a way that, when in series, they produce graduated noises. As with the other sense-materials, the method of using the boxes for noises is to mix them all together and then arrange in pairs those boxes which give out the same noises. Then, trying to estimate the difference among the boxes in one series, the children use the evidence to place the things in graduated order.

For the education of the musical sense, there was adopted a series of bells which Signorina Anna Maccheroni had prepared with great accuracy. The bells, each mounted on a stand and separate from each other, constitute a group of objects identical in appearance, but which, when struck with a little hammer,

produce the following notes, so that the only difference perceptible is that of sound:

The individual bells, which constitute a double series, are
moveable; they can therefore be mixed together, precisely as are
the other objects used in sense education.

The bells are handled by the stand and made to vibrate by
a small hammer. The first exercise consists in recognizing two
bells which produce the same sound and placing them side by side
(semi-tones being excluded). Then comes the learning of the notes
of the scale, in their order, and in this case it is the mistress who
arranges in the desired order one set of bells, leaving the other
series mixed up. The exercise is again one of making up pairs,
for it consists in sounding one of the bells in the fixed series, and
then finding by trial among the mixed group the bell which gives
a corresponding note. In this exercise, however, the pairing is
guided in a prescribed order.

When the ear is sufficiently accustomed to recognizing and
memorizing the succession of simple sounds in the scale, the child
may possibly be able, without any guidance, to put the displaced
and mixed group of bells into the successive order of the diatonic
tones guided solely by his own musical ear; afterwards he may add
the semi-tones.

As in the case of the other systems of objects, the name is
added to the sensation after that has been clearly perceived (smooth,
rough, red, blue, etc.). So here the name of the note is made to
accompany the sound, after the latter has been distinguished with
certainty.

The greatest limit possible for a child six or seven years old
is that of recognizing and naming an isolated sound.

To the tones are added the semi-tones, which, to prevent waste of energy, are recognizable by the bell-stands, which are black instead of white (recalling the keys of the pianoforte). The exercise consists in placing the semi-tones in connection with the respective tones.[1]

One must not confuse the sense-education of the musical sense in general technique, which delimits it, with musical education.

One may carry out the exercises in identifying tones without entering at all into the field of music, just as, in another field, the scientific, they make studies in physics, which are concerned with the vibrations of matter including that special form which produces musical notes.

The sense-exercise represents the essential base for musical education. The child who has done such exercises is extremely well prepared for listening to music, and therefore for making more rapid progress.

It is not necessary to say that, for this very reason, music itself will continue and strengthen the sense education, just as the study of painting will continue the study of colours, etc. The exact base of a " classified perception " which is fixed within the child like a foundation stone for comparison, possesses an inestimable initial value for continued progress.

[1] It was in the course of these exercises with the bells that notice was taken of the maximum number of repetitions of the same exercise in a single round; there were counted as many as 200 repetitions by children between six and seven years of age.

Pairing the bells reproducing one octave of the scale lays the foundation for musical education and leads to writing, reading, singing and many original compositions. Amsterdamsche Montessori School, Holland.

GENERALIZATIONS ON THE EDUCATION
OF THE SENSES

THE method of educating the senses of normal children from three to six years of age opens, I believe, a new way for psychological research which promises rich results.

Up till now experimental psychology has aimed at perfecting instruments of measurement, that is, the graduation of stimuli; but it has not attempted to prepare the individual methodically for the sensations.

Instead of that, I consider that psychology will owe its development more to the preparation of the individual than to that of the instrument.

But leaving out of account this purely scientific interest, the education of the senses is of the highest pedagogic interest.

We set before ourselves two objects in general education, one biological and one social. The biological object is to help in the natural development of the individual; the social is to prepare the individual for his environment, and into this there enters also professional education which teaches the individual to utilize his environment. The education of the senses is of the highest importance for both purposes; the development of the senses precedes that of the higher intellectual powers, and in the child between three and six years of age it is in the formative period.

We can, then, help the development of the senses during this very period, graduating and adapting the stimuli, just as we ought to aid the acquisition of speech before it is completely developed.

All the education of early childhood ought to be based on this principle—to aid the natural development of the child.

The other part of education, that of adapting the individual to the environment, will become more important, when the period of intense development is past.

The two parts are always interlaced but the predominance of either of them depends on the age.

The period of life which lies between three and six years is a period of rapid psychical growth and of building up the sensorial mental faculties. The child of that age is developing his senses; his attention is therefore directed towards the observation of his surroundings.

It is the stimuli for things, not the reasons, which attract his attention; it is, then, the time to direct sense stimuli methodically, in order that sensations should evolve rationally. In this way is prepared a basis on which may be built up a positive mentality for the child.

Besides, through the education of the senses it is possible to discover and correct casual defects which today are not noticed in the schools, at least until the time in which the defect shows itself by a definite and then irreparable inadaptability to the surroundings (deafness, shortsight).

It is this physiological education which prepares for mental education, by perfecting the organs of the senses and the nervous tracks of projection and association.

But the other part of education also, touching the adaptation of the individual to the environment, is indirectly affected because in this way we are preparing the infancy of the humanity of our time. Men of our present day civilization are pre-eminently observers of their environment because they must utilize to the utmost extent all its riches.

Today, art also is based, as in Greek times, on the observation of truth. The exact sciences progress directly through observation; all discoveries and the applications of them which for a century have been the means of transforming the world in which we move were arrived at by this very route. We ought, therefore, to prepare the new generations for this attitude of mind which is rendered necessary as a form of modern civil life and as the indispensable means for continuing efficiently the work of human progress.

We see as the result of observation the discoveries of the Rontgen rays, the Hertzian waves, the vibrations of radium, and similar great applications from the Marconi telegraph. Meanwhile, in no epoch to such a degree as in ours, has thought, based upon positive research, thrown so much light on philosophical speculations and on spiritual subjects. The theories of matter themselves, after the discovery of radium, have led on to metaphysical ideas.

So it might be said that by training the power of observation we have also prepared ways leading to spiritual discoveries.

The education of the senses, by producing keen observers, not only fulfils a generic office of adaptation to the present epoch of civilization, but also prepares directly for practical life.

Up till now, I consider we have been holding very imperfect views about what is necessary for practical life. We have always started off with ideas and followed up with practical work. The educational method has always been to teach intellectually, and then proceed to action. Generally speaking, in teaching, we speak of the object which interests *us*, and try to induce the pupil, when he has understood, to carry out a piece of work connected with that object. Very often the child who has grasped the idea finds enormous difficulty in carrying out the work which has been assigned to him, because there is lacking in his education a factor of prime importance—the training of the senses.

It is worth while to illustrate the principle by several examples. We tell a cook to buy some fresh fish; she understands the idea and proceeds to carry it out. But if the cook's sight and smell have not been trained to recognize the signs of freshness in fish, she will not be able to carry out the order.

Such a deficiency will be still more manifest in culinary operations. The cook may be able to read and may be wonderfully well acquainted with the quantities and times set out in a cookery book; she may be able to carry out all the manipulations necessary to give the required form to the dishes; but when it comes to testing by smell the right moment in the cooking, or to deciding by sight or taste the moment when a certain condiment should be added, then the performance will break down if the cook's senses have not been sufficiently trained. She will have to acquire this skill through long practice and such practice is no other than late education of the senses, which in the adult is very often no longer effective.

The same thing can be said concerning manual work and generally for the training for all the crafts of the labourer. Everybody must " learn by means of repeated exercises," and this ' learning ' includes a training of the senses which has to be undergone at a later age. For instance, those who spin have to acquire the capacity of using the tactile sense of their fingers to discriminate the threads; those who weave or embroider have to acquire a refinement of the eye to discriminate the particularities of their work, specially for the discernment of colour.

Finally, learning a craft, specially if it is an artistic or refined craft, means undertaking a development of the senses and of the movements of the hand, and this movement of the hand is then helped by a subsequent refinement of the tactile sense.

If this training is undertaken at an age in which in nature the formative period is over, it becomes difficult, imperfect. The secret of preparing anybody for a craft lies in the utilization of that period of life, between three and six years of age, when there is a natural tendency to perfect the senses and movement.

The same principle holds true, not only for manual work, but also for all those higher professions to which a practical activity is associated.

The medical profession gives us an example. The medical student studies theoretically the symptoms of the pulse, and goes to the patient's bedside prepared and eager to recognize them, but if his fingers are not capable of making the recognition his studies and his goodwill will be useless. To become a doctor he is deficient in the discriminative capacity for sense stimuli. The same may be said about heart-sounds which the student learns about in theory but which his ear cannot distinguish in practice; the same applies to trembling and vibrations to which the hand is insensitive. The thermometer is the more indispensable to a doctor when his cutaneous system is badly adapted to perceive stimuli from heat.

It is well known that a doctor may be learned and extremely clever and yet not be a good practical man, and that to become so long experience is required. In reality this long experience is nothing but belated and often ineffective training of the senses. After having mastered brilliant theories, the doctor finds himself condemned to the unprofitable labour of collecting symptoms of diseases, if he is to obtain practical results from these theories. Here we have then the beginner who proceeds methodically by feeling, by tapping, by listening, in order that he may recognize the vibrations, the resonances, the tones, the murmurs, the noises which alone can enable him to form a diagnosis. In this way there arises the deep and sad discouragement, the disillusion of these early years; besides this, there is the wrongness of carrying on a profession of such grave responsibility whilst uncertain of discerning the symptoms. The whole art of medicine is founded on sense-activity, yet the schools prepare doctors by way of classical studies! Thus the wonderful intellectual equipment of the doctor is made of no avail owing to the defective development of his senses.

One day I heard a surgeon giving popular lectures to mothers on how to recognize the early symptoms of rickets in children, with the intention of inducing them to bring their rickety children to the doctor in the early stages of the complaint, when curative treatment might still be efficacious. The mothers understood the idea, but they could not recognize the early deformities because they had had no sense-training in fine discrimination of forms slightly divergent from the normal. Hence these lessons were rendered useless.

If we think carefully we shall perceive that almost all the adulteration of food substances is made possible because of the sluggish state of the senses in most people. Industrial fraud is fostered by the lack of sense-education among the masses, just as the fraud of the swindler depends upon the guilelessness of the victim. We often see buyers relying upon the honesty of the seller or putting faith in the trustworthiness of a firm when deciding on purchases; and this is because they lack the physical ability to gain knowledge directly, the power to distinguish by the senses the differentiating characters of substances.

Finally in many cases intelligence is rendered useless through lack of practice, and this practice is almost always education of the senses. It is a fundamental necessity for everyone, in practical life, to obtain exact knowledge of the stimuli derived from the environment.

But pretty often in the adult sense-education is difficult, as is the education of the hand of an adult who wishes to become a pianist. The education of the senses must begin in the formative period of life, if we wish later on to raise it to a high level through education and to apply it to some special form of culture. For this reason the education of the senses ought to begin methodically in childhood, and then be continued during the period in which the individual is being educated for the practical life of the world he will live in.

Otherwise, we isolate the man from his surroundings and prolong the time necessary to acquire a professional ability. In fact, when we believe that we are completing education through intellectual culture we are making thinkers fit to live only outside

the world, not practical men.   And when, wishing to provide education for the practical part of life, we confine ourselves to
practising actions, we neglect the fundamental part of practical
education, that which places man in direct contact with the external
world.   And so professional work is preparing a man to utilize
his surroundings.   He must then, of necessity, fill up the great gap
in his education, by beginning again, now when his education is
completed, the training of the senses necessary to put himself into
direct contact with the world around.

Aesthetic and moral education also is linked up closely with
that of the senses.   By multiplying the sensations and developing
the capacity for assessing the smallest differential qualities among
stimuli, the sensibility is refined, and pleasure is intensified.   Beauty
dwells in harmony, not in contrasts, and harmony means affinity,
hence delicacy of the senses is required in order to perceive it.
The aesthetic harmony of nature and of art escapes those whose
senses are dull.   The world is then restricted and common place.
In the world around us there exist inexhaustible sources of aesthetic
enjoyment, in the midst of which men move about as if they
possessed no senses, or like the lower animals, seeking enjoyment
in strong, sharp sensations, since only these come within their
powers of perception.

Very often wicked habits arise out of gross pleasures; it is a
fact that strong stimulants do not make more acute but rather
tend to weaken the senses, which, as a result, demand stronger
and stronger excitement.

From the point of view of physical education, the importance
of education of the senses is emphasized when we look at the
scheme of the reflex arc which represents in principle the functions
of the nervous system.

The senses are organs designed for the apprehension of images
from the external world necessary for the intelligence, as the hand
is the organ used to gain a knowledge of the material things
necessary for the body.   But both the senses and the hand can
be perfected far beyond such simple offices, becoming more and

13

more worthy servants of the great internal motor which keeps them in its service.

The education which improves the intelligence ought to increase these two faculties which are capable of indefinite improvement.

THE TEACHER

THE mistress who wishes to equip herself for this special education must, above all, keep clearly in front of her this idea—that her aim must not be to fill the child with knowledge about the qualities of things, such as dimensions, shape, colour, etc. by means of objects. Neither should the object be to train the child to be able to use without mistake the material which is presented to him so that he does an exercise *well*. That would place our material in competition with that of anybody else, of Froebel for example, and it would demand continually the active super-vision of the teacher, who would have to be supplying infor-mation and hastening to correct every mistake until the child has learnt. Finally, the material is not a new means which is placed in the hands of the old laborious teacher to help in her task as teacher.

With us, it is a matter of transference of activity, with which the teacher is at first invested, but which, by our method, is left mainly to the child.

The work of education is divided between the teacher and the environment. For the old teaching mistress there is substituted a much more complex combination, that is, there exist along with the mistress many objects (the means of development) which co-operate in the education of the child.

The profound difference which separates this method from the so-called ' object lessons ' of the old style, is that the objects are not an aid for the mistress who has to explain, that is they do not constitute means of teaching.

But they are an aid for the child who chooses them himself, takes possession of them, uses them and employs himself with them according to his own tendencies and needs and just as long as he is interested in them. In this way the objects become means of development.

The objects and not the teaching given by the mistress form the principal agent and as it is the child who uses them, it is he, the child, who is the active being and not the teacher.

The mistress, nevertheless, fulfils many functions. Her co-operation is very far from being excluded, but it becomes prudent, delicate and takes a varied form. There is no need for her words, her energy, her severity, but what is needed is wisdom, keen-eyed in observing, in serving, in approaching and in withdrawing, in speaking and in keeping silent, in accordance with the occasions and needs. She must acquire a moral alertness which has not been demanded by any other method, a mingling of calm, patience, love and humility. Virtues and not words form her main qualification.

Summing up her principal duty in school practice, one may state it thus—the mistress must explain the use of material. She is, in the main, a connecting link between the material (the objects) and the child. A simple, modest duty and yet much more delicate than when, in the old schools, the material was, on the other hand, a simple connecting link helping to establish intellectual correspondence between the mistress who had to pass on her ideas and the child who had to receive them.

In our system, the mistress does nothing more than facilitate and make clear to the child the very active and prolonged work which is reserved for him in choosing objects and employing himself with them. It is somewhat similar to what takes place in a gymnasium, where teacher and apparatus are necessary. There, the master teaches the use of the parallel bars and the swings, shows how weights are to be handled, etc. The pupils use these objects, and through the use of them are developed strength, agility, and all that can be developed when muscular energy is put in connection with the various means which the gymnasium offers for exercising it.

This gymnastic teacher is not a lecturer, he is a guide. And, as he would never succeed by speeches on the theory of gymnastics, in making robust a single one of his pupils, so the old school failed absolutely in strengthening the individuality and the personality of the children. On the contrary, in our schools, where the mistress limits herself to pointing out and directing, and there is placed at the child's disposal a gymnasium of mental exercises, he grows stronger, becomes an individual of robust character, is properly disciplined and acquires an inward health which is the direct and brilliant result of the liberation of the mind.

The study which the mistress must carry out is twofold in character, for she must know very well the work which is expected from her, and the function of the *material*, that is the means of development. It is difficult to train theoretically such a teacher, who ought to fashion herself, who ought to learn to observe, to be calm, patient and humble, to restrain her own impulses, and who, in her delicate mission, has a task which is eminently practical. She, in her turn, has more need of a gymnasium for her mind than of a book for her intelligence.

Yet what she has to do can be learnt easily and without mistake, that part of it which regards the mistress as a person who places the child in a position of activity. She ought to be able to choose the appropriate object, and place it before him in such a way as to make him understand it and arouse his keen interest in it.

The teacher must therefore be well acquainted with the material and keep it present in the forefront of her mind at all times. She must acquire exact knowledge of the technique which has been experimentally determined for the presentation of the material and for the treatment of the child that he may be guided aright. This is the part with which the training of the teacher is chiefly concerned. She will be able to study theoretically certain general principles of the highest importance for guiding her in practice, but only through experience will she acquire those delicate variations which vary in the training of different individuals. She will learn that she must not hold back minds already abnormally developed by giving to them material less than their individual powers can handle, which creates boredom; she will learn not to offer objects which are beyond the capacity of the child, thus discouraging and destroying the first childish enthusiasm.

KNOWLEDGE OF THE MATERIAL

In order to know the material the mistress ought not to content herself with looking at it, studying it with a book as guide, or learning the use of it through the explanations of a teacher. She must exercise herself with it for a long time, trying in this way to form an estimate by her experience of the difficulties or the interest which every piece of material may present, trying to interpret, however imperfectly, the impressions which the child may receive from it. If the mistress has sufficient patience to repeat the exercise as often as a child might do, she is able to measure in herself the energy and the endurance of which a child of a definite age is capable. For this last purpose, the mistress will be able to grade the materials and thus test the activity which the child is able to exert at successive ages. (vide later chapter on the order for the exercises.)

MAINTENANCE OF ORDERLINESS

The mistress, besides putting the child in touch with the material, also puts him in touch with the arrangement of his surroundings. She imposes on him the rule on which is based an external, disciplinary organization, very simple in character, but sufficient to ensure peaceful work. It is that every object must have a definite place, where it is kept and where it remains when it is not in use. The child may take a piece of material only from the place where it is exposed for free choice, and when he has finished using it he must put it back in its place, in the same condition in which he took it out. That is to say, no child may leave off just when he has satisfied his own desires, but must continue the work to the end, giving willing attention to the environment and the rules which keep it in order. He must never pass on his material to a companion, still less take it from one.

In this way, from the start, all competition is eliminated. The object which is not exposed does not exist for any one who is seeking it. If he desires it intensely there is nothing to be done but be patient and wait till the companion has finished using it and has put it back into its exhibition place.

INVIGILATION

Finally, the mistress keeps watch so that the child who is absorbed in his work is not disturbed by any companion, and this office of guardian angel of minds concentrated in efforts which are to elevate them is one of the most solemn duties of the teacher.

GIVING LESSONS

The mistress, whilst she is guiding the work of the child with the material (the lessons of the mistress) must distinguish between two different periods. In the first, she puts the child into communication with the material, initiates him into its use. (Time of initiation.)

In the second, she intervenes to enlighten the child who has already succeeded through his spontaneous exertions, in distinguishing the differences between things. It is then that the teacher can best make definite the ideas acquired by the child by himself, if that be necessary, and supply the terms relative to the differences observed.

THE TECHNIQUE OF LESSONS

First Period: Initiations

Isolating the Object.   The mistress, when she is giving a lesson, or wants to help the child to use the sense-material, regards it as being essential that the attention of the child should be isolated from everything except the object of the lesson; to that end, she will be careful to clear a table of all else and place upon it only the material which she wishes to present.

Working exactly.   The help which the mistress has to give consists in presenting to the child the material so as to show him how to use it, performing the exercise herself once or twice; for example: displacing the cylinders of the solid insets, mixing them up and putting them back in position by trial; or mixing up the colour spools to be matched up, then taking one of them by chance in the proper way without touching the silk, and placing it alongside the identical spool; and so on.

Rousing Attention.   When the mistress offers the object to the child she must never do it coldly, but must display some vivacious interest as she calls the attention of the child to it.

Prevention of Errors in Using Material. The most efficient prevention of misuse of the material lies in its presentation at the right moment of the child's development. Another guarantee of proper use lies in the exactness of the presentation. If, notwithstanding this, a mistress sees material being used in such a way as to render it valueless for its purpose, that is, that it does nothing towards the development of the child's intelligence, she must put a stop to the work. She will do this with the utmost sweetness if the child submits quietly and with good temper, but if he shows a tendency to behave badly she will restrain him energetically, not so much as a punishment for noise and disorder, but offering him the help of her authority.

Authority, in fact, becomes in such a case the support which is needed by the child, who having lost control of himself owing to temporary lack of balance, needs a strong support to which he can cling, just as one who has stumbled needs to hang on to something to maintain his balance. The work of helping means, at such a moment, the friendly hand of the strong held out towards the weak.

When the child is working he is like a person poised in perfect equilibrium, and it is material which he needs with which to employ himself, just as the body striving after perfect mobility would require a gymnasium.

We must distinguish clearly between two kinds of mistakes which the child may make. First, we have the error which is controlled by the material itself, and which arises from the fact that the child, quite willing to carry out exactly an exercise which he knows well, yet does not succeed because of his immature power of execution or because his senses do not appreciate the various stimuli, or because he cannot execute definite movements for which his mechanism is not yet far enough developed. For example, he makes a mistake in putting the cylinders into the holes, because he does not yet distinguish the differences between them; or for a similar reason, he places a large cube over a small one in building the tower, and so on.

Such errors are controlled by the material, which does not allow the mistake to be continued without being found out; they can be corrected only through the growth of the child's powers, through that modification, which will follow as a consequence of long and correct manipulation of the material. Such errors may be placed in the category described when we say that we learn by making mistakes; they are overcome by determination, with the aid of the means which are offered from the outside.

The second mistake can be traced to naughtiness, or to careless teaching as for instance, in dragging about the whole stand of solid insets like a wheelbarrow, or in building houses with the tablets of coloured silks, or in walking on the rods when laid out in a row, or in wrapping one of the cloths used for fastenings round the head like a scarf, and so on. Abusive use of material which corresponds to disorder or to needs different from those which the material can satisfy, means making no use of it; it results in waste of energy, uproar; all the actions which prevent the child from concentrating and therefore from improving and developing. It is as if a hemorrhage of the body shed that blood which ought to concentrate in the heart in order to maintain health and life. It cannot be said of the above-mentioned errors that ' one learns by making mistakes '; the longer the mistake is kept going, the farther off is the possibility of learning.

It is in conditions such as these that the authority of the teacher succours the erring little soul, extending to him, now gentle, now energetic help.

Respect for useful Activity. If, instead of using the material wrongly, the child uses it either in accordance with the instructions of the mistress or in some other way invented by himself which shows intelligent modifications, then the teacher will leave the child to go on repeating the same exercise or making his own attempts and experiments. She will let the child have as much time as he wants without ever interrupting his activity, neither for the purpose of correcting small errors, nor by stopping the work through fear of tiring out the child.

A Good Finish. When the child has voluntarily given up his work, which means that the impulse which urged him to make use of the material has been exhausted, the mistress, if need be, may, indeed *must* intervene in order to see that the child puts the material back in its place and that everything is returned in prefect order.

SECOND PERIOD: THE LESSONS

The second period is that when the teacher intervenes in order to fix more securely the ideas of the child, who after having been started, has already carried out many exercises and has succeeded in identifying the differences presented by the sense material.

The first intervention consists in teaching the exact names of things. This helps the child to speak correctly, which is easily done at this tender age.

By our method one of the most delicate tasks of the teacher must be that of presenting words which are exactly fitted to convey the idea which the material has to fix in the mind of the child. In giving these words the teacher pronounces them correctly and clearly, breaking them up into their component sounds, without however, adopting a style differing from ordinary speech, that is without any exaggeration.

THE LESSON IN THREE STAGES

For this purpose I have found to be excellent even for normal children the lesson divided into three stages, used by Seguin, to obtain in the defective child the association between the object and the corresponding word; this form of lesson has been adopted in our schools.

First Stage: The Association of Sense-perception with the Name. The teacher must first of all pronounce the necessary names and adjectives, without adding another word, pronouncing the words very distinctly and in a loud voice, so that the various sounds of which the word is composed may be distinctly and clearly apprehended by the child.

Thus, for example, in the first exercises on the senses, the smooth card and the rough card having been touched, she will say: " It is smooth," " It is rough," repeating the word a great many times, with various modulations of the voice, but always with clear vowel tones and with distinct enunciation, " Smooth, smooth, smooth," and " Rough, rough, rough ".

In the same way, when dealing with heat sensations, she will say: " It is cold," " It is warm," " It is frozen," " It is tepid," " It is burning." Then she will begin to use the generic term " heat "; also " more heat," " less heat ".

In this way the lesson in nomenclature ought to consist in establishing the association of the name with the object or with the abstract idea which the name itself represents. The object and the name must appeal to the child's understanding at one and the same time. It is, however, imperative that no word other than the name should be pronounced.

Second Stage: Recognition of the Object Corresponding to the Name. The mistress ought always to test the success of the lesson which she has given.

The first test will be that of finding out whether or not the name has remained associated with the object in the memory of the child. For that, she will have to allow a requisite time to elapse between the lesson and the test, that is, several moments of silence should intervene between them. Then she will ask the child, pronouncing slowly and with very clear pronunciation only the name (or the adjective) which had been taught: " Which one is smooth? " " Which one is rough? "

The child will point to the object, and the mistress will know whether or not the association has been established.

This second time is the most important of all and contains the real lesson, the real mnemonic and associative aid. When the mistress is satisfied that the child is in touch with her, has understood and is interested, she will repeat over and over again the same questions: " Which one is smooth? " and " Which one is rough? "

In repeating the question a great many times the teacher repeats that word which finally will be remembered, and at every repetition the child, responding by pointing to the object, has repeated the exercise of associating with it the word which he is learning and fixing in his mind. If, however, the mistress notices at the very start that the child is not disposed to pay attention to her and makes mistakes in answering without making any effort to do well, she ought, instead of correcting and insisting, to suspend the lesson and start it again at another moment, on another day. Why should she correct him? If the child did not succeed in associating the name with the object, the only way in which he can succeed will be to repeat the act of sense stimulus as well as the name, namely to repeat the lesson. But when the child has made a mistake, it means that, at that moment, he was not disposed towards the mental association which was hoped for from him; therefore it would be necessary to choose another moment.

Supposing that along with the correction one had said: " No, you have made a mistake, it is this," all these words which contain a reproof, would have made much more impression on him than the other (e.g. smooth, rough); they would have remained in the child's mind, retarding the learning of the names. Instead of that, the silence which follows the error leaves clear the field of the child-mind and the next lesson will follow on the first successfully.

Third Stage: Remembering the Name Corresponding to the Object. The third stage is a rapid verification of the lesson taken first. The mistress asks the child: " What is this like?" and if the child is ready to do so he will reply with the correct word: " It is smooth," " It is rough."

Since the child is often uncertain in his pronunciation of these words, often new to him, the mistress may insist on having them repeated once or twice, exhorting the child to pronounce them more clearly, saying: " What is it like?" " What is it like?" If the child shows marked defects in speech, this is the time to make them perfectly clear so that definite corrective exercises in pronunciation may be given afterwards.

ILLUSTRATIVE APPLICATIONS: GUIDE TO THE
MATERIAL SOLID INSETS

Dimensions. The teacher, after the child has had long practice
in handling the three solid insets and has acquired confidence in
the exercise, takes all the cylinders of equal height and spreads
them out on the table close together. Then she chooses the two
extremes saying: " This is the thickest," and " This the thinnest ".
She places them side by side to make the comparison more telling,
and then, taking each one of them by the knob, she places them
base to base in order to mark the extreme difference. Then she
places them close together again and upright, in order to show
that they are of equal height. Meanwhile she may be repeating
many times: " Thick, thin ". She must every time follow the
other stages of verification in which she asks: " Give me the
thickest, the thinnest," and finally the language test: " What is it
like? " In later lessons the teacher removes the two extremes and
repeats the lesson with the two remaining at the extremities.
Finally, she uses all the pieces, chooses one of them by chance,
and asks: " Give me one thicker than this, or thinner than
this."

The teacher proceeds in the same way with the second set of
solid insets. In this case she places the pieces upright, all of them
having a base wide enough to maintain them in this position.
She says: " It is the tallest, it is the shortest." Then she places
the extreme pieces in juxta-position, having removed them from
the row; she places their bases, end to end, showing that they are
equal. From the extremes she passes to the middle pieces, as in
the first exercise.

With the third set of solid insets, the teacher, after having
placed all the pieces in a graduated row, points to the first, saying:
" It is the largest," and to the last saying: " It is the smallest."
Then she places them close together and points out how they differ
in height as well as in the size of the base. The proceeding is
similar to that in the two preceding exercises.

The same plan is followed with the graduated systems of prisms, rods and cubes. The prisms are thick or thin in one set, and high and low in another and of equal length. The rods are long and short and of equal thickness. The cubes are large and small and differ in all three dimensions.

Form. The teacher, after the child has shown that he can with certainty identify the shapes of the flat insets, begins the lessons in nomenclature with the two contrasted forms, the square and the circle, following the usual method. She will not teach all the names relating to the geometrical figures but only some of the principal ones, such as the square, circle, rectangle, triangle, oval, pointing out specially that there are narrow, long, rectangles whilst others are wide and short, and that the squares have equal sides and can only be large and small. This is pretty easily shown with the insets; no matter in what direction the square piece is turned, it always enters its hole. Instead of that, the rectangle, if placed across the hole, will not fit into it. The child works away very cheerfully at this exercise, for which he arranges in the frame a square and a series of rectangles having the longer side equal to the side of the square, and the other side gradually decreasing in the five successive pieces.

By similar procedure there is demonstrated the difference between the oval, the ellipse and the circle. The circle can be embedded in its socket, however it may be turned round; the ellipse does not enter when placed crosswise, but, provided that it is placed lengthwise it can be reversed as regards its ends; the oval, on the other hand, not only will not enter when placed across, but its ends are not interchangeable, and it must be placed with the wide curve towards the wide part of the cavity, and the narrow towards the narrow part. The circles, large and small, enter their beds when turned all ways. I advise teaching the difference between the oval and the ellipse at a much later stage, and not to all the children, but to those who show themselves particularly interested in form either by their frequent choice of the game or by their requests. (I would prefer that such a difference should be recognized by the children spontaneously much later, for example, in the elementary schools.)

The Child's Guide. The work of the new mistress is that of a guide. She guides in the choice of material, in finding exact words, in facilitating and explaining work, in preventing waste of energy, in quelling chance disturbances. Thus she affords the help necessary for proceeding surely and swiftly along the road to intellectual development.

A sure guide on the path of life, she neither urges forward nor holds back, satisfied that she has done her work when she has guaranteed to this precious traveller, the child, that he is on the right road.

In order to be a sure and practical guide the mistress needs a great deal of practice. Even after she has grasped the fact that the periods of initiation and intervention are very diverse, she very often is uncertain about the condition of the child's mind in passing from one to the other. She waits too long whilst the child is finding out differences by himself before intervening to teach nomenclature.

I once found a child five years old who could already make up all the words, knowing the alphabet very well (he had learnt it in fifteen days); he could write on the blackboard; in free drawings he showed not only that he was an observer but that he intuitively grasped the idea of perspective by the way in which he had drawn a house and a table. As for the exercise in colour sense, he mixed together the seven shades of the nine colours we used, that is, he mixed sixty-three tablets each covered with silk of one colour of a different shade; he rapidly separated all the groups, and then arranged in a graduated scale the individuals of each group, filling up a whole table with the classification of them and partly extending it over a coloured mat. I made the experiment of showing the child in the full light of a window a coloured card, telling him to look at it well that he might remember; I then sent him to the table on which were spread out all the shades in order to find the same shade. He made only very slight mistakes; often he selected the identical tint; very often, the nearest; very rarely, a tint two tints removed. He possessed a discriminating power and a memory for colours which were almost prodigious. This child, like most others, was devoted to the colour exercise.

Having been asked the name of the colour white, the child hesitated a long time, and only after a number of seconds did he say uncertainly " white ". Now so intelligent a child, even without special help from the mistress, might have learnt the name in the family life.

The Directress told me that having noticed that this child had special difficulty in naming the colours of things, she had limited him up till now to the sense exercises. She thought it better not to intervene yet in the teaching.

Certainly the education of this child was somewhat confused, and the control left excessively free the spontaneous explanations of mental activity.

Although it is most praiseworthy to give to ideas a basis of sense education, it is nevertheless essential to associate language and perceptions at the same time. The mistress ought to avoid the superfluous, but not forget the necessary. The existence of the superfluous and the absence of the necessary are the two principal mistakes made by the teacher; the middle course between the two marks the level of her perfection.

The end to be attained is the orderly stabilization of the spontaneous activity of the child. As no master can give the pupil the agility which he acquired by gymnastic exercise but the pupil must improve himself by his own efforts, so it is here by close analogy for the education of the senses and for education in general.

We think of what the teacher of the pianoforte does. He teaches his pupil how to place his body, teaches him the notes, shows him the relation between the written note and the key to be touched, as well as the position of the fingers; then he leaves him by himself to practice. If from this pupil there is to be produced a pianist, there will have to intervene between the instruction

14

given by the teacher and the musical performances a long patient course of the exercises which serve to give flexibility to the finger-joints and to the tendons, to render automatic the co-ordination of special muscular movements, and to strengthen by repeated use of the organ the muscles of the hand.

The pianist will therefore have to make himself by his own efforts, and will have succeeded in doing so in the proportion in which his natural genius would induce him to persist in his exercises. Nevertheless the pianist would never have created himself by practice alone, without the guidance of the master.

One might say that the same thing happens in every branch of education; a man's value depends not on what masters he has had, but on what he has done.

One of the difficulties met with in teaching our method to mistresses of the old style is that of hindering them from interfering when the child is worried for a long time about some mistake and is making repeated attempts to put it right. Then the old-time mistresses are seized with pity, and nothing can prevent them from coming to the child's assistance. When one prevents this interference, they speak pityingly of the small pupil; but very soon the latter shows in his smiling countenance the joy of having overcome an obstacle.

Normal children repeat these exercises many times more or less, according to the individual; some are tired of them after five or six times, but others go on for more than twenty times displacing and rearranging the pieces without ever losing their keen expression of interest.

On one occasion, after I had counted sixteen exercises done by a little girl of four, I had a hymn sung to her in order to distract her attention; but she continued, unperturbed, to displace, mix up and replace the cylinders.

An intelligent mistress might carry on interesting studies in individual psychology, and up to a certain point, measure the times of resistance of the attention to different stimuli.

Indeed, when the child is educating himself, and the control and correction of error is given over to the material, there is nothing left for the teacher to do but to observe.

With my methods, the mistress teaches little, observes a great deal, and above all, hers is the function of directing the mental activity of the children and their physiological development. For this reason I have changed the name of teacher to that of *directress*.

In the early days this name made people smile, for everybody asked who it was that this mistress would direct since she had no one under her sway and had to leave her little pupils at liberty. But her direction goes much deeper and is more important than what is commonly understood, since she directs life and souls. The directresses of the Children's Houses must have a very clear conception of two factors—the guidance which is the function of the teacher, and the individual exercise, which is the work of the child.

Only after having fixed in their minds this idea can they proceed rationally to the application of a method for guiding the spontaneous education of the child and for imparting the necessary ideas.

The personal skill of the educator is revealed by the opportuneness and the efficiency of her intervention.

OBSERVATIONS ON PREJUDICES

THE training of the teacher for our method is greatly simplified, as compared with that of ordinary teachers. The necessary is pointed out; she is taught to avoid the superfluous, which is harmful as being an obstacle to the progress of children; there is indicated a limit as perfection. Ordinary teachers, on the other hand, are preoccupied with many things, tire themselves out by doing many things whilst one thing only is necessary.

In order to help the teacher to free herself from old preconceptions and prejudices I will refer briefly here to some of the needless difficulties which dissipate the energy and the attention of the teacher. They are particularly concerned with the degrees of difficulty which the pupil must overcome and with the repose of the child.

Prejudices respecting the ease and difficulty of learning form one of the stumbling-blocks from which we have saved the teacher. Ease and difficulty in doing things cannot be judged through preconceptions, but by direct experience after difficulties have been analysed one by one.

For example, it strikes many people that in teaching geometrical forms we are teaching geometry, and that this is premature in infant schools.   Others are of opinion that if we wish to present geometrical forms we should use solids instead of plane figures.

I think a word is necessary to combat such prejudices. Observing a geometrical form is not analysing it; it is with analysis that the difficulty begins.   When, for example, we talk to the child of sides and angles, and explain to him, perhaps by the objective method as Froebel chooses, that the square has four sides and can be constructed with four equal rods—then we really enter the field of geometry; and I think that early childhood is too immature for this step.   But observation of form cannot be unsuitable at this age; the plan of the table at which the child sits to eat his soup is probably a rectangle; the plate which contains the meat he likes is a circle; and we certainly do not consider that the child is too immature to look at the table and the plate.

The inset pieces which we present simply call attention to form.   As for the name, it is analogous to other names in nomenclature.   Why should we find it premature to teach the child the words " circle," " square," " oval," whilst, if at home he repeatedly hears the word " round " applied to plate, it does not strike us that this is an injury to his tender intelligence? Very often too at home he will hear spoken of the square table, the oval table, etc.; and these common words will remain confused in his mind and in his language for a long time, if there is not interposed assistance similar to that given by us in the teaching of form.

One must remember that very often the child when left to himself makes an effort to understand the language of adults and the things which surround him; teaching, when applied at the right time, forestalls this effort and therefore the child is not wearied out, is given rest, and has his craving satisfied.

In this case also there is to be found prejudice—that when the child is left entirely to himself his mind is at rest.   If that were so, he would remain a stranger to the world; instead of which we see him, little by little, by his own efforts, acquiring ideas and language.   He has come as a traveller into life, one who takes notice of the new things which present themselves to him and tries to learn the unknown language of those around him; he makes great spontaneous efforts to understand and to imitate. The teaching given to the little ones ought to be directed to lessening such efforts, changing them into the enjoyment of easier and more extended success. We are the guides of these travellers who are making their entry into the human life of thought, and we help them to avoid wasting time and strength over useless things.

The other prejudice to which reference has been made is that it is more suitable to present to the child geometrical solids rather than plane figures—sphere, cube, prism, etc.

Leaving aside the physiological question, which shows how the vision of solids is more complex than that of plane figures, let us restrict ourselves to the more pedagogic field of practical life.

The objects which present themselves to our vision in the greatest numbers in our surroundings are comparable with our plane insets. In fact, the cupboard doors, the panel-work, the window and picture frames, the wooden or marble top of a table, are certainly solid objects but have one of the dimensions greatly reduced so that the two more noticeable dimensions determine the shape of the plane. As a result the shape of the plane surface predominates, and we say that such and such a window is rectangular, such a frame is oval, a certain table is square.

The solids determined in form by the surface which shows the greatest dimensions are those which really and almost solely meet our eyes. And it is precisely these solids which are represented by our solid insets. The child will very often recognize in his surroundings the forms thus learnt, but very rarely will he recognize the forms of geometrical solids.

That the long prismatic legs of a table is a prism, and the rotunda is a truncated cone or an elongated cylinder, he will see much later than the rectangular top of the table on which he places the objects whilst at the same time he looks at it. We do not speak then of the fact of recognizing that a cupboard, and much less a house, is a prism or a cube. For the time being there never exist pure geometrical solid forms in the objects around, but

combinations of forms.   There is enormous difficulty in embracing
with the eye the complicated shape of a cupboard; the child ought
to recognize in it an analogy of form, not an identity.

On the other hand he will recognize the geometrical forms
perfectly represented in all the windows, doors, surfaces of the
solid domestic objects, the pictures which adorn the walls, the
walls themselves, the floors, the tiles of the floor.

In this way the knowledge presented to him in the flat insets
will be for him a kind of magic key for the interpretation of all
the surroundings, and he will be able to give himself the consoling
illusion that he knows the secrets of the world.

I once took with me for a walk on the Pincian Hill a boy
from an elementary school who was studying geometrical drawing
and was familiar with the analysis of flat geometrical figures. When
we reached the lofty terrace from which one looks down on the
Piazza del Popolo and the wide expanse of the city, I said to him:
" See how all man's work forms a great collection of geometrical
figures." Very plain to be seen were the rectangles, ellipses,
triangles, semicircles, which perforated and adorned in a hundred
different ways the gray rectangular facades of the buildings. Such
widespread uniformity seemed to prove the limitation of human
intelligence. In contrast, in a neighbouring plot, grass and flowers
displayed in supreme degree the infinite variety of Nature's forms.

The child had never made these observations; he had studied
the angles, the sides and the construction of the geometrical figures
drawn, without thinking of anything else, and feeling only bored
by the dull work which he had to do. At first he laughed at the
idea of man piling up geometrical figures, then he grew interested
and gazed for a long time; I saw in his face a keen expression of
thought.

To the right of the Ponte Margherita a building was in the
process of construction, and the body of it consisted of rectangles.
" How hard they are working," I said, alluding to the workmen.
Then we went to the grass-plot, and remained silent for a time
looking at the grass which grew spontaneously. " It is beautiful,"

said the boy, but that ' beautiful ' referred to the inner movement of his own mind.

I thought then that in the observation of the geometrical forms in the flat insets, and in that of the plants cultivated by the children and seen growing under their own eyes, there exist precious sources of spiritual education also.

Another preoccupation of the ordinary teacher is that she has to widen the knowledge of the child through continual applications to the surroundings, or through generalizations. " Making him see everything," " reflect on everything " is an anxious business, and unfortunately destroys his youthful energy, deprives him cruelly of everything which would create interest in him. It is the spiritual part of that fatal intervention of the adult who wants to substitute herself for the child and act for him, and in doing so, erects the most serious obstacle to his development. Beauties which, when discovered by the child himself in the world which surrounds him, would bring him time after time, joy and satisfaction, give rise to the tedium of mental inertia when the gay flowery path becomes the subject of instruction by an adult.

Let the mistress then cease from worrying herself about ' applications,' urged by the fear that the child, as so many want to insinuate, will be miserably held up by the material which we have limited and which we have substituted for the greatness of variety in the things offered by nature and by the vast environment which surrounds the child in the school and at home.

If the child, by exercising himself with the sense-material, has strengthened his power of distinguishing one thing from another, and has opened up the pathways of his mind to a continually growing avidity for work, he has certainly become a more perfect and intelligent observer than at first, and anyone who is interested in things on a small scale will be the more interested in great things.

We ought to expect from normal children the spontaneous enquiry into the surroundings, or as I put it, the voluntary exploration of the environment. In this case the children are overjoyed with every new discovery which they make; that gives them a sense of dignity and satisfaction, which encourages them to go on indefinitely to seek new sensations in the surroundings and renders them voluntary observers.

The teacher ought to limit her efforts to keeping watch with the utmost vigilance for the time when the child reaches generalizations in ideas. For example, on one occasion one of our little ones aged four whilst he was running on the terrace, stopped to cry out, " Oh, the sky is blue! " and stood still for a long time to gaze at the expanse of the heavens.

One day, on entering one of the Children's Houses, five or six little ones came to a standstill round me, all silent, gently caressing my hands and my dress, saying—" It is smooth," " It is velvet." Then many others drew near and all of them with serious countenances and expressions of intense attention said, as they touched me, the same words. The mistress wanted to interfere to set me free; I made a sign to her not to move and I myself stood motionless and silent, admiring that voluntary activity of the little ones. The greatest triumph of our educational method will always be this—to obtain the spontaneous progress of the child.

On one occasion when a child was making a drawing by filling in with coloured pencils a figure already drawn in outline—a tree, to be precise—he laid hold of a red pencil with which to fill in the colour of the trunk. The mistress was about to intervene saying, " Do you think trees have red trunks? " I restrained her and allowed the child to colour the tree red. This drawing was precious for us because it revealed the fact that the child was not an exact observer of his surroundings. But he continued in class the exercises in colour sense. He used to go with companions into the garden and had many chances of observing the colour of treetrunks; when the action of the senses became strong enough to direct the attention of the child naturally to the colours around him there would come one wonderful moment when he would see that the trunk of a tree is not red; just as the other child, whilst racing about, discovered that the sky was blue. Indeed, one day he took up a brown pencil to colour the trunk and made the branches and the leaves green. Later on, he coloured all the branches brown also, using green only for the leaves.

In this way we gain proofs of the intellectual progress of the child.

We do not create observers by saying, " Observe," but by supplying the means of observation; and this material educates the senses. Once this connection between the child and his environment is established, his progress is assured, because the more acute senses enable him to observe his surroundings better, whilst the latter, attracting his attention by their variety, continue the sense education.

If, instead of this, we leave out sense education, recognition of the properties of bodies comes to form part of culture, which is limited precisely by recognitions learnt and remembered; and they remain sterile. That is to say, when the teacher has taught, according to the old methods, the names of the colours, she has imparted knowledge about determinate qualities, but she has not developed the interest in colour. The child will learn those colours forgetting them over and over again, and he will not go beyond the limits of the teacher's lessons. When the teacher in the old style has suggested the generalization of the idea by saying, for example, " What is the colour of this flower, of this ribbon?" probably the attention of the child will remain fixed in dull fashion on the specimens offered him by the teacher.

If we compare the child with a watch or any other complicated mechanism, we may say that the old method can be likened to what we do when we press with the thumb on the teeth of the motionless wheels to make them go round, in which case the ' turning ' corresponds exactly with the driving force applied by the thumb. This is the equivalent of the culture which is limited to the work of the teacher. The new method, however, resembles winding-up, which sets into independent motion all the mechanism, motion which is directly dependent on the machine and not on the work of the person who has wound it up. Similarly, the

independent mental development of the child continues indefinitely
and is in direct dependence on the mental powers of the child
himself and not on the teacher's work.

The movement which is independent mental activity, arises in
our case, from the education of the senses, and is maintained
by intelligence as an observer. The sporting dog owes his
cleverness to the special acuteness of his senses and not to
education given by his master; moreover, the practice which he
gets in hunting by continually sharpening the sense faculties, gives
the dog pleasure in the chase and then a passion for it. The same
may be said of the pianist who, improving his musical sense as
well as his manipulative skill, develops a growing love for extracting new harmonies from his instrument whilst the exercise is still
further strengthening the sense and the dexterity. He is thus
launched on the way to a perfection which will have as its limits
only his own personal powers. A physicist, on the contrary,
might know all the laws of harmony which will form part of his
scientific training, yet he may not be able to execute the simplest
musical composition; his culture, however extensive, will have
limits defined by the branch of his science which deals with
acoustics.

Our educational aim for early childhood should be that of
helping development, not conferring culture. Therefore after having
offered to the child the material suitable for the development of
the senses, we ought to wait for the faculty of observation to
unfold itself.

The Touchstone. Very often one is amazed by the fact that
children not only make independent observations on their environment, noticing things which at first they did not distinguish in it,
but that they seem to observe and to compare them with what
they remember. They express opinions which seem marvellous,
for they reveal to us that some children form within themselves a
kind of 'touchstone' which we do not possess. They compare
external things with the images which they have fixed in their
minds, and they show judgment which is surprising in its accuracy.

On one occasion in a classroom in Barcelona, a workman entered carrying in his hand a pane of glass which was to be replaced in one of the classroom windows. A child, five years old, called out: "The glass does not fit, it is too small." Only when he applied the glass did the workman find that it was too short by about a centimetre.

Two children of five and six in a Children's House in Berlin, carried on the following discussion: "Do you think that the ceiling is three metres high?" "No, it is about three metres, twenty-five centimetres." When measured the distance proved to be somewhat over three metres.

A child, five years old, on seeing a lady enter, said to her, "The colour of your dress is exactly the same as that of the flower which is out there." The lady went into the next room where she found a flower which was not visible from the room she had entered, and comparing the flower with her dress, found the two colours to be amazingly alike. Apparently the lady's ability was limited to recognizing the identity of the colours when they were placed side by side; but the child possessed a power beyond this; he had an inward fixed standard to which he could refer both the flower and the dress, just as we have a fixed unit of measure which permits us to judge the relationships between things to be measured and a fixed stone of comparison by which other stones can be judged.

The touchstone, which produces such wonderful results in children and which sets them on a plane very different from ours and often inaccessible to us, is worthy of being considered as a fact unknown until today. It seems that at certain periods in life there exist possibilities of making mental acquisitions which are no longer possible at other ages. A fact which is clearly evident to everybody is the capacity many times mentioned which little children have for remembering and reproducing the sounds of language and for learning the words of it.

The age at which language is imprinted in indelible fashion is the period at which nature has established an extraordinary sensitivity adapted to fixing accents and words. In life one cannot go backwards, and what the mind acquired during its sensitive period is a permanent possession for all life, one which can never be acquired at any other period. Thus in the early acquisition of sense impressions and in the fixation of movements there are periods in childhood which, if they pass without bearing fruit, can never be replaced in their effects.

Once our attention is directed to this fact, we will see small variations which often illustrate it. The child of three is able to repeat forty times in succession an exercise (e.g. the solid insets) which the child of six cannot repeat more than five or six times in succession. However, the child of six can do things of higher standing than those possible to the child of three, things of which the very small child would not only be incapable but which would be quite strange to him.

This interesting fact is repeated in normal matters. The intensely formative period of early childhood is also that in which there may be established a form of perfect obedience, the external element of which was fixed as a tendency to imitation. When, however, one goes deeply into this phenomenon and when surrounding circumstances are favourable to the development of the child and therefore to his deepest expressions, one sees that there exists in the child a tendency towards a wonderful adaptability to the human beings who surround him, a trait in which we ought to seek to establish a base for love and good feeling towards all human beings. Later on, except in cases of unusually lofty moral perfection due to exceptional forces, there will no longer exist this form of obedience; there will be only reasoned agreement or enforced submission.

The same phenomenon is shown with extraordinary clearness in the development of religious feelings. The little child has a tendency which one cannot describe better than by calling it the sensitive period of the soul when it has intuitions and religious urges which are surprising to anyone who has not observed the child to whom it was made possible to express the needs of his inner life. It seems then that little children are exceptionally endowed with supernatural intuitions, are miraculously called by divine grace, though rationally it is not possible to give them that religious education which later, in the so-called age of reason, the child can absorb, whilst the man will grow greater through intelligence illuminated by faith.

The sensitive period is always a base for wonderful acquisitions which the man will no longer be able to gain at a different age.

Mental Order. The mind of the little child is certainly not void of knowledge or ideas when the education of the senses begins, but the images are confused together on the edge of the abyss. That chaos of the mind has no need of other new things, but it does need order among those which exist in it. It begins to distinguish all the characters of things. It distinguishes quantity from quality, and separates what is form from what is colour. It distinguishes dimensions according to their frequency of occurrence, in objects long and short, thick or thin, large or small. It separates colours into groups calling them by their names—white, green, red, blue, yellow, violet, black, orange, brown, pink. It distinguishes colour in its intensities, calling the two extremes light and dark. Taste is separated from odours; smoothness from softness; sounds from noises.

As the child had learnt to put everything in its place in its surroundings, one result of the education of the senses was the orderly arrangement of mental image. That is the first orderly act which has to be done in the mind; it is the first point of departure because mental life unfolds by avoiding obstacles.

The conquest of the external world in its sense aspects will now be easy and orderly. The orderliness which has been started has prepared the conditions.

This was what was done by those men who have become brilliant in the opinion of the world. They began by distinguishing things, grouping them, classifying them, inventing names by which to identify them, and deciding to what uses they could be put. They wedded exact knowledge with scientific language.

And this was the beginning of all the sciences which deal with existing things, was the first chapter in the history of future discoveries. It was the man trained in this knowledge of the world who proceeded in the light of knowledge to create progress, the man who looked across the darkness of ignorance, a dark abyss, impassable and immutable.

ELEVATION

Silence: Abstractions Materialized

One of the differences between our method and those generally used in the schools for the education of normal children bears reference to the way of education.

Perhaps the ' silence ' may serve to illustrate the idea.

In the ordinary schools there is discussed a state of normal order which is accepted although it has never been defined. It is that state in which the behaviour of the class makes it possible for the master to give a lesson.

As, however, the class is acting under compulsion the tendency is to drift from that mediocre state of order into a disorder in which movements of all kinds, unco-ordinated and purposeless, create noise and restlessness which make the giving of a lesson difficult or impossible; that is, it disturbs the working order. There must in such a case be an energetic call for ' silence ' indicating with this very word the working order.

So the ' medium order ' is not only something already attained, but is normal and customary; a simple command suffices to obtain it.

By our method, the medium order (which, however, has another form which results from the individual labours of the pupils) is a point of departure for climbing to a higher level by means of a step not yet reached and unknown. Silence is then a positive victory which must be gained through knowledge and experience.

Knowledge, therefore, is applied to considering the slightest movements, to controlling actions in every detail in order to obtain the absolute immobility which leads to silence—a striking idea, new, never before evaluated. In the ordinary schools the call for silence is intended to bring back affairs into their normal condition.

By contrast, the silence of immobility suspends the normal life, suspends useful work and has no practical aim. All its importance, all its fascination, springs from the fact that by suspending the communal life it raises the individual to a higher level where utility does not exist but where it is the conquest of self which calls him.

When we find that little children of three or four ask ' to have the silence' or when having been invited, they respond at once with the keenest interest, we have plain proofs that children have a tendency towards elevation and that they enjoy the higher pleasures. Many people have been present on some one of these astonishing occasions when a mistress having begun to write on the blackboard the word ' silence' in order to obtain it, even before she has completed the word they perceive that profound silence has invaded the place where, an instant before, forty or fifty little ones had been intent on their occupations.

The motor life was suspended by contagion instantaneously. Some child had read the first letters and had understood that the order for silence was coming; by suspending his own movements, he started the performance which each of the others at once guessed at and joined in with him. And so silence called for silence, without a single voice having asked for it by speech.

Similar comparisons may be made with respect to all the activities of the two different types of schools.

15

A certain medium level represents ' good ' in the ordinary schools—a ' good ' which is not defined, but which as a matter of custom restricts the scholastic level aimed at.

In our schools we set out from a medium ' good ' which is that attained spontaneously by individual work, in order to rise to a higher condition, towards a goal of perfection.

It is evident that if the tendency which renders this elevation possible does not exist in the child as a matter of necessity it will never be reached in practice.

If it does exist and if it shows itself in undoubted success, we ought, as educators, to feel that a new duty illumines our mission.

The education of the senses may serve to illustrate this idea. It is known that many educationists have considered education of the senses to be a mistake. That is because, by taking the ' medium ' life as the end, the education of the senses causes a deviation from the natural way of learning.

Objects are regarded in their entirety as a combination of qualities, as possessing many characters. The rose will have its colours and its odours; the marble vase its form and its weight, and so on. The lesson on actual objects just as they are is then the correct thing. This is the reasoning which regards as finality the medium order of things.

If, however, we consider the medium order not as a fixed end but as a point of departure we may find out by intuition that little children notice spontaneously much more than the object lessons dream of explaining, because, naturally, they are left free to observe in accordance with their own instinct; they are not hindered by organic inhibition, that is, by the fear of acting by themselves.

I say " intuition " because even if we have not studied methodically spontaneous child reactions we can understand such a truth empirically. The child possesses a vital tendency to explore his surroundings, however great, as he also tends to listen to language; he must get to know the external world, he must learn to speak, driven by a pressing instinct. It is, we say, a period of the senses in his life which makes him observe in this way the things around him like the sounds of the human voice.

There is no need to illustrate objects for him; the only need is to refrain from stifling the instinct of observation which nature has given him.

If we want to help him we must place ourselves on a higher level. We must give him more than he could obtain by his unaided efforts.

May I be permitted to make a strong assertion that we ought to give him the philosophy of things?

Let us begin with abstraction. Abstract ideas are synthetic conceptions of the mind which, detached from actual objects, abstract from them some qualities held in common which do not exist of themselves but exist in the actual things. For example, weight is an abstraction; it does not exist by itself; only heavy objects exist.

In the same way one considers form and colour. These words stand for abstractions which are synthetic in themselves because they mass together in one single idea in an abstract manner, a quality scattered in various ways over an infinite number of real things. The children who love to stroke things materially rather than just to look at them appear to have minds which are less open to abstract ideas. But here comes in a fine distinction. Is it the absence of the object which makes the abstractions inaccessible to the child, or is it real mental incapacity for grasping that synthesis of many things which is an abstract idea of quality?

If we succeed in materializing the idea, presenting it in a form adapted to the child, that of tangible objects, will his mind be capable of grasping it, of interesting himself deeply in it?

The sense material may certainly be considered from this point of view as materialized abstraction. It presents colour, dimension, form, odour, sound, in a tangible and distinct manner and arranged in grades which permit of the classification and analysis of qualities.

When the child finds himself in front of the material he applies himself to it with a serious, concentrated effort which seems to draw out the best there is in him. It actually appears that children are found making conquests greater than their minds are capable of; the material opens up to their intelligence ways otherwise inaccessible in the age of childhood.

It is by way of this material that concentration is attained, for it includes things fitted to absorb the intense attention of the child.

A COMPARISON BETWEEN THE EDUCATION OF NORMAL CHILDREN AND THAT OF THOSE MENTALLY DEFICIENT

Knowing that this educational method for normal children has its origin in the method which Itard and Seguin elaborated for children mentally deficient, many have objected that it is impossible to apply one and the same treatment to the two classes of children. At the present time more and more is the tendency to distinguish mental levels with increasing accuracy, recognizing and treating differently those who from the point of view of intelligence are differently endowed, e.g. the supernormal.

I think it well, therefore, to point out the difference which our method recognizes so clearly between children rich in vital spirit and those who are poor in it. The same means used in both cases provoke different reactions and serve to establish an extremely illustrative comparison.

The first and fundamental difference between a child mentally inferior and a normal child, when placed in front of the same material, is that the defective child does not show spontaneous interest. It is necessary to ask for his attention continually and actively, inviting him to observe, to compare, exhorting him to do something.

Let us suppose that we are using as our first object a piece of the solid insets. The exercise, as we know, consists in taking the cylinders out of their places, putting them on the table, mixing them up, and then replacing them, each in its own place.

For the child who is apathetic and mentally weak, it would be necessary, however, to begin with exercises in which the stimuli are more strongly contrasting and would be reached in this exercise after many others had been taken.

For normal children this is the first object which may be presented, and from among all the sense material this is the object preferred by little children of two and a half to three and a half years of age.

For defectives, when they reached this object, it was necessary to attract their attention continually and firmly, inviting observation and comparison; the child, having gathered all the cylinders once into their places, stopped, and the game was finished. When the defective made mistakes, he had to be corrected, or urged to correct himself, and even when he managed to recognize a mistake it generally left him indifferent.

It is different with the normal child who of his own free will takes the liveliest interest in the game, corrects himself, while the correction itself leads to an intensification of his attention on the differences in dimensions and in making comparisons among them.

When the normal child is absorbed in his work he refuses interference from those who want to step in and help him; he wants to be left alone with his problem. The result is a voluntary activity which has a much higher value than simply clearing up the differences between things. Used in this way the material reveals itself as a key which puts the child in communication with himself and opens his mind to expression and activity.

Concentration on a voluntary exercise repeated a great many times is the index to the superiority of the normal child.

Another difference is found in the distinction which the normal child is capable of making between essential things and secondary things which often serve to throw the others into relief.

It has been said that there enters into the education of the senses the isolation of the sense which is to be exercised. Thus, when establishing tactile differences, it is a good plan to isolate the child from visual impressions either by making the surroundings dark or by covering up his eyes with a bandage. In other cases, silence is what is required.

All these methods are instrumental in helping the normal child to concentrate on one isolated stimulus; they strengthen his interest in it.

On the contrary, the defective child is easily distracted by these very methods; he is led away by them from the principal subject which ought to be claiming his attention. In darkness, he easily falls asleep, or he becomes unruly. It is the bandage which attracts his attention instead of the sense stimulus on which he was expected to fix his mind; thus the exercise degenerates into a useless game or an outburst of meaningless joy.

Finally, there is another fact specially worthy of notice; it is that both among defectives and normal children, excellent results are produced by Seguin's ' lesson in three stages,' which so simply and so clearly links up the word with the idea acquired.

That ought to make us reflect that the difference between the higher and the lower mentality diminishes and becomes less noticeable when the child is in a condition to receive, like a passive creature, lessons based on the activity of the teacher who acts over him.

The simple and psychologically perfect lesson of Seguin succeeds in its aim in both cases.

This is clear and eloquent proof that individual differences are revealed and intensified only through spontaneous work and in expression which has not been incited—that is, in the direct manifestations of the inner impulses.

The association of the name with the sense perception in Seguin's lesson succeeds not only in fixing that association in the mind of the defective child, but also partly in increasing his perceptive power. The defective is helped by that lesson to observe the object better; it seems now to be doubly attached to him—by appearance and by name.

The normal child has no need of this help in observing. His observation is at a stage preceding the need for the lesson. He

receives the lesson with great joy when he has already fixed the
sense distinctions. The lesson on the name then clarifies and
completes his own voluntary work. The idea is known, it lives
through his own work; and now comes the baptism, the name, the
consecration. It is interesting to watch the child's intense joy
when he has associated a name with something about which he
has learnt something through his senses.

I remember having taught one day to a small girl who was
not yet three the names of three colours.

I got the children to place one of their little tables in front of
the window and having seated myself in one of their chairs, I
made the child sit down in a similar one, on my right hand. I had
on the table six pieces of colour, in pairs of the same colour—red,
blue and yellow. As a first exercise I put before the child one of
the tablets and asked her to find its match; and this I repeated for
all three colours, getting the similar pairs arranged in a column.
Then I passed on to Seguin's three stages. The little one learnt
to recognize the respective names of the three colours.

She was so delighted that she looked at me for a long time
and then began to dance about. As I watched her dancing in
front of me, I said to her laughing: " Do you know the colours? "
And she always replied as she danced on: " Yes ". This joy of
hers had no end; she continued to dance round that she might
hear the same question repeated, and answer it with her enthusiastic
" Yes ".

The defective child, on the contrary, is helped by the lesson
to understand the material; his attention is directed insistently on
the contrasting differences, and in the end he gets interested in
them and begins to work; the object in itself did not possess a
stimulus strong enough to rouse his energy.

A COMPARISON BETWEEN OUR TEACHING AND EXPERIMENTAL PSYCHOLOGY

There is generally neglected a very interesting comparison
between the research of Itard on the education of children who

are deaf-mutes and defectives, and that attempt which was made much later through the work of the Germans, Fechner and Weber and then Wundt, to subject psychology to experimental research made by means of instruments and measurements.

Itard, who lived about the time of the French Revolution, was led by his scientific studies on diseases of the ear to experiment the education on a positive basis, looking for reactions which, by exciting the senses systematically, would stimulate attention and awaken intelligence and motor activity. The objects which he had in mind had therefore the real meaning of stimuli.

Later, Fechner, Weber and Wundt tried to found a psychology on experimental basis, beginning by testing the sensitivity which existed in normal individuals in respect of minimum stimuli; aiming at determining with mathematical exactitude what times of reaction to the stimuli were displayed by the various subjects which were acted on. Importance was given to the objects by the possibility of their being more or less directly a means of measurement. They formed the instrumentarium of *estesiometry*, the measurement of sensibility.

The two lines of research, born independently, were carried on independently, the first creating, as it expanded, schools for deaf-mutes and mental defectives, the second founding institutes of estesiometry which had for their purpose experimental research directed to the building up a new science.

All these research workers, however, seeing that they based the construction of their instruments on the sensitive reactions of the man, arrived at a determination of objects for the most part analogous and similar to one another, although they would constitute in the one case material for the education of the senses and in the other a kind of arsenal for psycho-sensational measurements.

The aim of the two lines of research, so much alike in the matter of their constructive bases, is therefore quite opposite.

As a matter of fact, estesiometry is seeking for the smallest stimuli perceptible to a man already fully developed or to a child developed to a standard corresponding to his age, by pure and simple demonstration.

The importance of such demonstrations was to show that mental facts are susceptible to mathematical measurement. And it included the idea, which was considered almost as an axiom, that the manner of feeling, or rather of perceiving (that is recognizing) stimuli was an absolutely natural quality, not dependent on knowledge, or on the methodical working of the mind, or on intellectual education; that is, it was not dependent on those artificial mental differences which result from education.

Seeing if one thing is larger or smaller than another, feeling if a minute object has come into contact with our skin, etc. are experiences common to all, and individual differences are characters derived from nature which normally creates its own variations, and which therefore make men more or less sensitive just as they make them more or less intelligent, more or less markedly dark or fair. Its judgments therefore were considered as judgments on the man in his natural mental development. In fact psychology is intended later to determine the characters corresponding to the various mental levels associated with each age and associated with individual variations (of normal, sub-normal people, etc.).

In place of this method, Itard proposed to set up maximum stimuli which were in strong contrast in order to attract to them the sense faculty of children shut out from their environment and incapable of obtaining in the ordinary way precise knowledge of it; he meant to lead them on by repeated exercises, to perceive, step by step, contrasts less abrupt and differences more minute in the separate qualities presented to them. In this case it is not a simple test which is being carried out on the subject in order to demonstrate his mental condition but a modifying action which is directed towards the intelligence in order to awaken it, to kindle contact with the external world, to estimate its characters with precision and to bring into a harmony of interests the intellect and the outer realities.

A modifying action which increases the power of discrimination is a true and proper educational action.

Education of the senses leads to a perfecting of the differential perception of stimuli by means of repeated exercises.

There exists, therefore, a sense education which generally is given no consideration in researches made in mental development, but which is a factor which has to be considered.

For example, I have often seen used as mental tests cubes varying in size and placed at different distances. From among these the child had to recognize the smallest and the largest, whilst the chronometer was measuring the time of reaction which elapsed between the command and the response, and the error was noted.

I used to repeat that in such an experiment the factor of education was forgotten, and by that I meant sense education.

Our children have, among the teaching material used for the education of the senses, a series of ten cubes graduated in their dimensions. The exercise consists in placing on the ground on a dark-coloured rug all the cubes which are coloured pale pink, and then building up the 'tower,' placing at the base the largest cube and then the others in succession up to the smallest. The child must choose from the carpet, every time, the largest cube. This game is found to be most amusing even by children of two and a half years old, who, directly they have built up the tower, knock it down with little blows, admire the pink shapes as they lie on the dark background, and begin the construction all over again, for an indefinite number of times.

If one of my children between three and four years of age, and one of the children from the first class in the elementary school between six and seven years of age were exposed to these tests, mine would undoubtedly show a shorter reaction period and would be much readier to choose the largest cube and the smallest from the heap, and would make no mistakes.

The same may be said about tests in colour sense, tactile sense, etc.

This fact, in a fundamental manner, strikes at the intentions of psychometry (and in general of all experimental psychology based on tests), because it displays in age the mental levels which it considered absolute as a natural variation in individuals.

This educational method may also be taken into consideration by the advocates of experimental psychology who hope to estimate by means of instantaneous reactions the level of mental development, almost making an absolute measure of the whole through one detail, as one would do if one were to calculate the growth of the body at various ages by measuring the height. Systematic exercise of the senses would upset these proportions, showing that they have not demonstrated an absolute feature in mental growth.

If it is desired to obtain from experimental psychology a practical application, wherever it may be attempted, to the reform of educational methods in schools, then the mistake in principle becomes all the clearer.

If scientific pedagogy is to be established it will have to take as the starting-point active and modifying stimuli and not measuring stimuli.

This standard constituted the very beginning of my researches. In practice it succeeded in establishing an experimental pedagogy for normal children, and at the same time, in revealing mental qualities which had not previously been known in children.

The psychology of the study, with its reactions and its tests, introduced into elementary schools to reform them, has not succeeded in influencing the practical work in the school itself or changing its methods of education.

The logical consequence has merely been to catch a glimpse of the possibility of modifying examinations, that is tests of the scholar, and for a time English-speaking America seemed very keen on considering seriously the substitution of the scientific examination of individual attitudes for the old examination for testing of what had been learnt. There was thus placed at the end of the studies the same examination as that adopted in institutes of a professional character for the admission of men to work.

On the other hand, Itard's studies had immediate practical results in the heart of education and resulted in the curing of partly deaf children, who regained their hearing by the strengthening of their auditory faculty by means of exercise; and at the same time they regained speech. From this beginning there arose the education of the real deaf-mutes and then of the defectives.

The schools established throughout Switzerland, Germany, France and America spread this work of redemption of unhappy children and raised the mental and social level of all the children who were affected by them.

And directly the same methods were introduced into the schools for normal children, a profound change in the school was the result, an elevation of the personality of the child which has spread through the whole world the social conception of independence and the liberation of the child.

WRITTEN LANGUAGE

OUGHT our pedagogic conception of aiding the natural development of the child to be arrested by an artificial acquirement derived exclusively from the work of civilization; by this I mean written language? How does this concern writing and reading? Here we have clearly a question of teaching, and this teaching does not take into account the nature of man. We have reached the moment in which it is necessary to face in education the problem of culture and therefore of the effort necessary to acquire it, even by the sacrifice of natural impulses. Every one knows that reading and writing form the first tasks of the school; the first affliction of the man who has to sacrifice his own nature to the requirements of civilization.

With regard to this question, those who were concerning themselves with the child himself, came to the conclusion that it was best to delay as long as possible so painful a task, and they considered the age of eight years just suitable for so difficult a problem. Generally speaking, the teaching of the alphabet and of writing begins at the age of six, it being considered almost a sin to introduce early childhood to the alphabet and written words. Written language is in fact, like the second dentition, of use only in an advanced stage of development. It is language which enables us to express thought which is already logically organized, and to obtain from books the ideas of a vast number of distant, unseen people, or of those who have died in ages long past. As long as the child is incapable of using this language because of his immaturity, he may be excused from the hard labour of learning it.

We, however, believe that the solution may be arrived at through a more profound study of the problem. Above all there will have to be considered an infinite number of errors in the method of teaching writing. This is not the place to discuss them, but one example, that of the method used by Seguin to teach writing to defectives, will suffice to illustrate our point. Another problem for study is that of considering writing in itself, analysing it into its factors. By trying to separate them into independent exercises, they can be adapted to various ages and thus distributed according to the natural powers of the child. This is the principle inspiring our method which will be illustrated in the following pages.

THE OLD METHODS OF TEACHING READING AND WRITING

CRITICISM OF SEGUIN'S METHOD OF TEACHING WRITING

Seguin does not present in his treatise on teaching any reasoned out methods for teaching writing. Here is the substance of his way of teaching writing.

" In order to carry a child on from drawing, strictly so-called, to writing which is the immediate application of it, the teacher needs only to call the letter D a portion of a circle supported at its extremities against a vertical line, and A, two sloping lines joined at the top and crossed by a horizontal line, and so on."

" It is no longer then a question of knowing how the child will learn to write; he draws, *then* he will write. After that it is not necessary to say that the letters must be drawn according to

Disagrees w/ Seguin
& therefore criticises

the laws of contrast and similarity; thus O next to I, B opposite P, T along with L, etc."

According to Seguin, then, it is not necessary to *teach* writing; the child who draws, will write. But writing is, for this author, the printed capital letter! Neither does he go on to tell us whether or not the idiot will write in any other way. Instead, he enlarges on a description of the teaching of the drawing which prepares for writing and which includes writing—teaching which is full of difficulties and which is methodized by the joint efforts of Itard and Seguin.

" Chapter XL. *Drawing.*—In drawing, the first ideas to be acquired, in the order of their importance, are that of the plane surface intended to receive the drawing, and secondly, that of the lines traced on it.

" Within these two ideas are comprised all writing, all drawing, every linear creation.

" These two ideas are correlative; their relationship generates the idea, the capacity for producing lines in this sense, because lines deserve their name only when they follow a methodical and rational direction; the mark made without a direction is not a line; it is produced by chance, it has no name."

" The rational mark, on the contrary, has a name, because it follows a direction, and since all writing or drawing is none other than a mixture of different directions which a line follows, it is necessary, before dealing with writing properly so-called, to insist on these notions of plane and line which the normal child acquires by intuition, but which one has to make precise and clear for idiots, in all their applications. Through methodical drawing they will come into rational contact with all parts of the plane, and will produce, at first by imitation, simple lines at first, complicated later on.

" In successive stages they will be taught—(1) to draw different kinds of lines, (2) to draw them in various directions and in positions differently related to the surface, (3) to join these lines so as to form figures graduated from the simple to the complicated.

Hence they must be taught at first to distinguish between straight lines and curves, verticals and horizontals and between the vast variety of sloping lines; then, lastly, the principal points of union of two or more lines to form a figure.

"This reasoned analysis of drawing, from which writing will be born, is so essential in all its parts that a child who was able to draw many letters before being entrusted to me, spent six days in drawing a perpendicular and a horizontal line, fifteen days before he could reproduce a curve and a sloping line. Most of my pupils are for a long time incapable of imitating the movement of my hands on paper before being able to draw a line in a definite direction.

"The more imitative or the less stupid produce a mark diametrically the opposite of that which I have shown them, and all of them confuse the points where two lines meet, even the easiest to understand like the top, the bottom, the centre. It is true that the thorough teaching which I have given them about the plane, the lines and configuration makes them later prepared to grasp the relationships which have to be established between the plane and the different lines with which they must cover the surface; but in the research made necessary by the abnormalities of my pupils, the progression from the vertical to the horizontal, the oblique and the curve, must be determined by consideration of the difficulties of comprehension and of execution which each one of them offers to a dull intelligence, and to an unsteady and unsure hand. Here one has no longer merely to make them carry out a difficult job since I have prepared myself to help them to overcome a series of difficulties. I have, therefore, asked myself if these difficulties might not vary in degree and if sometimes they might not originate in theories. Here are the ideas which have guided me in this matter.

"The vertical is a line which the eye and the hand follow directly, raising and lowering themselves. The horizontal is not natural either to the eye or the hand, which lower themselves and follow a curve (like the horizon from which the name is taken) starting from the centre to go to the lateral extremities of the plane if they are not kept in proportion to the distance which they traverse.

" The sloping line involves ideas comparatively more complex; and curves exact steadiness and differences with respect to the plane so variable and difficult to grasp that it would be a waste of time to begin the study of lines with these. The simplest line is therefore the vertical, and this is how I got the children to grasp the idea.

" The first geometrical formula is this: from one point to another we can draw only one straight line. Starting from this axiom, which the hand alone can demonstrate, I fixed two points on the blackboard, and joined them with a vertical line. My children tried to do the same between two points which I had marked on their papers; but some came down with the vertical to the right of the lower point, others to the left; there were others whose hand wandered over the page in all directions. In order to get rid of these various divergences, which are very often due more to intelligence and sight than to the hand, I thought it would be a good plan to restrict the usable area of the surface, by drawing two verticals, one to the right and one to the left of the points which the child was to join with a line parallel to and intermediate with the other two, which serve, so to speak, as banks. If these two lines were not enough I fixed vertically on the paper two rulers which completely stopped the hand from wandering. But these material barriers are not useful for long. We first remove the rulers and then turn to the use of the parallel lines, between which the idiot is not long before he interposes the third vertical. Then one of the directive verticals is taken away, and there is left sometimes that on the right, sometimes that on the left, in order that they may prevent any deviation which presents itself. Finally the last line is suppressed, then the points, beginning by cancelling that at the top which indicates the starting point of the line and of the hand; the child learns in this way to draw a vertical line, alone, without any assistance, without any points of comparison.

16

"The same method, the same difficulties, the same means of direction apply to the straight horizontal lines. If by chance they are begun fairly well the child may be expected to curve them, tending to go from the centre to the extremities, as nature compels him, for the reason which I have explained. If points marked at intervals are not enough to keep his hand up, it is kept within limits by parallel lines which are drawn on the paper, or by rulers.

"Finally, the child will be made to draw the horizontal line whilst a set-square is placed against a vertical line forming with it a right angle. The child will thus begin to understand the meaning of the vertical line and the horizontal line, and will be able to catch a glimpse of these first two ideas for drawing a figure.

"From the order in which the lines are introduced it might appear that the study of oblique lines should follow immediately after that of the vertical and horizontal, but it is not so. The oblique, which shares with the vertical in its inclination and with the horizontal in its direction, and which shares with both in its character because it is a straight line, presents, because of its relationship both with the plane and with other lines, too complex an idea to be appreciated without preparation."

In this way Seguin continues for several pages to speak of lines sloping in all directions, which he has drawn between the parallels. He goes on to the four curves, which he has drawn to the right and to the left of a vertical, and above and below a horizontal. He concludes: "In this way were solved the problems which I was investigating—the vertical, the horizontal and the sloping lines, and the four curves the union of which forms the circle, the whole containing in principle all the lines possible in writing.

"Having arrived at this point, Itard and I stopped for a long time. The lines being known it was a suitable time to get the child to draw some of the regular figures, beginning of course with the simplest. Speaking from his experience, Itard had advised me to begin with the square, and I followed this advice for three months without succeeding in making myself understood."

After a long series of experiments and following the guidance of ideas about the origin of geometric figures, Seguin found out that the easiest figure to draw was the triangle.

" When three lines meet together in this way, they always form a triangle, whilst four lines may meet in a hundred directions, without keeping exactly parallel, and therefore presenting an imperfect square.

" From these experiments and observations, confirmed by many others which it would be superfluous to quote, I deduced the first principles of writing and drawing for idiots—principles the applications of which is too simple for me to dwell longer on it."

The above describes the methods used by my predecessors in teaching writing to defectives. To teach reading, Itard proceeded in the following way. He hung from nails on the wall geometrical figures like triangles, squares, circles; then he drew the exact reproduction of them on the wall. After that, having removed the figures, he had them replaced on their respective nails by the Savage de l' Aveyron, who had to be guided by the drawings. It was from these drawings that Itard took the idea of the flat insets. Finally, Itard made letters of the alphabet in printed capitals and used them in a way similar to that which he had used for the geometrical figures; that is, he drew them on the wall and placed nails at such a height that the child could hang up letters over the drawings. Later on, Itard used a horizontal plane instead of the wall, drawing the letters on the bottom of a box and getting the drawing covered with the solid letters.

Twenty years later, Seguin had not changed his method.

Criticism of the method used by Itard and Seguin for teaching writing and reading seems to me superfluous. There are inherent two fundamental mistakes which make it inferior to the methods in use in schools for normal children. The first is that of teaching writing with printed capital letters; the second lies in preparing for writing a study of rational geometry, which we reserve today for pupils in secondary schools. In doing this Seguin really confuses ideas in a way which surprises us. He suddenly jumps from the psychological observation of the child and his relationship to his environment to a study of the origins of lines and figures and of their connection with the plane surface.

He says that the child will draw a vertical line easily but the horizontal will very often become a curve because ' nature orders it '; and that this command of nature is represented by the fact that man sees the horizon as a curved line!

Seguin's example is valuable as being an illustration of the necessity for special education fitted to train man in observation and to direct logical thought. Observation ought to be absolutely objective, free from all preconceptions. Seguin's perception in this case is that geometrical design must prepare for writing, and that prevents him from discovering the truly natural method necessary for such preparation. Another of his preconceptions is that the deviations of the lines or the inexactitute with which the child draws them, is due to the mind and the eye, not to the hand; therefore he wearies himself out for weeks and months in explaining the direction of the lines and in directing the vision of the idiot.

Seguin's idea seems to be that a good method ought to start from above; geometry, the intelligence of the child, and certain abstract relationships are alone worthy of being taken into consideration.

Is this not a common mistake?

A great deal of time and intellectual energy are lost in the world because falsehood seems to be great and truth small.

Seguin's method of teaching writing illustrates the tortuosity of the paths which we follow in teaching, and that because of an innate tendency to complicate things, analogous to that which makes us attach value only to complicated things. So we have Seguin teaching geometry in order to teach writing, and making the child-mind undertake the great effort of understanding geometrical abstractions in order to relieve him from the much simpler task of drawing a printed *D*. Further, will the child not have to make the effort of forgetting the printing, in order to learn cursive writing? And would it not have been simpler to begin with cursive writing?

Would many not believe that in order to learn to write it is necessary to make children draw little strokes? This used to be a deep-seated conviction. It actually seemed natural that, in order to write the letters of the alphabet which are all round, it was necessary to begin with straight lines and with strokes giving a bend at an acute angle. Need we really marvel then that the beginner experienced such great difficulty in getting rid of sharp angularity when attempting the beautiful curves of the letter *O*, or how much effort he and we expended in getting him to make strokes and write with acute angles? Who is it who revealed to us that the first drawing to be made ought to be a straight line? And why are we so determined to use angles to prepare the way for curves?

Let us rid ourselves for a moment from such preconceptions, and let us travel along a simpler track. Perhaps it will bring us great relief, sparing future humanity every effort needed to learn to write.

Is it necessary to begin with strokes? Logical thought at once answers " No ". The child expends too painful an effort in such an exercise, for the strokes must form only the minor difficulty which has to be overcome.

Also, if we notice carefully, the stroke is the most difficult exercise to accomplish; only a first-class writer can complete with regularity a page of strokes, whilst a person who writes moderately well could offer a page of presentable writing. In fact, the straight line is unique, indicating the shortest distance between two points. On the contrary, every deviation from this direction means a line which is not straight; the infinite deviations are therefore easier than the unique line, which represents perfection. If the order is given to draw on the blackboard a straight line without any other limitation, every one will draw a long line, in different directions, beginning sometimes on the one side, sometimes on the other and almost all will succeed in it. If one asks for a straight line to be drawn in some particular direction and beginning from a definite point, then the ability first shown will be much less, and there will appear a pretty big series of irregularities, that is mistakes.

Almost all the lines will be long, because the individuals have to make a dash in order to carry out their intentions.

Let us now give directions that the lines must be short and kept within defined limits; the errors will increase because the dash which had helped to keep the direction straight is prevented. Now let us add that the writing instrument must be held in a particular way, not as each one chooses.

In this way do we approach sensibly the first attempts at writing which we expect from children—attempts which also demand the preservation of parallelism among the separate lines drawn, and which will make a dull, very difficult piece of work, because they have no aim for the children who do not understand them.

I noticed in the copybooks of deficient children visited in France (and Voisin also mentions this fact) that the pages of strokes, although they begin as such, finished with the lines of the letter C; that means that the defective child whose attention is less resistant than that of the normal child exhausts, little by little, his first effort at imitation, and natural movement is gradually substituted for that which was imposed. Thus the straight lines are changed into curves often resembling those of C. Such a phenomenon does not appear in the copy-books of normal children, because they maintain their effort up to the end of the page, and, as so often happens, they cover up the error in teaching. But let us examine the spontaneous drawings of normal children when, for example, they are drawing lines on the sand of the garden paths with a branch which has fallen from a tree; we will never see short straight lines, but long curved lines variously interlaced. Seguin saw the same thing when he made the children draw horizontals which at once became curves, an occurrence which he considered was due to imitation of the horizon.[1]

---

[1] An obstacle arises here, when there have to be analysed alphabetical orms which include both straight lines and curves.

The labour which we had thought necessary to learn to write is quite artificial work, demanded not by writing but by the methods of teaching it.

MY FIRST EXPERIMENTS WITH DEFECTIVE CHILDREN

Let us discard for the moment all the old dogmatism which pertains to the subject. Let us disregard culture. Let us drop all interest in the question of how man began to write as well as in the genesis of writing itself. Let us drop the conviction which established custom has given us of the necessity for beginning writing with strokes; and let us imagine ourselves to be stripped bare in spirit, like the truth which we want to discover.

Let us observe an individual who is writing, and try to analyse the moves which he makes as he writes—the mechanism which is concerned in writing.

This would mean carrying out a psycho-physiological study of writing; it would mean studying the individual who is writing—the subject, not the object.

It was always by beginning with the object, by beginning with the writing, that a method was built up.

A method which started from the study of the individual rather than from that of the writing would really be original, very different from any method which has preceded it.

If I had thought of giving a name to this new method when I undertook the experiments on normal children, before I had learnt the results of it, I would have called it a psychological method, because of the source of inspiration. But experience has given me, as a surprise and as a gift from nature, another title —the method of spontaneous writing.

During the time when I was teaching defectives I happened to notice the following fact. An idiot girl, eleven years old, whose motive power and strength of hand were normal, could not learn to sew, could not even master the first stage, that of pushing the needle in and out in succession under and over the cloth, taking and leaving a few threads.

Then I set this girl to work at Froebel's weaving exercise which consists in threading a roll of paper transversely through vertical rods also of paper, fixed at the top and the bottom. I was led to think of the analogy between the two kinds of work, and was greatly interested in my observations. When she had become skilful in Froebel's weaving I put her back to her sewing and was pleased to see that she succeeded in executing the needlework.

I considered that the necessary movement of the hand had been prepared for the sewing *without sewing*, and that really it is necessary to find out the way to teach before having it done. Especially is this true when it is a question of preparing movements which might be stimulated and also limited by repeated exercises, outside the direct work for which they are preparing. In this way it would be possible to be able to carry out the work when they attack it, without having yet put a hand to it directly and to accomplish it perfectly at the first attempt.

I thought that this idea might usefully be applied to writing. The thought interested me intensely and I wondered at its simplicity. I was surprised that I had not thought at first of the plan which the observation of the girl who could not sew had suggested to me.

Since I had made the children touch the outlines of the geometrical figures in the plane insets, there remained only to make them trace with their fingers the shapes of the letters of the alphabet.

I had made for me a splendid alphabet, the letters being in the form of cursive script, the body of the writing 8 cms. high, the rest in proportion. The letters were made of wood, $\frac{1}{2}$ cm. thick, in coloured enamel, red for the consonants and blue for the vowels, except underneath where there was a very elegant brass cover fixed by small studs. To correspond with the alphabet (of which there was only one example) cards were made on which were painted the letters of the alphabet in the same colours and of the same size as the movable letters, and grouped according to contrasts and similarities of shape.

To every letter of the alphabet there corresponded a picture painted by hand in water-colour, in which was reproduced in colour and size the cursive letter; and, close by, much smaller, was painted the same letter in small printed character. In the picture were represented objects the name of which began with the letter in question; for example, for *m* there was *mano* (hand) and *martello* (hammer), for *g*, *gatto* (cat), etc. These pictures served to fix the sound of the letter in the memory.

The pictures certainly do not represent a new idea, but they complete a whole which did not exist previously.

The interesting part of my experiment was this, that after the movable letter had been superposed on the corresponding letter drawn on the cards on which they were grouped, I made the children trace the letters in imitation of cursive writing many times over. These exercises were then multiplied on the letters drawn simply on the cards; in this way the children succeeded in mastering the movements necessary for reproducing the forms of the graphic signs *without writing*. At that stage I was struck by an idea which had not entered my mind before: that in writing are employed two different kinds of movement, namely besides the already mentioned movement which reproduces the form there is that of handling the instrument of writing. Indeed, when defective children had become expert in tracing all the letters of the alphabet according to their forms, they were not yet able to hold the pen in their hand. Holding and manipulating a rod with certainty needs a special muscular mechanism which is independent of the movements involved in writing; it is in fact contemporaneous with the movements necessary for tracing all the different letters of the alphabet. It is, therefore, a unique mechanism which ought to exist along with the motor memory of the separate graphic signs. There remained the preparation of the muscular mechanism for holding and manipulating the instrument of writing. That I tried to obtain by adding to what has already been described two other exercises. In the first, the letters were touched not only with the index finger of the right hand, as on the first occasion.

but with two fingers, the index and the middle finger; in the second, the letters were touched with a wooden rod held like a pen in writing.

In the main, I had the letters repeated sometimes with and sometimes without the addition of holding the instrument.

It is to be noted that the child must follow with his finger the visible image of the letter drawn. It is true that this finger has already been exercised in touching the outlines of the geometrical figures, but this practice does not always appear to be sufficient for the work. We ourselves, for example, when making a drawing clearer, cannot follow perfectly the line we see and on which we have to retrace the drawing. It would be necessary that the drawing should possess some special property which attracted the point of our pencil, in magnet fashion, or that the pencil should find a mechanical guide on the paper where it is drawing, in order to follow with precision the trace which is apparent to the eye. Defectives did not, therefore, always follow the drawing, either with the finger or with the rod; the teaching material did not offer any control to the work done; or offered only the untrustworthy control of the eye of the child, who certainly could not see whether or not the finger was following the lines. I thought that, in order to get the movements of writing carried out more exactly, and to guarantee or at least to guide execution in a more direct manner, it would be necessary to prepare hollow letter shapes, so that they were represented by a groove, in which the wooden rod might move. I made a plan for such work, but as it was too costly I was not able to carry it out.

I spoke at length about this method to teachers in the course of my lessons on teaching at the College for Training Teachers of Defectives. In the second year of the course, lithographed leaflet were distributed and I have preserved up till now about a hundred copies of them as documents of the past.

Here are the words which, spoken in public twenty-five year ago remained in lithographed form in the hands of two hundred elementary teachers without any one of them, as Professor Ferrer said with astonishment in an article,[1] extracting one profitable idea from them.

(Summary of the lectures on teaching by Dr. Montessori, in 1900, Lith. Romano, Via Frattina 62, disp. 6a, p. 46, " Simultaneous Reading and Writing.")

" At this point there is presented the card having the vowels coloured in blue; the child sees irregular figures drawn in colour. The blue vowels are offered to him to be placed over the drawings on the card. He has to trace the wooden vowels in the same way as writing them, and name them; the vowels are grouped according to similarity of shape—

o, e, a,   i, u.

" Then one says to the child, for example: ' Bring me the letter *o*,' ' Put it into its place.' Then, ' What letter is this? ' Here it will be found that many children make mistakes because they only look at the letter; they guess without touching it. Observations may be made which reveal various individual types, visual and motor.

" The child is then made to touch the letter drawn on the card, first with the index finger only, then with the index and middle fingers, then with a wooden rod held like a pen. The letter must be followed as in writing it."

" The consonants are drawn in red and are placed on cards according to similarities in shape; there is added a movable alphabet of red wood, to be placed over the cards as with the vowels. Along with the alphabet is a series of other cards where alongside the consonants similar to those of wood there are painted one or two figures of objects the names of which begin with the letters drawn. In front of the cursive letter there is also painted with the same colour a smaller letter of printed character.

---

[1] G. Ferreri, " On the Teaching of Writing " (System of Dr. Montessori), Bulletin of the Roman Association for the medico-pedagogic care of abnormal children and poor defectives, vol. I, no. 4, Oct. 1907, Rome (Tip. delle Terme Diocleziane).

" The mistress, naming the consonants in the phonetic manner, points to the letter, then to the card, pronouncing the name of the object which is painted and dwelling on the first letter thus: ' m. . . . . .*mela*,' ' give me the consonant *m*, put it in its place, touch it.' In this way the defects in the child's language are studied.

" Tracing the letters as in writing begins the muscular exercise which prepares for writing. One of our children of the ' motor ' type, taught by this method, has reproduced all the letters with the pen, about 8 mm. high, before she could yet recognize them, and this with surprising regularity. This child succeeded very well also in manual work."

" The child who looks at, recognizes and touches the letters in the manner of writing is prepared for reading and writing simultaneously.

" Touching the letters and at the same time looking at them fixes their images more quickly, owing to the co-operation of the senses; later, the two acts are separated—looking (reading), touching (writing). Some learn to read first, others to write; it depends on the type of individual."

I had, then, started many years ago, in its fundamental characters, my method of teaching, writing and reading. It was with great surprise that I noticed the ease with which, one fine day, after a piece of chalk had been put into the hand of a defective, he drew on the blackboard, firmly and in good handwriting, the letters of the whole alphabet, writing for the first time; this was done much more quickly than one would have expected. As is said in the leaflets, children used to write even with the pen all the letters of the alphabet before they were able to recognize any one of them. I have noticed this quite as much in normal children, and I am led to say that the muscular sense is the most highly developed in childhood, wherefore writing is very easy for children. It is not the same with reading, which involves a very long period of instruction and calls for higher intellectual development, since it means interpreting signs, modulating the accents of the voice

that the meaning of the word may be understood. All that consists of purely mental work, whilst in writing, as is shown below, the child translates sounds into signs in a material way; and he moves, which to him is easy and pleasant. Writing is developed in the small child easily and spontaneously, in the same way as speech, which is also a motor translation of sounds which are heard. On the other hand, reading forms part of abstract intellectual culture which is the interpretation of ideas represented by graphic symbols, and is acquired only much later.

FIRST EXPERIMENTS ON NORMAL CHILDREN

My first experiments with normal children began in the first half of November, 1907.

In the two Children's Houses in San Lorenzo, from the 6th of January in one case, and from the 7th of March in the other, dating from their respective inaugurations, until the end of July, I had applied only exercises in practical life, and in the education of the senses. After July a month of holidays had interrupted the lessons. I was influenced by the prejudice that the teaching of reading and writing should be delayed as long as possible, certainly till the age of six years. But during the months which had elapsed, the children seemed to be asking themselves for some conclusion to the exercises which had already developed them intellectually to a surprising degree. They could dress and undress themselves and wash themselves; they could sweep the floors, dust the furniture, set the rooms in order, open and close boxes, turn keys in locks, replace objects in good order in the cupboards, water the flowers; they were able to observe objects by touching them; some of them came and asked us frankly to teach them to read and write. And, after we had refused, some children came to school able to draw *o*'s on the blackboard, and displayed their doings to us like a challenge. Afterwards a large number of mothers came to ask us as a favour to teach their children to write. " Because," they said, " here they wake up and learn so many things so easily that if

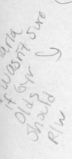

they were taught to read and write they would learn quickly and would be spared a great deal of trouble in the elementary school."

This belief of the mothers that with us the little ones would learn reading and writing without trouble struck me forcibly. And, thinking of the results obtained in the schools for defectives, I decided, during the August holidays, to make an attempt when the school opened in September. But then I reflected that in September it would be well to resume the interrupted teaching, and to begin reading and writing only in October when the elementary schools opened, which would give ours the advantage of beginning the same teaching at the same time as these.

In September, therefore, I began to look for some one to make the material, but found no workers disposed to do it. A professor advised me to place orders in Milan, and that led to a great waste of time. I wanted to make a fine alphabet like that for the defectives in wood, covered with enamel paint and metal. Then I would have contented myself with single letters of enamel similar to those used for inscriptions on shop windows, but I found none. In a professional school, I was on the point of obtaining letters hollowed out in wood (for touching along the groove with a rod), but the workers were discouraged by the difficulty of the work and it was suspended.

In this way the whole of October passed. Already the children of the first elementary class had filled pages with strokes, and mine were still waiting. Then I decided, in consultation with the mistresses, to cut out from simple sheets of paper very large letters of the alphabet, and one mistress coloured them roughly on one side with blue and red respectively. For the purpose of tracing the letters, I thought of cutting out the letters in sandpaper and gumming them on smooth paper, thus making objects very similar to those used in the first exercises in the sense of touch.

Only after having made these simple things did I realize the great superiority of this alphabet over the magnificent affair made for the defectives, which I had sought for in vain for two months. If I had been rich, I would have used for ever the superb but sterile alphabet of the past. We desire the old because we do not know the new, and we always look for the grandeur of things which have passed away without recognizing in the humble simplicity of new beginnings the germ which must develop in the future.

I understood then that an alphabet of paper could easily be multiplied into more copies, and so could be used by many children at the same time, not only for the recognition of letters but for the composition of words.

I also learnt that in the alphabet of sandpaper I had found the guide so much desired for the finger which touches the letter, so that not only sight but also touch was used directly in teaching the movement of writing, together with exact control. Full of the enthusiasm of this hope we set ourselves, the two teachers and I, in the evening after school, to cutting out a great number of letters of the alphabet from simple writing-paper, gumming some on smooth paper and colouring the others blue. We then spread them out on tables and found them dry next morning. Whilst we were working there took shape in my mind an exceedingly clear picture of the method in all its completeness, so simple that it made me smile to think that I had never thought of it before. The story of our attempts is very interesting.

One day when one of the mistresses was ill I sent as a substitute for her one of my pupils, Signorina Anna Fedeli, a teacher of pedagogy in a normal school. When I went to see Signorina Fedeli in the evening, she showed me two modifications made in the alphabet. One consisted in having placed above and below each letter a strip of white paper to enable the child to recognize the side of the letter, which he often turned about in all directions. Another change consisted in making a case out of cardboard, in which would be placed in every compartment a group of the same letters, whereas at first they were all mixed up together in a heap. I still keep that case made from the cardboard of a broken box which was found in the door-keeper's lodge and stitched together roughly with white thread. In showing it to me Signorina Fedeli was almost excusing herself for the disgraceful work, but I was filled with enthusiasm. I understood at once that the letters being in the case formed a precious aid to teaching; there was offered to the child's eye the possibility of comparing all the letters and choosing the one designated.

In this way there originated the method and the material which I will now describe.

Here it is enough to point out that at the time of Christmas holidays in the following December, or less than a month and a half after, when the children of the elementary schools were labouring to forget the strokes and angles learnt with so much trouble in order to prepare themselves for the curves of *o*'s and the other vowels, two of my little ones of four years old were writing in good style without corrections or smudges—writing which was later considered comparable with the handwriting which is common in the third elementary class.

THE MECHANISM OF WRITING

WRITING is a complex act which has to be analysed. One part of it is dependent on motor mechanisms, and the other represents real work of the intellect.

Among the movements, I have distinguished first of all two principal groups: one is concerned with the management of the instrument of writing; the other with the drawing of the different shapes of the separate letters of the alphabet. These parts constitute the motor mechanism of writing, which can be substituted for by an actual machine, and therefore, it is also mechanism although of another kind that would be developed if made for type-writing.

The fact that a machine may enable a man to write makes it possible for us to understand how the two things, that is, the mechanism and the higher function of the intelligence which uses written language to express itself, can be separated one from the other.

The physiological mechanisms are those which allow of accurate analysis, because by noticing how one writes and noting the various coefficients which take part in it, it is possible not only to distinguish but to separate them from one another.

17

Let us commence then to study the two groups of movements.

First we take that which refers to the manipulation of the instrument of writing, to the holding of the pen or pencil. This is grasped with the first three fingers of the hand, and is moved up and down with that sure uniformity which we are accustomed to call the style of the writing. The movement is so individualistic that each one of us, although using the same alphabet, imposes his own character on writing, and there are as many handwritings as there are men.

It is impossible to falsify handwriting, to write exactly like another person. The infinitesimal differences are unfathomable in their origin, but it is certain that they are fixed by the senses in each one of us when our own particular mechanism is established and that they hinder us from ever varying it much. They become a mark of identification, one of the clearest and most indelible in our personality.

In this way there will be fixed in us the modulations of the voice, the accent with which we pronounce our mother tongue, and all these mechanical requirements for motion which form our own functional characters, destined to survive even after many of our physical traits which are subject to continual though slow transformation.

It is in childhood that the motor mechanism is fixed, that the child is elaborating and stabilizing, by his own exertions, the characters of his individuality and in this he is obeying an invisible individual law. At this age the motor mechanism is in its sensitive stage, and is quick to obey the hidden orders of nature.

The child therefore experiences, in every motor effort, the joyous satisfaction of responding to one of the necessities of life.

It is necessary to find out the age in which the mechanism for writing is ready to be established; it will be established without effort, naturally, giving pleasure and stimulating vital energy.

This is certainly not the age in which they try, in the ordinary schools, to excite the motor mechanism of writing, asking from

With remarkably delicate and controlled movements this boy traces the outlines of the geometrical figures and their frames, the muscular impression completes visual recognition and is a remote preparation for writing. Photo by Mrs. A. V. Baker taken in an English Montessori School.

The activity illustrated in this picture is a sequence to the one illustrated in the picture on the previous page.

the little hand which is now adult because it has fixed many movements, the painful, almost deforming, effort of turning back in the
paths of its development. The hand of the child of six or seven
years old has lost its precious period of sensitivity to movement.
This delicate hand has left behind it the delightful time in which
movements were being co-ordinated, in which is created the functional hand and it is condemned to a painful and unnatural effort.

It is necessary to go further back and look for the baby hand
which is still unco-ordinated, still functionally ' soft '; it is the
enquiring little hand of the very small child of four who touches
everything round about him, in the irresistible and unconscious
attempt to stabilize definite co-ordinations.

Analysis of the Movement of a Hand which is Writing

In order to help the teaching of writing, it is needful first of
all to analyse the various movements which enter into it, and to
try to develop them separately, in a manner independent of actual
writing. In this way we will be able to suit various ages, each
having its own possibilities, co-operate in constructing that
mechanism which is so difficult and complex.

In the sense exercises, which are accompanied by fine movements of the hand and which interest the child so much that he
is led to an indefinite repetition of the same actions, we will find
the psychological time and the external means which are precisely
adapted as a remote preparation for the mechanism of writing.

The Hand which Writes

One must be capable of holding in the fingers some instrument
of writing (pen, pencil, etc.) and of guiding it with a light hand to
draw definite symbols.

Holding the instrument requires not only the work of the three
fingers which grip it, but also the co-operation of the hand which
has to travel lightly over the surface on which the writing is being
done.

Indeed, the first difficulty of ordinary scholars is not so much that of holding the pen as the accompanying one of keeping the hand light, of lifting instead of leaning on the hand. (The scholar makes the chalk screech on the blackboard, the pen scrape on the paper, and often breaks the chalk and the pen; he has grasped and dragged the instrument convulsively, but his effort is that of struggling against the unsupportable weight of his feeble hand.)

Besides, the quite unco-ordinated hand cannot execute signs so precise as those of the letters of the alphabet. Such an act is suited only to a hand which is already capable of guiding itself steadily. What is called ' firm hand,' a hand under the control of the will, is a condition necessary to fit it for writing.

To acquire these long exercises, patiently repeated, are required and if they have to be mixed up with learning to write, that is, if the hand, clumsy and unfitted for writing, has to be trained by writing, it will constitute the greatest obstacle to the progress of writing.

By our method, however, little children have acquired a hand which is practised and ready to write.

When in the course of the sense exercises they move the hand in various directions and with various objects in view, but repeating in the same way the same actions, they unconsciously are preparing for writing. Let us consider some of the exercises already carried out by our children.

The Three Fingers which Move the Instrument

As the age of three the children disarrange the cylinders of the solid insets, holding with the three fingers the grip-button which is nearly of the same size as a writing implement. The three fingers carry out, for an infinite number of times, that exercise which co-ordinates the motor organs intended for writing.

The Light Hand

Watch the little one of three and a half, who bathes the tips of his fingers in tepid water, and with bandaged eyes devotes his energy to one single object, that of moving his hand, lightly poised, so that the fingers barely slip over the surface of a smooth or a rough tablet. This effort to move the hand whilst holding it lightly is accompanied by a sharpening of the tactile sensibility of those fingers which will have to write some day. In this way there is being perfected the most precious instrument of the human will.

THE FIRM HAND

There is something underlying the ability to draw a figure; it is the possibility of moving the hand with a purpose, of being able to direct it in an exact manner. This power is a generic property of the hand, because it refers to the greater or lesser possibility of co-ordinating movements.

Consider the exercise with the flat insets which consists in touching exactly the outlines of the various geometrical figures and their frames, using as a guide a wooden rim which helps the unpractised hand to keep itself within the prescribed limits. In the meantime the eye is growing accustomed to seeing and recognizing the forms which the hand is touching.

This preparation, so remote and indirect, is a preparation of the hand *to write*; it is not a preparation of writing; the two preparations must not be confused with each other.

DIRECT PREPARATION FOR WRITING

ANALYSIS OF ITS FACTORS

What we must now do is to make an analysis of the factors of writing, using as illustrations things already mentioned. Writing consists of a complex set of difficulties which we can separate one from the other, and which we can overcome one by one by different exercises, and also at different moments and epochs in life. The exercises for every factor, however, must be kept independent of writing. Looking for an analogy in chemistry, we find that the oxygen and hydrogen which are derived from the analysis of water are no longer water; they are two gases, each possessing its own properties and being able to exist alone. When we speak then of the analysis of factors, we mean separating out the elements of which writing is composed into interesting exercises which may by themselves constitute motives to induce activity in children. This is a very different thing from the analyses which have been intended to break up a whole into parts considered as incomplete details of the whole and therefore devoid of interest, (strokes, curves, etc.). Instead of that, our analysis of factors makes every factor live in an independent exercise. It separates, but it seeks in the separation for elements which can exist by themselves, and which can be applied to exercises having a rational end in view.

First Factor:
Mastery of the Instrument of Writing: Drawing

I profited by that childish liking for filling in figures drawn in outline by means of marks made with coloured pencils. This is the most primitive form of drawing, or rather it is the precursor of drawing, and our children had already done this filling in drawings given in their outline. But now to make such work more interesting, I arranged that the children themselves should draw the outlines of the figures to be filled in so as to secure for the outlines an aesthetic order, allowing the child to make its own. For this purpose I prepared certain material, the iron insets, (the description of which will follow later) which provide for the tracing of the geometrical figures. That has given place to a decorative design which we have called ' the art of the insets ' and which in no way seems to be included in direct preparation for writing.

Second Factor: The Execution of Alphabetic Symbols

For the other group of movements, that is, for the drawing of graphic signs, I offer to the child material which consists of smooth cards on which are applied letters of the alphabet in sand-paper; these are traced repeatedly following the direction taken in writing. There are thus fixed the relative movements of the hand and the arm, which in this way have become capable of reproducing any sign which the eye, at the same time, has the opportunity of fixing gradually. There is thus memorized in a two-fold manner the symbols of the alphabet—by sight and by touch.

Summing up, the two mechanical factors of writing are resolved into two independent exercises: drawing, which gives the hand skill in handling the writing instrument; and touching the letters of the alphabet, which serves to establish the motor memory together with the visual memory of the letters.

Description of the Material for Carrying on Drawing at the Same Time as Writing

I made two similar desks having slightly sloping wooden tops and supported on four short legs also of wood; at the lower edge of the sloping top there is fixed a transverse bar which prevents things from slipping off the support. Fitting exactly into each desk there are four square plaques with insets, each of 14 cm. sides, of iron, coloured pink. In the centre of every plate there is an inset piece, also of iron, blue in colour and provided at the centre with a brass knob.

Exercises

When the two desks are put together, they look somewhat like a single desk which contains eight figures; this may be placed, for example, on a ledge, on the mistress's table, on a cupboard, or even on the edge of the child's table.

The object is elegant and attracts the child's attention. He may choose one or more figures, and he takes the inset piece along with the frame.

The similarity with the flat insets already noticed is complete, only here the child has at his free disposal pieces which are very heavy and thin. He first of all takes out the frame and places it on a sheet of white paper; then with a coloured pencil he draws the outlines of the empty centre of the frame. Next the frame is removed, and on the paper there remains a geometrical figure.

This is the first time that the child reproduces a geometrical figure by drawing it; up till now he has done nothing but superimpose the plane insets on the cards of the first, second and third series.

Then, on the figure which he himself has drawn, the child places the inset piece, as he did with the plane insets on the cards of the third series. He outlines it with a pencil of a different colour; then he takes it away: on the card there remains the figure doubly outlined in two colours.

After that, the child, with a coloured pencil of his own choosing, held like a writing pen, fills in completely the outlined figure. He is taught not to pass outside the outline.

The exercise of filling in a single figure demands that the child should carry out and repeat hand-movements such as would be needed to fill ten pages with ' strokes '; and it would be done without causing weariness, for the child, in thus co-ordinating precisely the muscular contractions necessary for the work, does it of his own free will and in any way he pleases, whilst under his eyes there comes to life a big, beautifully coloured figure.

At the beginning the child fills many sheets of paper with these great squares, triangles, ovals, trapeziums—in red, orange, green, purple, blue, pink.

When we examine the successive figures executed by the same child, a double form of progress is revealed. First, by degrees, the lines begin to project less beyond the outline, until they are perfectly enclosed, and the filling-in is steady and uniform all round the edge as well as in the central part. From being short and confused the lines of filling become longer and more nearly parallel, until sometimes the figures are filled with a perfectly regular system of strokes which go across from boundary to boundary. In any case, it is certain that the child is *master of the pen,* and the muscular mechanism necessary for wielding the writing-instrument has been established. From an examination of such drawings it is possible to come to a safe conclusion about the child's readiness to hold a pen in his hand.

As alternative exercises are also used the above-mentioned outline drawings which represent combinations of geometrical figures and various decorative subjects such as flowers and scenery. Such drawings perfect the handwork, because they oblige the child to draw lines of varying lengths and make him more and more skilful and sure in the use of his hands.

Now if we were to reckon up the lines produced by a child in filling in the figures and if they were translated into the graphic lines of writing, there would be filled many dozens of copybooks. Hence the mastery of the sign in the writing of our little ones could be compared with that which is attained in the third elementary class by the common methods.

When they take a pen into their hand for the first time, they will be able to handle it almost like a writer.

I consider that no means could be found which could be more efficacious in making such a conquest in less time, and which could give so much amusement to the child. The old method which I used with the defectives—of touching the outlines of the letters on the card with a rod—was, by contrast, very poor and sterile.

Even when the children can write, I always continue with these exercises, which allow of indefinite progress, for the drawings can be varied and complicated in all sorts of ways, and the children, always practising essentially the same exercise, see accumulating a gallery of varied pictures of increasing merit, which are the pride of every one of them. Thus I not only start, but improve writing, by the very exercises which I call preparatory; for example, in the present case the holding of the pen will be made more and more secure, not with repeated exercises in writing, but with those of filling in drawings. So my children perfect themselves in writing *without writing.*

MATERIAL FOR TRACING THE LETTERS

This consists of small cards bearing the letters of the alphabet in sandpaper and large cards with letters grouped according to similarity of form. A copy of each letter cut out of fine sandpaper is fixed on a small card, the dimensions of which are adapted to each letter; the cardboard is covered with smooth pink paper for the consonants whilst the sandpaper is light grey; or the mount is of blue paper (or wood) for the vowels; the colours help the form of the letter to stand out more distinctly from the background.

Similar mounts, but much larger, of cardboard or of wood, carry groups of letters which are identical with the corresponding letters on the small mounts, but they are combined in groups according to contrast or similarity of form.

The letters must be beautifully shaped, attention being paid to light and dark strokes. They are in the vertical style, if that is in use at the moment in the elementary schools. It is the writing in common use which determines this character of the material, which does not aim at reforming the style of writing, which would be something quite different from the intention which animates us. That is to obtain facility in writing, whatever may be the style of it.

EXERCISES

One begins at once with teaching the letters of the alphabet, beginning with the vowels and going on to the consonants, which are pronounced according to their sound. The sound is at once joined up with a word so that it is clearly associated with the spoken language.

The teaching proceeds according to the three stages already mentioned.

FIRST STAGE. VISUAL AND TACTILE-MUSCULAR SENSATION ASSOCIATED WITH ALPHABETIC SOUND

The teacher presents to the child a letter and says: " This is ' *i* '; " she will go on to deal with the other letters in the same way.

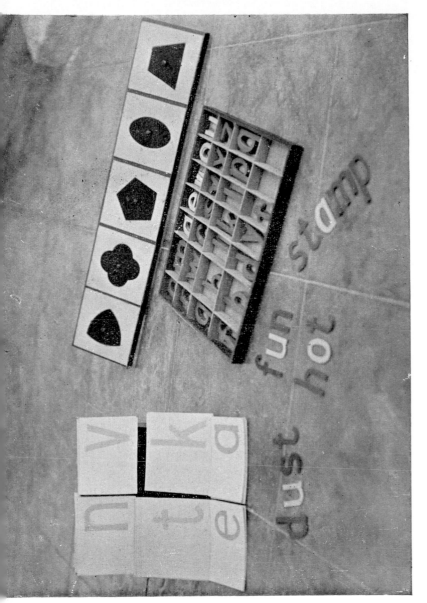

Sandpaper letters, moveable alphabet and drawing insets form part of the apparatus preparatory to the "explosion into writing". Its continued handling perfects calligraphy and orthography.

Then she at once has the letter touched, saying " Touch "; without any other explanation she shows the child how to trace the letter, and if necessary, she guides the index finger of the child's right hand over the sandpaper, in the direction followed in writing.

Knowing how to trace and not knowing how to trace will consist in knowing the sense according to which one draws a definite graphic form.

The child learns at once and his finger, already expert in tactile work, is guided, by the texture of the fine sandpaper, over the exact trace of the letter. He is then able to repeat by himself indefinitely the movement necessary to produce the letters of the alphabet, without fear of making mistakes while following the form of the handwriting. If his finger wanders, the smooth surface of the mount at once makes him aware of his error.

Little ones between 3½ and 4½ years of age, as soon as they become rather expert in this tracing, are very fond of repeating it with closed eyes; in this way they let themselves be guided by the sandpaper in following the shape without seeing it. One may say truly that perception of the letters by direct tactile muscular sensation will form a great contribution to final conquest of difficulties.

If, on the other hand, the exercise is offered to children who are too old (e.g. five or six years old) the interest of seeing the letter which reproduces the sound and composes words is so strong that touching no longer attracts him sufficiently to induce him to do the movement exercise; he will write less easily and less perfectly, having already missed the delight in movement which belongs to an earlier age.

With the very small child, it is not the visible image which leads him to trace the shape with such great interest; it is the feeling of touch which induces his hand to perform this movement, which will then be fixed in his muscular memory.

Three contemporary sensations take part when the mistress has the letters looked at and touched—the visual sensation, the tactile and the muscular. Hence the image of the graphic symbol is fixed in a much shorter time than when, by the usual methods, it is acquired only through the visual image.

We notice then that the muscular memory is most tenacious in the small child, and at the same time the readiest. Sometimes he does not recognize the letter when he looks at it, but does so when he touches it.

These images are at the same time associated with the hearing of alphabetic sounds.

SECOND STAGE: PERCEPTION

The child must be able to compare and recognize the figures when he hears the sounds corresponding to them.

The mistress asks the child in the case mentioned above (and analogously she will proceed with the other letters): " Give me ' o '! Give me ' i '! " If the child cannot recognize the signs when he looks at them, he is invited to trace them; but, if even then he does not recognize them, the lesson is finished and will be taken up again some other day. (The need not to stress an error and not to insist on the lesson when the child does not respond at once has been already dwelt upon in another chapter.)

THIRD STAGE: LANGUAGE

The child must know how to pronounce the sound corresponding to the alphabetic signs.

After the letters have been in use for some time and the second stage has met with success, the child is asked: " What is this? " He ought to answer: " o," " i," etc.

In teaching the consonants the mistress pronounces only the *sound*, and directly she has pronounced it she links it up with a word and she goes on pronouncing several words with that letter, always emphasizing the sound of the consonant. Finally she repeats the sound by itself " m, m, m ".

It is not necessary to teach all the vowels before passing on to the consonants, and as soon as one consonant is known it is made up into words. Other details of the same kind are left to the teacher's judgment.

I have not found it practical to follow any definite rule in teaching the consonants. Very often the child's curiosity about a symbol leads to the teaching of the consonant which he desires; the sound of a name may awaken in the child a wish to know what consonant is necessary to build it up. And this wish of the child is a more useful means than any reasoning for deciding upon the order to follow.

When the child pronounces the sounds of the consonants he evidently experiences pleasure. He regards as a novelty this series of sounds so varied and so well known, which come to life on the presentation of an enigmatic symbol like a letter of the alphabet. There is some mystery about it and it raises intense interest. One day I was on the terrace while the children were playing freely around, and had near me a little one two and a half years old, left there for a moment by his mother. I had scattered on several chairs some complete alphabets mixed up together, and was sorting them into their respective cases (*v.* below). When I had finished the work, I placed the cases on little seats. The little one was watching. I drew near and took a letter of the alphabet in my hand—*f*. The boys at this moment were running in a line; on seeing the letter they all uttered the sound belonging to it and passed on. The child paid no attention. I put away the *f* and took up an *r*; the boys as they ran looked at it laughing and began to shout to him—r, r, r! r, r, r! Little by little the small child began to understand that when I took a letter in my hand those passing uttered a sound. That amused him so much that I made up my mind to observe how long the game would go on without wearying him; I waited quite three quarters of an hour. The boys had become interested in the affair and stopped in groups, pronouncing the sounds in a chorus, and laughing at the wonder of the child. Finally the baby, because I had more frequently taken the letter *f* and held it up, always receiving from the groups the same sound, took it up, showed it to me and himself said—*f, f, f*. He had learnt that one from among the great confusion of sounds which he had heard; he had been impressed by the long letter which, seen by the running file of children, had made them burst into a shout.

It is not necessary to explain how pronouncing the alphabetic sounds separately reveals the state of speech. The defects, almost all connected with the incomplete development of speech itself, are made manifest to the teacher who can easily make a note of them one by one. Here there may be created a standard of progress for individual teaching, based on the state of development reached by the speech of the child.

For the correction of speech, it is useful to follow the physiological rules of its development and to graduate the difficulties. But when the child's speech is already developed sufficiently and he pronounces all the sounds, it is a matter of indifference whether we make him pronounce one rather than another in teaching graphic language with the reading of symbols.

A great many of the defects which remain permanently in the adult are due to functional errors in the development of speech in the period of childhood. If instead of correcting the speech of adolescents we trained its development in childhood we would accomplish a most useful work of a preventive character. Besides these there are many defects due to dialects, which are almost impossible to correct later, but which could very easily be eradicated if education directed itself specially to improving the speech of the child.

Let us ignore here the real defects in speech due to anatomical and physiological anomalies, as well as to pathological facts disturbing the functioning of the nervous system; let us confine ourselves to those defects arising from the persistence of faulty childish pronunciation, from the imitation of wrong pronunciation, including that of dialect. Such defects, grouped under the term *blaesitas*, may affect the pronunciation of every consonant. And no more practical means of correcting speech methodically can be suggested than that exercise in pronunciation necessary for learning graphic language by my method.

But this most important question deserves a separate chapter. All the mechanism of writing is prepared for. Turning now directly to the method for teaching writing, we notice that it is already included in the two stages described, since the child is given by these exercises the opportunity of learning and fixing the muscular mechanism necessary for holding the pen and for making the graphic symbols. After the child has had long practice in these methods he will be potentially ready to write all the letters of the alphabet and simple words, without ever having taken pen or chalk in his hand for the purpose of writing.

Reading and Writing Are Fused from the Beginning

By this method, the teaching of reading goes on at the same time as that of writing. When a letter is presented to the child and its name is pronounced, the child fixes the image of it with the visual and with the tactile-muscular senses, and associates the sound with the symbol without fail; that is, it makes acquaintance with written language. When it sees and recognizes, it reads; when it touches, it writes; thus it begins its acquaintance with two actions which later on, as they develop, are separated to form the two diverse processes of reading and writing.

The contemporary character of the teaching, or better, the fusion of the two initial actions, presents the child therefore with a new form of language, without it being decided which of the two constituent acts will take precedence.

We must not trouble ourselves as to whether the child, as the process goes on, learns reading first or writing first, as to whether the one way or the other will be the easier for him. We should learn this from experience keeping our minds free from prejudices, waiting for the appearance of probable individual differences in the prevalent development of either of the two actions. That gives an opportunity for a very interesting study in individual psychology, and for a continuation of the practical direction of our method which is based on the free expansion of individuality.

But in the meantime it is certain that if the method is applied at the right age, that is, before the age of 4, the little child will write before it reads, whilst the child already too far developed (5 years) will read first, finding great difficulty in setting in motion his clumsy mechanism.

INTELLIGENCE FREED FROM MECHANISM

Writing and reading are quite distinct from simple knowledge of the signs of the alphabet. They really come into existence when the word rather than the graphic symbol comes to be fixed as an element. In spoken language also the beginning is marked by the first appearance of words having a meaning, as distinct from sounds which might be represented by vowels and syllables. When intelligence is expressing itself in the loftiest medium, it will make use of the mechanism which nature or educational art has placed or prepared for its service, for the composition of words.

This is something quite different from what has been described up till now in the analysis of movements for writing which represents the preparatory action for the establishment of this super-language which is the real writing and reading. It means the composition of words. The building up of words from graphic signs need not necessarily be done along with writing and reading; it is even useful to keep separate this act which may be distinctly independent of the higher utilizations of it.

The intelligence of the child may find intensely interesting this marvellous fact that it is possible to construct a word by putting together those symbolic signs which are the letters of the alphabet.

To create words is much more fascinating at the beginning, than to read them, and much easier than to write them, because for writing them there is necessary the controlling mechanism which is not yet established.

Therefore, as a preparatory exercise, we offer to the child an alphabet which will be described below, and he, by choosing the letters of the alphabet and placing them one beside the other, composes words. His manual work is only that of taking known shapes from a case and spreading them out on a mat. The word is built up, letter by letter, in correspondence with its component sounds. Since the letters are movable objects it is easy to correct by displacements the composition which is made. This represents a studied analysis of the word and an excellent means for improving spelling.

It is a real study, an exercise of the intelligence free from mechanism; it is not mixed up with the interesting exercise of the necessity for producing writing. Hence the intellectual energy devoted to this new interest may be expended without weariness in a surprising amount of work.

MATERIAL

This consists essentially of the alphabets. It includes letters of the alphabet identical in form and dimensions with those of sandpaper, though here they are cut out of coloured cardboard.

The letters are loose, that is, they are not gummed on cardboard or on anything else; hence every letter is an object which can be handled.

At the bottom of each compartment is fixed a letter which cannot be taken out; so no trouble is wasted over putting the letters back into the case, seeing that the fixed letter forms a guide.

The letters are distributed in two boxes, each one of which contains all the vowels. The vowels are cut out of blue cardboard, and the consonants out of pink. These letters carry at the bottom of the back a strip of white cardboard fixed transversely, which indicates the position of the letter as well as the level at which the various letters should be placed according to shape (corresponding to the line on which we write).

THE COMPOSITION OF WORDS

Directly the child knows some vowels and consonants there is placed before him one of the big boxes containing all the vowels and half of the consonants, some known, others unknown, marked

18

on the back with the white strip. With this material words can
be composed by putting on the table one after another the letters
of the alphabet which correspond to each of the successive sounds
that make up the spoken word. These letters are taken from the
compartment in the big box where they are kept. In order to
initiate the child to this exercise the mistress gives a practical
demonstration. E.g. she says the word " mano," and then she
analyses the sounds pronouncing them separately: " m " . . . and
she takes the letter ' m; ' " a ". . . and she takes the ' a ' placing
it next to the other; " n ". . . " o ". . . ; she picks the letters one by
one pronouncing the sounds and thus she composes the word with
the alphabet. Now there are on the table the four letters in
successions; m—a—n—o.

Sometimes the child, having understood the procedure, rushes
in to finish the word himself instead of leaving the mistress to do
so. Almost all begin to compose words on their table after a few
lessons. They " ask " for words to be composed, and thus a kind
of *dictation* takes place.

The composition of words revealed facts that were a real
surprise. As if the spoken language already existing in the child
had been excited he showed great interest for his own language
and tried to analyse it. Children were seen walking by themselves murmuring something; one said: "to make Zaira, z a i r a
are needed" and he pronounced the alphabetic sounds without
material. He therefore did not aim at composing the word, but
merely at analysing the sounds that made it up. It seemed a kind
of discovery: "The words we pronounce are composed of sounds."
This activity can be aroused in all the children of about 4 years
of age. I remember a gentleman who asked his son on his return
from school, if he had been good (" buono "). The child answered:
" Buono? b u o n o," i.e. instead of answering he started analysing
the word.

In the box of the movable alphabet the signs corresponding
to those sounds are clearly seen; there we find the vowels distinguished from the consonants by their colour and every sign has its

own compartment. The exercise is so fascinating that the children begin to compose words long before they know all the letters of the alphabet. Once a girl asked the mistress: " How is the letter ' t '? " The mistress who wished to follow a certain order in their presentation had not yet shown the letter ' t ' which is one of the last letters of the alphabet. The girl then explained: " I want to make ' Teresa ', but I do not know which is ' t '." The teaching of new letters was thus often stimulated by the ambition of the children who went faster than the mistress!

Once the interest is aroused, i.e. when the principle of the alphabet, " each sound can be represented by a sign," has come into contact with the inner deposit of spoken language, a kind of spontaneous procedure is liable to follow which promotes progress in the teaching of the written word. The mistress finds her position changed, she is no longer a teacher, but has merely to ' correspond ' to the needs of the children. Indeed, many children were convinced that they had learned by themselves.

This fact of finding an intense interest in the analysis of one's own words and an immense pleasure in seeing them translated into objects placed in a row, will perhaps not be met with in children of older age.

This phenomenon can be explained only when realizing that the child of four years of age finds himself still in the formative period of language. He lives in a ' sensitive period ' of his psychic development. All the marvellous phenomena that revealed themselves in our experience in this field will be understood only when this fact is admitted; a creative period, an intensification of life is building up and completing the language of man.

At five years of age already this sensitivity is diminishing, because the " creative period " is about to end.

Another phenomenon that amazed many people was that such small children composed entire words without being in need of having it repeated as soon as they heard it dictated in a clear manner. This was the case also with long words, or with words that in themselves were incomprehensible to them, e.g. with foreign words. The children translated phonetically these words after having heard them only once. As soon as they had been pronounced clearly they were translated into alphabetic signs on their table.

It is very interesting to watch the child at this work; he stands looking at the box most intently, his lips moving slightly, then he takes the required letters one by one, without making any errors in spelling (if they are phonetical). The movement of the lips is due to the fact that the child is repeating to himself an infinite number of times the word, the sound of which he is translating into signs.

Many people came to witness this fact, especially inspectors of schools who know how difficult dictation is in elementary schools, where the teacher has to repeat many times the word she dictates so that it may not be forgotten.

Here children of four years of age remember it exactly, and yet they had to do a work quite liable to distract their attention and to exhaust the energy necessary to finish the word. They have in fact to look for the letters of the alphabet in the boxes by means of their eyes, to take those they need with their hands and so on until the word is finished.

During the first period of this marvellous experiment an inspector of schools came to visit us and wished to dictate a word that seemed to him very difficult. He pronounced it clearly, laying stress, in his Italian pronunciation, on the two last letters so similar in sound: Darmstadt. The child composed the word as he heard it pronounced. Another time an official in the Ministry of Public Instruction dictated: ' Sangi accato di Novibazar ' to a child of four and a half years of age, who translated it on his table and produced the word composed of the letters of the movable alphabet.

Then there is the anecdote of the Chief Inspector of Schools of Rome who wished to do a simple and serious experiment. He dictated only his own name ' Di Donato '. The child began to compose it, but he had not clearly heard all the sounds, because

The apparatus leading to writing adapts itself to any language. On top a group of children handles the Tamil alphabet (Montessori School, Adyar. Photo by C. T. Nachiappan). Below the same apparatus is used for English. (Karachi)

he made a mistake and put ' dito '. The Inspector repeated ' dido '. The child was not in the least perturbed, he took the ' t ' he had previously laid down, but did not place it back in the box, but left it on one side of his table. ' Dito ' thus became ' didona . . .' and then the child took that ' t ' that he had put aside and used it to finish the word: ' didonato '. The entire word therefore was as if sculptured in his mind. He knew from the start that a ' t ' was necessary at the end. His certainty was so great that he was not in the least confused by the remark of the inspector. The latter was really amazed. "This ' t '," he said, "makes me believe that a miracle in the history of education is about to take place."

Not one child alone, but many were there who showed the same surprising psychological phenomenon. They revealed a particular ' sensitivity ' for words, almost a ' hunger of their age ' for an instinctive acquisition of language.

The child evidently re-composed these words with the movable alphabet, not because he ' remembered ' them with the help of an ordinary memory, but because he had ' sculptured ' and ' absorbed ' it in his mind. It was from this sculptured and absorbed image that he ' copied ' the word, as if he ' saw ' it in front of him. However long or strange the word might be, it was simply reflected and fixed so that the child could reproduce it. It should also be remarked that this exercise was absolutely fascinating to the children who repeated it without fatigue, because it was a *vital* exercise.

The children who thus composed words did not know either to write or to read. They were not ' interested ' in the written word. They acted, or rather re-acted, to a stimulus that instead of provoking an inferior reflex, produced a response corresponding to a creative sensitivity.

THE EXPLOSION INTO WRITING

Children who are able to retain in their mind, as if it were sculptured or photographed, a word and the corresponding alphabetical signs, should be able to write and to read too.

In fact, they are ' potentially ' able to do so.

Their hand is trained and prepared for writing by means of ever so many exercises. Only an occasion is needed, one might say. A kind of magic touch that brings into actual, exterior reality, this inner potential capacity for writing.

Our children of the Quarter of San Lorenzo have in fact given this marvellous reaction.

On one winter day in December, a day full of sunshine, we climbed with the children to the terrace.[1] They ran about freely, playing; some stayed round me. I was sitting near a chimney-stack, and I said to a child of five who was near me, offering him a piece of chalk, " Draw this chimney ". He sat down on the ground obediently and drew the pot on the floor, reproducing it so that it was quite recognizable. Then, as I always do with my little ones, I was loud in my praises.

The child looked at me, smiled, stood for a moment as if he would break out into some joyous act and then shouted " I write, I write! "; then, bending down, he wrote on the ground ' man ' (hand); then, growing very enthusiastic, he wrote again ' camino ' (chimney), then ' tetto ' (roof). Whilst he was writing he continued to shout aloud " I am writing, I can write," so that all the others were attracted by his cries and made a circle round him staring in astonishment. Two or three of them in great excitement said to me " Chalk, I will write too." And in fact they set about writing various words: mamma, mano, gino, camino, ada.

Not one of them had ever had in his hand chalk or anything else used for writing; it was the first time that they had written, and they were writing a whole word, just as, when they spoke for the first time, they spoke a whole word.

If the first word pronounced by the child gives ineffable joy to the mother who has chosen this first word, mamma, as her own

---

[1] The meaning of " terrace " (terrazza) differs in Italy from that which we associate with it in England. The term is applied to a flat roof, or to a wide, open balcony with which an upper storey of the dwelling communicates.—M.A.J.

name, almost as a reward due to motherhood, so the first word written by my little ones fills them with inexpressible joy. They see spring into being, by their own act, a power which seems to be a gift from nature, for they cannot link up what they are doing with the preparatory acts which have led them up to their performance.

Hence they imagine almost that on one fine day, when they have reached it they become able to write. And so it is in reality. The child, when it begins to speak, has also prepared beforehand, unconsciously, the psycho-muscular mechanism which will lead him to the articulation of the word. In the case of writing, the child does nearly the same; but direct aid given by teaching and the possibility of preparing almost materially for the movements of writing, which are much simpler and coarser than those necessary for the pronouncing of the word, result in written language developing much more rapidly and perfectly. Since the preparation is not partial but complete, that is, the child is equipped with all the movements needed for writing, therefore written language is not developed gradually, but in a sudden outburst; the child is able to write every word.

In this way we shared in the moving experience of the first development of written language among our children. We were stirred into deep emotion during those days; we felt as if we were in a dream, and that we had seen miraculous events.

The child who was writing a word for the first time was consumed with joy; I compared him at once with a hen which had laid an egg. Indeed, no one could escape from the noisy demonstrations of the little one; he called everybody to look and if the person did not come he pulled him by the dress to make him come. Everyone had to go there, stand round the written word and admire the wonder, adding his exclamations of surprise to the joyous shouts of the fortunate performer. Generally speaking, this first word was written on the ground, and then the child used to kneel down to get nearer to his work and to gaze on it more closely.

After the first word, the child continued to write with a kind of frenzy everywhere, though generally on the blackboard. I have seen children crowding round the blackboard eager to write, and behind the standing children there was lined up another row of children mounted on chairs who were writing above the others, whilst some more were behind the blackboard. I saw other children who were left outside running about in disorder in their vexation and upsetting the chairs on which their companions were standing in order to find a little space. Finally, the losers in the struggle bent down and wrote on the floor, or ran to the window shutter or the door and filled these with writing. In these early days we had almost a tapestry formed of written signs on the floor—a tapestry of writing. At home the same thing happened, and some mothers, in order to save the floors and even the bread, on the crusts of which they found written words, gave their children paper and a pencil. One of these children brought to school one day a kind of copybook filled with writing, and the mother told us how the child had written all day and all evening and had gone to sleep in bed with paper and pencil in his hand.

Such impulsive work, which I could not curb in the early days, made me think of the wisdom of nature which develops spoken language little by little, and develops it at the same time as ideas are gradually taking shape. If instead of that, nature had acted as unwisely as I had done, had allowed to develop from the senses a rich and orderly stock of material, and had allowed a wealth of ideas to develop, and had thus prepared completely for articulate language, so that she might say to the child, mute up to this point, "Go, speak," we would have been faced with a sudden, mad outbreak of torrential speech, in which the child would begin to speak without a pause and without possible check, until its lungs were exhausted and its vocal cords were worn out with pronouncing words which were very difficult and strange to it.

Yet I think that between the two extremes there exists a mean which embodies the really practical way. We must, then, encourage written language less suddenly; but in bringing it into existence by degrees we must encourage it as a spontaneous act which is carried on from the very first in an almost perfect manner.

MANNER OF APPLYING THE METHOD

The latest development of our experiment has led us to set up a calmer, more orderly procedure, due to the fact that the children see their companions writing, which, through imitation, incites them to write as soon as they can. Then the written words are no longer a surprise, but an achievement. This is the case also with children who see people write in their homes, whilst this was not so with the first children whose parents were all illiterate. Hence, when the child writes his first word, he has not the whole alphabet at his disposal; there is a limit to the number of words which he can write, and he is not capable of finding out all the possible combinations of words with only the letters which are known to him. He never loses the great joy of the first written word, but that no longer constitutes a stupifying surprise, because he sees something similar happening every day, and he knows that sooner or later it will happen to him also. That leads to the establishment of a calm atmosphere, orderly and at the same time wonderful because of its sudden, natural achievements.

Paying a visit to the Children's House, where I had also been the day before, I chanced upon new facts. I saw two very small children who were writing quietly, though vibrant with pride and joy; the day before they were not yet writing. The Directress told me that one of them began to write at eleven o'clock on the previous morning and the other in the afternoon at three.

The occurrence is now regarded with the indifference which custom brings, and is easily recognized as a natural form of development in the child.

The judgement of the mistress will decide if and when it is suitable to encourage the child to write, when he, having passed through the three stages of the preparatory exercise, does not yet do it of his own accord. That is because, by keeping back writing too long, the child may break out into a frenzy of impulsive work, which, owing to his knowing the whole alphabet, can no longer be curbed.

The signs which the mistress may use in making a diagnosis of the preparedness for spontaneous writing are: the parallelism and straightness of the marks used in filling in the geometrical figures; recognition of the sandpaper letters of the alphabet with the eyes closed; certainty and readiness in the composition of words. Before intervening to encourage writing with an invitation, it is, however, always well to wait for at least a week for the spontaneous launching out into writing, after the readiness for it has been judged to be found existent.

Only when the child has begun to write of his own accord ought the mistress to intervene to guide the progress of the writing.

The first help which she will give is that of ruling the blackboard so that the child may be guided in keeping right the direction and the dimensions of the writing.

The second is that of urging the hesitating child to repeat the tracing of the sandpaper letters, without ever correcting him directly about the writing which he has done. The child will not improve himself by repeating the actions of writing but by repeating the acts preparatory to writing. I remember a little beginner who, in order to give his letter a beautiful shape on the ruled blackboard, went to the thin cards, traced two or three times all the letters which were necessary for the words he had to write, and then he wrote; if a letter did not seem to him to be beautiful enough, he rubbed it out, again touched the letter itself on the card, and again went to write it.

Our little ones, even those who have been writing for a year, always carry on the three preparatory exercises, which, as they led up to, also improve written language. Our children then learn to write and also to improve their writing, without writing. Real writing is an experience, the outbreak of an inner impulse, an act in compliance with a higher activity: it is not an exercise.

It is also an educational idea to prepare oneself before making attempts, and to perfect oneself before going further. To go on correcting one's own errors encourages one to attempt imperfectly things for which we are not ready, and it also deadens the sensitiveness of the mind towards its own mistakes. My method of teaching writing includes as an educational conception teaching the child the prudence which makes one avoid error; the dignity which gives foresight and is a guide to perfection; and also the humility which keeps one constantly in touch with the sources of goodness, from which alone one obtains and maintains mastery over oneself; getting rid of the illusion that, once success has been reached, it is quite enough to go on just as we have been doing.

Because all the children, those who have just begun the three exercises, as well as those who have already been writing for many months, are always repeating the same movements, they are united and fraternize on an apparently equal level. Here there are no classes for beginners and advanced; they are all to be seen filling up figures with coloured pencils, tracing sandpaper letters, composing words with the movable alphabets; the smallest work alongside the biggest, the latter helping the former—all imagining that they are doing the same thing. There is no one who is preparing himself, there is no one who is perfecting himself; all are moving along the same road; running deeper than any social differences there exists a similarity in which all men are brothers, just as on the spiritual path all, whether aspiring or perfect, are carrying on the same exertions.

Writing is learnt in a very short time, because we begin to teach it only to children who show a desire for it, paying voluntary attention to the lessons which the mistress is giving to other children and to the doings of other children. Some learn without ever having received lessons, merely by having heard the lessons given to others.

In general, children from four years of age onwards are keenly interested in writing. Some of our children have even begun at three and a half. Lively enthusiasm is shown specially in tracing the sandpaper letters.

THE PROCESSION OF THE ALPHABET

During the first period of my experiment, when the children saw for the first time the letters of the alphabet, I asked Directress Bettini one day to carry to the terrace, where the children were playing, the various types of cards which she had made. Directly the children saw her, they crowded round the teacher and myself with their fingers held out, and in dozens the small fingers were soon touching the letters, whilst the babies were pressing against each other. Finally some of the taller children succeeded in getting some of the cards out of our hands, pretending to touch them like teachers, but the crowd of little ones hindered this performance. I remember with what a joyous rush the possessors of the cards, clasping them in both hands, raised them like standards and began to march followed by all the other children, who clapped their hands and uttered loud cries of joy.

The procession passed in front of us, and all, big and little, laughed loudly, whilst the mothers, attracted by the noise, watched the scene through the windows. This was like a homage paid to the material that had worked miracles.

The average period which elapses between the first attempt at preparatory exercises and the first written word is, for children of four, a month and a half. For children five years old, the period is much shorter, about a month; but one of ours learnt to write, with the letters of the alphabet, in twenty days. Children of four years, after two and a half months, write some words under dictation, and are able to pass on to writing with ink in copybooks. Generally, after three months, our little ones are proficient, and those who have been writing for six months may be compared with children in the third elementary class.

Writing constitutes one of the easiest and most enjoyable *achievements* gained by our children.

If learning were as easy for adults as it is for children under six years of age, illiteracy could be got rid of in a month, but perhaps two obstacles would interfere with so brilliant a success. In the adult, however, there is no longer this enthusiasm which, in small children, is given by psychical sensitivities that exist only during the constructive period provided for by nature for the formation of language. Besides, the hand of the adult is by this time too stiff to acquire easily the delicate movements needed in writing.

But I know that when the procedure used by us in the education of children was applied to adults (to the recruits and soldiers of the United States of America), the struggle against illiteracy was considerably facilitated. Montessori teachers, in fact, dedicated themselves to the instruction of soldiers.

Later I learned that in Rome, in bygone ages, the hand of adults was trained in order to improve their penmanship by having them *trace* very large letters of perfect shape, and not by having them *write* with a model before their eyes as is done nowadays in exercises for penmanship.

To trace letters and compose phonetically entire words with a movable alphabet, therefore, facilitates everybody's effort to learn how to write. Many months, however, are certainly needed when an adult tries to learn what a small child already indirectly prepared can achieve in only one month.

So much for the time needed for learning. As for the style of execution, our children, from the moment they begin, write well, and one is surprised by the shape of the letters, bold and rounded, resembling in every way the sandpaper models. The beauty of their writing is scarcely ever attained by any pupil in the elementary schools who has not had special lessons in calligraphy.

I, who have studied calligraphy closely, know how difficult it is to get boys of twelve and thirteen in the secondary schools to write whole words without lifting the pen except for the letter ' *o*,' and how drawing the lines of the various letters with a single stroke often forms an insuperable difficulty, the parallelism between the component strokes being lost.

On the contrary, our little ones, of their own accord, with marvellous certainty, write whole words with a single effort, keeping the parallelism between the strokes perfect, and the distances between the various letters equal. More than one competent visitor has exclaimed, "If I had not seen it, I would not have believed it."

Calligraphy, indeed after teaching, is needed to correct defects already acquired and fixed; it is extra work, heavy and long because the child whilst looking at the model has to execute the movement required to reproduce it, whilst between such a sensation and such a movement there is no direct relationship.

Besides, penmanship is taught at an age when all defects have been stabilized, and there has passed the physiological period in which the muscular memory is particularly alert. One does not speak of the fundamental error which makes calligraphy pursue the same course of learning as writing from strokes and its continuation.

We prepare the child in a direct manner not only for writing, but also for penmanship regarded in its two main attributes— beauty of form (by touching beautiful letters) and freedom of execution (by exercises in filling in figures).

READING

EXPERIENCE has taught me to recognize a distinct difference between writing and reading and has shown me that the two acquirements need not necessarily be made at the same time. In our first experiment, writing precedes reading, though I know that this is in contradiction to the common practice. I do not call 'reading' the attempt which a child makes when he is verifying the word which he has composed with the movable alphabet, that is when he is translating signs into sounds, as at first he translated sounds into signs, because in such a verification he already knows the word, having repeated it to himself many times as he composed it. (That is, in a phonetic language.)

I call reading the interpretation of an idea by means of graphic signs.

The child who has not heard the word spoken, but who recognizes it on seeing it put together on the table in movable letters and can tell what it means (the name of a child, a city, an object, etc.), that child *reads*. This I say because the word ' read ' corresponds in written language to the word we listen to in spoken language, which serves to receive the language transmitted to us by others.

Until the child obtains from written words transmission of ideas, he does not read.

We may say that writing, as it has been described, is an act in which the psycho-motor mechanism predominates; in reading, on the contrary, we reach purely intellectual work. But it is evident that our way of teaching writing prepares for reading so as to render the difficulties involved almost unnoticeable. Writing prepares the child for interpreting mechanically the union of the letter-sounds which are the components of the word which he sees written. The child, therefore, can already read the sounds of the word. We notice that when the child composes the word from the movable alphabet, he has time to think of the signs which he must choose or make; the writing of a word takes a long time compared with that needed for the reading of it.

The child who can write, when he is confronted with a word to be interpreted by reading, is silent for a long time, and generally reads the component sounds as slowly as if he were writing them. The sense of the word is grasped when it is pronounced not only in a hurry but with the necessary phonetic accents. Now in order to place the phonetic accents, it is necessary that the child should recognize the word, the idea which it represents; therefore a higher activity of intelligence must be brought into play.

For practice in reading I, therefore, proceed in the following way, and what I am about to describe is a substitute for the old spelling-book. I prepare labels from sheets of ordinary writing-paper, on each of which there is written in running hand one centimetre high, some well-known word which has already been pronounced many times by the child, and which represents objects present or well-known. If the word refers to an object which is present, I place this under the child's eye, in order to make the meaning of the reading easier. In this connection I may mention that most of these objects are toys. The Children's Houses possess not only the kitchen utensils, the kitchen, the balls and the dolls which I already have had occasion to mention, but also cupboards, divans, beds—all furniture necessary for a doll's house;

also, houses, trees, flocks of sheep, animals made from papier-mache, ducklings and geese made of cellulose that float on water; boats with sailors, soldiers, railways which will work, factories, a country house, stables for horses and cattle within spacious enclosures, etc. For one House in Rome an artist made me a present of splendid fruit in ceramics.[1]

If writing serves to direct or rather to direct and perfect the mechanism of spoken language in the child, reading serves to aid in the development of ideas, thus making a connection with the development of language. Finally, writing helps physiological language, and reading, social language.

The beginning is, as I have pointed out, nomenclature, that is, reading the names of objects known, and, possibly, present.

I do not choose words on the ground of their being easy or difficult, because the child can already read the word as being composed of sounds. I allow the child to translate slowly into sounds the written word, and if his interpretation is exact, I confine myself to saying, " More quickly." The child, the second time, reads more readily, often still without understanding. I repeat, " More quickly, more quickly." The child reads still more rapidly, repeating the same group of sounds and finally he guesses. Then he puts on a look of recognition and beams with the satisfaction which so often appears in our children. In this consists the whole reading exercise, a very speedy exercise and one which presents to the child, already prepared through writing, very little difficulty.

Truly, all the terrors of the spelling-book are buried along with the ' strokes '!

When the child has read he rests the card used against the object the name of which it bore and the exercise is finished. The children having been taught in this way, more for the purpose of understanding thoroughly which exercise attracted them most than for practice in actual reading, I thought of the following game.

---

[1] The first Children's Houses were rich in toys; but practice had gradually led to their being forgotten, for the children did not seek them, but even now there are many objects which can be used for the above-mentioned purpose.

19

It was intended to make more pleasant the various exercises in reading which have to be repeated so often; as a result the reading is made clear and fluent.

GAME FOR READING WORDS

I spread out on the big table the most varied and attractive collection of toys; corresponding to each of them is a label on which its name is written. I fold the labels and roll them up, mix them together in a box, and have them drawn by lot by the children who can read. They must carry the labels to their places, unfold them very, very slowly, read them mentally without showing them to their neighbours, so that what they contain remains an absolute secret, and then go up to the table with the label enclosed in their hand. The child must say aloud the name of a toy, and present to the teacher the label that it may be verified; such a ticket then becomes like a piece of money with which the toy named may be acquired. The child, if he pronounces the word clearly, pointing out the object with his finger (and the teacher can check the accuracy by the card), takes the toy and can do what he likes with it for as long as he likes.

This stage being finished, the teacher calls upon the first child and then all the others, in the same order in which they took the toys, and makes them draw lots for another label, which the child must read at once and which bears the name of one of his companions, who cannot read yet and, therefore, has not had a toy. And then, politely, he must offer as an act of courtesy to his unlearned companion the toy which he possesses as his right. The offer must be made with kindly gestures, gracefully, accompanied by a salute. In this way there is eradicated any idea of grade, and there is inculcated the feeling that one must give out of kindness to those who have no claim to possession, as well as the sentiment that everyone, whether he deserves it or not, must share equally in pleasures.

The reading-play was a marvellous success; think of the satisfaction which these poor children felt over the idea that they possessed such beautiful toys and that they could play with them for such a long time.

But what was my surprise when the children, after having learnt to understand the written cards, refused to take the toys and to lose time in playing and in making these friendly gestures to their little companions; with a kind of insatiable desire they preferred instead to take out the cards one after another and read them all. I watched them, and pondered over the enigma of their minds, which had been hidden from us. As I stood watching them and meditating over the discovery that children, through some human instinct, love knowledge better than meaningless play, I was impressed by the loftiness of the human mind.

We then put away the toys and set ourselves to make hundreds of written labels—names of children, of objects, of cities, of colours and of qualities made known through exercises of the senses. We placed them in more boxes and let the children search as they pleased among them. I expected that at least they would hunt indiscriminately and without any order in one box and in another, but no, every child finished emptying the box which he had under his hand, and only after that did he go on to another, truly insatiable for reading. One day I went out on the terrace and found that they had carried the tables and chairs there, setting up school in the open air. Some little ones were playing in the sun, others were seated in circles round tables covered with letters and sandpaper cards; at one side, in the shade of a dormer window was seated the mistress, who had a long, narrow box, full of labels; the whole length of the box was occupied by little hands searching within it. A group of children were opening, reading and refolding the labels. "You would not believe," said the mistress to me, "that this has been going on for more than an hour, and still they are not satisfied." I made the experiment of having balls and dolls brought out, but with no result; these futilities had no value compared with the joy of *knowing*.

When I saw this surprising result, I was already thinking of trying to get them to read print, and I proposed to the mistress to write the same word in the two types on the same label. But the children forestalled me. There was in the school a calendar on which many words were written in printed characters and some in Gothic characters. In their mania for reading, some children began to look at this calendar, and to my indescribable surprise, they read both the printed and the Gothic matter.

So we had nothing more to do but present them with a book; in fact, they read the words in it. At first, in the Children's Houses, I gave only one kind of book, one in which, under the figures of all the objects they had seen, were printed the names.

The mothers at once profited by the progress of the Children. We actually surprised in the pockets of some of them pieces of paper roughly covered with the prices of things—macaroni, bread, salt, etc.: some of our little ones were going marketing with the note! The parents told us that their children no longer hurried along the street, because they stopped to read the shop signs.

Educated according to this method in a private house, a child, a little marquis of four and a half, did the following. His father, a member of parliament, received a great deal of correspondence. He knew that his child had begun exercises two months before, and that they were enabling him to read and write at a precocious age; but he did not pay much attention, and had not much faith in the assertions. One day the marquis was reading and the child was playing near him when a servant entered and placed on the table the voluminous correspondence which had just come by post. The little one turned his attention to it, began to turn over the letters and to read aloud all the addresses. The marquis thought it was almost a miracle.

It may be asked what is the average time which is needed for learning to read. Experience tells us that, counting from the moment at which the child can write, the passage from this lower form of written language to the higher one of reading is on an average about fifteen days. Accuracy in reading, however, almost always comes later than perfection in writing. In most cases the child writes very well and reads just fairly well.

Not all the children reach the same standard at the same age, and since none of them is, I do not say forced, but not even invited, or in any way attracted, to do what he does not want to do, it happens that some children, not having offered themselves for learning, have been left in peace, and can neither write nor read.

If the old method, which dominates the will of the child, and crushes out his self-expression, does not think that it ought to force him to learn to write before the age of six, no more do I think so!

However, I could not decide without long experience whether in every case the age of the full development of spoken language ought to be that which it is suitable to choose for encouraging the development of written language.

In any case almost all normal children brought up by our methods begin to write at four years of age, and at five they can read and write at least as well as children who have finished the second elementary class; that means that they could pass into the second or third class at an age a year or two below that of the present day admission to the first class.

THE EXERCISE FOR NON-PHONETIC LANGUAGES

The simple reading game described above was taken up again, modified and adapted for learning reading in languages which are not phonetic, like English, Dutch, etc.

The essential exercise, which in its general principle may be of general application as in phonetic languages, consists in preparing a series of objects and a corresponding set of labels on which are written the names relating to them; after the card has been read it is placed near the object which corresponds to it. For the phonetic languages, the exercise aims at raising interest in the written word; recognition of the object present makes the child feel that he has discovered a secret, and the act of placing the label satisfies him and opens up a round of intimate activity.

By this time the internal motor has been set going, interest has been kindled, and the communication between the source of life and mastery over externals has been established.

For the non-phonetic languages, something similar must constitute the first step. Search was made first of all (for teaching the English language) for a group of phonetic words, it being well known that words of this kind always exist even in non-phonetic languages. From among these were chosen all those which could be built up on the basis of about twenty different sounds, for it had been ascertained by experiment that this is about the number of isolated sounds which can be distinguished clearly by children between four and five years of age.

In trying to fix upon this definite number of words, we have not had to trouble ourselves about any difficulties other than those mentioned above, for the length of the word and the complications of sounds which enter into it present no difficulty to the child. In such early and fundamental research one needs only to interest the child; and for that it is enough that the word should be phonetic and that it should represent objects which are well known and under the eye. When this is done and interest in the written word is awakened it will be possible to go on to succeeding difficulties, preparing groups of words according to the spelling used in the language. In a word, one must proceed in the first instance with the aim of rousing keen interest in reading, and afterwards the way will be prepared for the long journey necessary to overcome the various difficulties of spelling. Then arises the necessity for research in grouping materially objects and words corresponding to objects, making up a series of successive exercises. Until there has been aroused in the child interest in difficulties themselves and in the grouping of words which illustrate them the only thing necessary is a proper classification of words. This leads the children to pure interest in reading words, as it is met with in phonetic languages.

In England, in adopting this procedure for the English language, it was found necessary to make small chests which, in different drawers, contain groups of words chosen according to some spelling difficulties, and groups of objects referring to them (as in the divisions for classification).

The child can, after having taken a drawer from the chest, take out the objects himself, apply the label to each one, and, having finished the work, replace it in the chest. He can then take another drawer, and so on. In this way he studies some of the difficulties relative to spelling and pronunciation.

REVERSAL OF THE EXERCISE

The practical advantages of such exercises have suggested another application, and so, reversing the object of these, there have been grouped together objects which have educational value; they are accompanied by labels on which their names are written. Whilst in the first exercise the objects were known and the difficulties of learning were connected with words, here one starts from a knowledge of words which is sufficient to teach the names of the objects which are grouped together for various educational purposes. In religious education, for example, prepared in miniature are various objects relating to the altar, the priest's vestments, the objects necessary for the Mass, etc. The development of this exercise has been extended to teaching the words relating to many parts of the material, as for example, the names of materials, of fastenings, of polygons, etc. Finally another application has been made to models of animals and plants, together with scientific terms relating to their classification, written on separate labels which must be placed on the objects when recognized.

These last applications, however, have carried us along a path different from that in which we are interested here—learning to read. Instead of that, they form an application of reading used as it is done by botanists and gardeners when they show the names of various plants on labels.

COMMANDS: READING SENTENCES

As soon as some visitors to the Children's Houses in San Lorenzo saw that the children were reading printed characters they sent us gifts of splendidly illustrated books, which formed the first nucleus of our library. Turning over the leaves of these books of simple stories, I realized that the little ones would not be able to understand them. The teachers, however, wanted to prove that they could, by making several children read, telling me that their reading was much more fluent and more correct than that of children who had finished the second elementary class. I did not allow myself to be convinced, and I applied two tests. The first was to get the mistress to tell some of the stories, and to notice how many children interested themselves voluntarily. After a few words the children's attention wandered; the mistress had to recall the inattentive ones to order and she was using old methods encouraging the children to understand. Little by little there developed in the class noise and movement, which were due to the fact that each individual was turning to his usual occupations and giving up listening.

Evidently the children who seemed to be reading the books with pleasure were not enjoying the meaning of them. They were enjoying the mechanical power which they had acquired, consisting of the translation of written signs into the sound of a word which they recognized. In fact they were reading the books with much less readiness than the cards, because in them they met with many unknown words.

My second test was to get the child to read the book without giving him the explanations which the mistress in the old fashion hastened to interpose, mixing them up with suggestive questions —" Have you understood? " " What have you read? " " The child went in a carriage, did he not? " " Read carefully." " Watch."

I then gave the book to a child, placed myself beside him in an affectionately confidential attitude, and asked him with the simple gravity with which I would have spoken to a friend: " Did you understand what you read? " The child answered, " No," but the expression on his face seemed to ask for an explanation of my question because he did not understand what was meant by ' reading '. The fact is that reading is not to read a series of words one after the other; but reading can put ourselves into communication with the complex thoughts of others and this was not the case with our children. Such a brilliant achievement was awaiting our children in the future, a new source of surprise and delight.

The book embodies logical language, not the mechanism of language; and for that reason, it cannot be understood by the child until he has mastered logical language. Between being able to read words and knowing the meaning of a book there may extend the same distance as between being able to pronounce a word and a speech.

I therefore had the reading of the books postponed and waited. One day whilst we were talking together, four children got up together with an expression of joy and wrote on the blackboard some sentences of this kind: " How pleased I am when the garden is in bloom." It was a great and moving surprise for us. They had arrived spontaneously at composition, just as they had spontaneously written the first word. The mechanism was the same; and the result followed logically. Logical spoken language one day led up to a sudden outbreak into written language.

I understood that the moment had arrived for going on to the writing of sentences, and I had recourse to the same means of writing on the blackboard.

" Do you like me? " The children read this aloud slowly, were silent for a moment, and then shouted " Yes ". I went on to write: " Keep silent and be quite still." They read it almost in a shout, and directly they had finished reading, deep silence fell in the room, broken by the movement of some chairs which the children made in settling themselves.

So there began between us communication through the medium of written language, which proved to be most interesting for the children. By degrees they discovered the great quality of writing, that it transmits thought. When I began to write they were eager in their haste to learn what I intended and to understand it without my pronouncing a single word.

Written language does not need speech; its full power is realized only when it is completely isolated from spoken language.

In these last days (in 1909) whilst the present book was for the first time in the press, we reached, in the Children's Houses, full enjoyment of reading by means of the following game.

I wrote on some sheets of paper long sentences describing actions which the children would have to carry out, for example: " Close the window shutters and go and open the entrance door; then wait a moment and put things back as they were at first." " Ask eight of your companions, politely to leave their places and stand in a line, in pairs, in the middle of the room; then make them march backwards and forwards on the points of their toes, very quietly, without making any noise." " Ask three of your oldest companions who sing very well to be kind enough to come to the middle of the room; group them in a row, and sing along with them any beautiful tune which you like." And so on.

The children, directly I had finished writing, almost snatched the cards from my hand to read them, placing them to dry on their little tables. They read them by themselves, with the most intense attention, in the deepest silence. I asked them, " Do you understand? " " Yes, yes." " Then go and do it." With what admiration did I watch the children as they each chose an action and carried it out at once. Great activity, movement of a new kind came to life in the room. Some closed and then opened the shutters, some set their companions running, some made them sing, some went to write, some took objects from the sideboard. Surprise and curiosity provoked general silence, and the scene was filled with the most intense commotion. It seemed as if magic strength had gone out from me stimulating activity which had been unknown before: that magic was written language, the greatest triumph of civilization.

How well the children understood the importance of it! When I left, they crowded round me with manifestations of gratitude and affection, saying: " Thank you, thank you for the lesson."

We had taken a great step; we had leapt from the mechanism to the spirit of reading.

Today, the following, which is the favourite among the games, is played in this way. First, absolute silence is established; then there is presented a box containing folded labels, on which is written a long sentence describing an action.

All the children who can read come up and draw a label by chance; they read it mentally once or oftener, till they are sure that they have understood it right, then they give the open label back to the teacher, and set about what has to be done. Since many of the actions require the assistance of companions who cannot read, and many lead to the using and moving about of objects, a general movement develops, which grows in a wonderfully orderly manner, whilst the deep silence is broken only by the subdued scuffle of little feet running lightly and by voices singing songs—an unexpected revelation of spontaneous perfect discipline.

Experience has shown us that composition must precede logical reading, as writing precedes the reading of words; and that the reading which conveys meaning must be mental and not vocal.

Indeed, reading aloud implies the employment of the two mechanisms of language, the articular and the graphic, which makes the work more complicated. Who does not know that an adult who has to read a passage in public prepares himself for it by getting the meaning of it beforehand by mental reading, and that reading aloud is one of the most difficult intellectual actions? Children, then, who are beginning to read in order that they may interpret thought, ought to read mentally. Written language, when it reaches logical thought, ought to be kept apart from articulate language. It really represents language which transmits thought from a distance, whilst the senses and the muscular mechanism are silent. It is spiritualized language which brings into communication all mankind.

Education having reached such a level in the Children's Houses, it follows as a consequence that the whole scheme of work in the elementary schools would have to be changed.

How to reform the lowest elementary classes, eventually carrying on our methods in them is a big question which does not call for investigation here. It is enough to say that the first as well as the second elementary class would be abolished completely by our child education which include it.

The elementary classes of the future would then receive children like ours, who already know how to look after themselves, to dress, undress and wash themselves, who know the rules of good manners, and are disciplined yet free, or as I may say, have set themselves free. They, in addition to articulate language completely developed and free from defects, have also mastered elementary written language which is beginning to develop into logical language.

That they speak with a good pronunciation and write beautifully, that their movements are full of grace, indicates that they belong to a humanity which has been educated under refining guidance.

It is the childhood of triumphal humanity, since they are intelligent and patient observers of their surroundings and possess as a form of intellectual liberty, spontaneous reasoning.

For such children there ought to be found an elementary school worthy to receive them and to guide them on the succeeding path of life and civilization, using the same general principles of respect for liberty and for the spontaneous manifestations of the child—principles which determine the personality of the little men.[1]

---

[1] These elementary Montessori schools now function fully in most of the places, where there are Children's Houses and the education imparted there is described in some of my books, notably: *The Advanced Montessori Method*, I and II.

THE SPEECH OF THE CHILD

WRITTEN language, which includes dictation and reading, involves articulate language in its complete mechanism (auditory, central and motor paths), and, in the way of development encouraged by my method, is based essentially on articulate language.

Written language may, therefore, be considered from two points of view:

(*a*) That of the mastery of a new language of great social importance which is added to the spoken language of the natural man. This is the cultural meaning which is usually attached to written language, which is, therefore, taught in schools without any regard for its relationships with spoken language, and only with the intention of offering to social man a means necessary for making contacts with the environment.

(*b*) That of the connection between written and spoken language, and the eventual possibility of using written language to improve spoken language—a new consideration on which I must insist and one which gives to written language physiological and psychological importance.

Besides, as spoken language is a natural function of man, and is also the means which he uses for social purposes, so this writing may be considered by itself, in its formation as an organic whole of new mechanisms which are established in the nervous system and as means usable for social purposes.

It is a question of giving to written language, apart from its physiological importance, a period of development which is independent of its other functions and which is destined to be completed later.

I believe that writing bristles with difficulties at the beginning, not only because up till today it has been taught by irrational methods, but because we have wanted to make it carry out, when it has barely been acquired, the lofty function of written language, which has been fixed by centuries of efforts made by the people.

Let us think of the irrationality of these methods. We have analysed the written signs rather than the physiological acts necessary to produce the alphabetic signs, yet the visible representations of the signs have no hereditary connection with the motor side of their execution, as for example, the auditory expression of the word has with the motor mechanism of spoken language. It is, therefore, always difficult to provoke an excito-motor action unless movement has already been prepared for its arrival. The idea cannot act directly on the motor nerves, which is all the more apparent when the idea itself is incomplete and incapable of sustaining a feeling which excites the will.

Thus the analysis of writing made in the ' curves ' and ' strokes ' has led to the child's being presented with a sign devoid of meaning, which for that reason does not interest him, and the making of which cannot determine a spontaneous motor impulse. The action expected constitutes an effort of the will, which in the child soon degenerates into weariness, into boredom and simple endurance. To such an effort there would be added that of setting up at the same time the muscular connections co-ordinating the movements necessary for holding and manipulating the writing instrument.

A combination of depressing feelings accompanies these efforts, leading to the production of imperfect and wrong signs, which the teachers have to correct, thus depressing the child's feelings still more, by the constant exposure of mistakes and imperfections in the marks made. So whilst the child is being urged to make efforts, his mental energy is being lowered rather than stimulated by the teacher. Whatever the method adopted to teach writing may be—excluding even the old way of proceeding by means of strokes and curves—the fact remains that the movements of the hand are not acted upon directly by either thinking or looking at a sample. A sign to be traced instead is the only direct guide to the establishment of movement.

Although acquired in such a mistaken way, the written language so painfully learnt, has at once to be used for social purposes; and, imperfect and immature, it is made to serve for the synthetic construction of language and the expression of ideas by the higher mental centres.

We remember that in nature spoken language is formed gradually, and is *already established* in words when the higher mental centres are using these words in what Kussmaul calls *dictorium*, that is, the grammatical, synthetic formation of the language necessary for the expression of complex ideas, that is, the language of the logical mind.

Finally, the mechanism of language must pre-exist the high mental activities which will have to use it.

There exist, therefore, two periods in the development of language—the lower one, which prepares the nervous tracts and the central mechanism which will have to link up the sensory and the motor tracts; and the higher one determined by the higher mental activity which is made evident by means of the pre-formed mechanism of language.

Thus, in the scheme of spoken language as given by Kussmaul, the most important fact to be noted is that there exists a kind of reflex cerebral arc which is established during the early stages of language formation.

Let us consider fig. 1.

Let *O* stand for the ear; *L* for the group of motor organs used for the words which make up language; *U* for the auditory centre

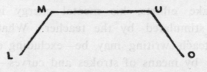

Fig. 1

of speech; and *M* for the motor centre. The paths *OU* and *ML* are peripheral, the first centripetal and the second centrifugal; the path *UM* is an intercentral connecting tract.

The centre *U*, in which are formed the auditory images of words, may be subdivided into three, as indicated in the figure 2.

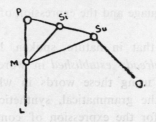

Fig. 2

Sounds are realized at *Su*, syllables at *Si*, and words at *P*.

That separate centres for sounds and syllables may be formed is confirmed by the pathology of language, in which in certain forms of centrosensory partial failure of speech the patients can no longer pronounce anything more than sounds, or sounds and syllables.

Small children are at first particularly sensitive to the simple sounds of language with which, especially with *S*, the mother fondles and calls for their attention, whilst later on the child is sensitive to syllables, with which also his mother caresses him, saying, " ba, ba, puf, tuf ".

Finally, the simple word which attracts the attention of the child is generally a dissyllable.

The same sub-division may be made for the motor centres, fig. 3. The child at first utters single or double sounds, e.g. *bl, gl, ch,*

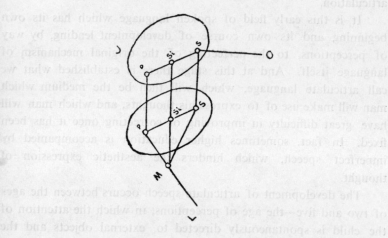

FIG. 3

expressions which the mother welcomes with tender invitations and with great delight. Then the child begins to produce sounds which are disyllabic, "*ga-ba*" and finally disyllabic words, mainly labial, e.g. "*mama*," "*baba*".

We say that spoken language is beginning in the child when the word which he pronounces represents an idea, when, for example, on seeing his mother and recognizing her he says "*mama*," or on seeing the dog, "*tete*," on seeing someone eating, "*papa*" (i.e. pap or food).

We consider language to be initiated when it is linked up with perception, whilst language itself is still, as regards its psycho-motor mechanism, quite rudimentary.

Language is considered to be initiated when, independently of the reflex arc, in which the mechanial formation of language is still unknown, there occurs the recognition of the word in such a way that it is associated with the object which it represents.

20

At this stage, therefore, one is perfecting language itself by degrees, as the hearing perceives better the sounds composing words, and the psycho-motor paths are becoming better adapted to articulation.

It is this early field of spoken language which has its own beginning and its own course of development leading, by way of perceptions, to the perfecting of the original mechanism of language itself. And at this stage there is established what we call articulate language, which will then be the medium which man will make use of to express his thoughts, and which man will have great difficulty in improving or correcting once it has been fixed. In fact, sometimes higher education is accompanied by imperfect speech, which hinders the aesthetic expression of thought.

The development of articulate speech occurs between the ages of two and five—the age of perceptions, in which the attention of the child is spontaneously directed to external objects and the memory is particularly retentive. This is also the age of mobility when all the psycho-motor tracts have become usable, and the muscular mechanism is fixed. At this period of life, by the mysterious linking up of the auditory tracts and the motor tracts of articulate language, it seems that the auditory perceptions have power to excite the complicated movements of articulate speech, which develops instinctively under these stimuli as if awakening from the sleep of heredity. It is well known that only at this age is it possible to acquire all the characteristic modulations of a language, which it is useless to try and establish later. The mother tongue is pronounced well because it is fixed in childhood, and the adult who learns to speak a new language must carry into it the imperfection which marks the language of the foreigner. Only children who, below seven years of age, learn several languages at the same time, are able to perceive and reproduce the characteristic modulations of accent and pronunciation.

In the same way, the defects acquired in childhood, like dialect errors, or others due to bad habits, cannot be cured in the adult.

That which develops later, the higher language, the *dictorium*, does not originate in the mechanism of language, but in intellectual development which makes use of mechanical language.[1]

As spoken language is developed by exercising the mechanism of it and is enriched with perceptions, the *dictorium* is developed

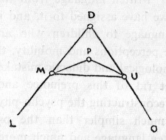

FIG. 4

with the mind, and is enriched with intellectual education. Referring back to the language diagram, fig. 4, we see that above the arc standing for the lower language there is placed the *dictorium D*, from which there now issue the motor impulses for the word which is established as spoken language fitted to express the thought of the intelligent man.

Up till now, owing to preconceived ideas, it has been thought that written language must be acquired only through the development of the *dictorium* as a means fitted to secure culture and to permit the grammatical analysis and the construction of language. Remembering that " spoken words fly away,' it is admitted that intellectual culture can advance only with the aid of a language which is stable, objective, and capable of being analysed, as is written language.

But why do we, who recognize the precious written language as an indispensable factor of intellectual education because it fixes the ideas of men and permits the analysis and assimilation of them through books in which they are indelibly written, like an

---

[1] So the typewriter has nothing to do with the intellectual thought of the person who uses it to transmit his thoughts.

ineffaceable memory of words therefore always present—why do we not recognize it as being useful for the humbler task of fixing the words which represent ideas, and of analysing them into their component sounds?

Under the influence of teaching prejudice we are not able to separate the idea of written language from that of the function which up till now we have assigned to it, and it seems to us that in teaching this language to children who are still at the age belonging to simple perceptions and mobility, there is being committed a grave psychological and didactic mistake.

But let us get rid of this prejudice and consider written language by itself, reconstructing the psycho-physiological mechanism of it. It is much simpler than the psycho-physiological mechanism of spoken language and much more directly amenable to education.

Writing especially is singularly easy. Let us consider dictated writing; we have a perfect parallel with spoken language, because to the word heard there must correspond a motor action. It is true that there does not exist here the mysterious hereditary relationship between the word heard and the word spoken; but the movements involved in writing are much simpler than those necessary for the spoken word and are carried out by muscles less fused in their function than those of the vocal cords and the tongue. They are all external and we can act directly on them in preparing movements.

My method prepares, in a direct manner, for the movements of the hand which writes; hence the psycho-motor impulse of the word heard finds the motor paths already established, and manifest itself in the act of writing like an ' explosion '.

The real difficulty lies in the written sign; but we must consider that we are here dealing with the age of perception, in which sensations and memory, like the early associations, are just in the characteristic expansion stage of natural development. Besides, our children have already been prepared by various exercises of the senses, and by the methodical building up of ideas and mental associations, to appreciate written signs. The child who recognizes a triangle and calls it a triangle, can recognize the letter ' *s* ' and call it by its sound *S*. This is obvious.

Let us stop talking about precocity in teaching. Let us rid ourselves of prejudices, and confine ourselves to experience, which shows how children actually carry on without any effort, even with distinct signs of pleasure and gratitude, with the recognition of written signs presented as objects.

With this preface, let us consider the relationships between the mechanical systems employed in the two languages.

The child of three or four years old has already, according to our diagram, begun spoken language some time before, but he is just at the stage in which the mechanism of spoken language is perfected—a period contemporaneous with that in which he masters the content of language with the inheritance of perceptions.

Perhaps the child has not heard perfectly in all their component sounds the words which he pronounces; and, if he has heard them perfectly, they may have been badly pronounced, and therefore have left a wrong auditory impression. It would be a good thing if the child, by exercising the motor tracts of spoken language, could establish exactly the movements necessary for perfect articulation, before faulty mechanism having been fixed and the age of easy motor adaptations being past, the defects become incorrigible.

To secure this, the word must be analysed. So wishing to perfect language, we first train the children in composition and then pass on to grammatical studies, and wishing to improve style we first teach them to write grammatically, and then we come to the analysis of the style; trying thus to perfect the word, it is first of all necessary that the word should exist, and then is the fitting time for attacking the analysis of it. It is when the child speaks that there has come the time for analysing the word in order to perfect it.

But as grammer and style are not possible with spoken language, but have to be referred to written language which presents to the eye the speech to be analysed, so it is with the word.

The analysis of that which is transient cannot be made.

It is necessary to materialize and stabilize language; hence the necessity for the written word, represented by graphic signs.

In the third factor involved in writing which I consider in my method, namely the composition of the word, there is included the analysis of the word by means of objects and alphabetic sign. The child breaks up the word heard, which he perceives in its entirety as a word knowing also its meaning, into sounds and syllables, and then translates it into the word composed with the movable alphabet.

Whilst in the development of spoken language the component sounds of the word may be imperfectly perceived, now in teaching the graphic sign corresponding to the sound—and this consists in presenting a sandpaper letter, naming it clearly, having it seen and touched—not only is there fixed clearly the perception of the sound heard, but this perception is connected with two others, the motor and the visual perceptions of the written sign, which permit external influences to affect the auditory images of words.

The following diagrams explain, stage by stage the sequence of events referred to above.

Let us consider, stage by stage, the three-stage lesson in its application to the first teaching of the alphabet.

First Stage

The mistress, showing a letter of the alphabet, says: " This is A, A, A." Then at once the mistress says a word which begins with A—" A," as in " Ada," adding some other words which have this sound and not necessarily as the first sound. When a consonant is being taught, the same thing is done, but by pro- nouncing the word which begins with that sound there is made a syllable, " This is M, M, M," as in " Mama ". Then the teacher turning to the child adds, " Touch A," or " Touch M ". The child traces the letter chosen as if writing it. Thus the motor image of the letter touched is associated with the auditory image of the alphabetic sound and with the visual image of it, and remains more strongly impressed in the memory.

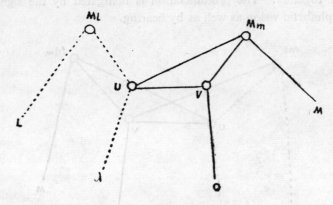

FIG. 5

A. . . . .the ear (auricle)
U. . . . .the auditory centre of the spoken word
Ml. . . .the motor centre of the spoken word
L. . . . .organs for the articulation of the word (tongue)
Mm. . .motor centre of language written
M. . . . .the hand
O. . . . .the eye (oculus)
V. . . . .the visual centre of the written word (visual)
The dotted lines refer to the reflex arc of spoken language.

SECOND STAGE

The mistress repeats many times—" Which is *A*? Point out *A*, touch *A*," or " Which is *M*?" In this second stage, by having the same exercise repeated over and over again, there is strengthened the association already reached during the first stage. This forms an association exercise.

THIRD STAGE

Pointing to a letter, the teacher asks the child: " What is this? " The child answers, " *A* " or " *M* ". The visual image of the written sign is associated with that of the pronunciation of the sounds, and the two languages, written and spoken, are associated together. The pronunciation is instigated by the sign, by the alphabetic vision as well as by hearing.

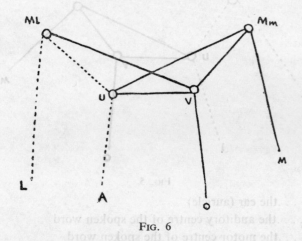

FIG. 6

The association set up is represented by the two triangles in fig. 6, *UVMm* and *UVMl*, which have the same base in the association between the two sense-centres, that is the auditory centre of the spoken word and the visual centre of the written word, whilst the apices correspond respectively to the two motor centres, one of spoken language (*Ml*) and the other of written language (*Mm*).

The lesson, as is well known, represents only a detail of initiation and enlightenment in comparison with the great work of the child, which consists of innumerable repetitions of the same exercise. When the child continues to trace the sandpaper letters for a long time, remembering the sound of them and pronouncing them to himself, he ends by establishing mechanically an association between the alphabet and the component sounds of the words.

The length of such exercises constitutes a real period of development by the fixation of the visual images of the letters of the alphabet, of the images of the movements necessary to reproduce them with the writing hand and of their associations with the images corresponding to spoken language—that is, the component sounds of words and the acts which reproduce them by means of the organs of speech. Then is practised a formative analytical work on a new language capable of setting up mechanically the analysis of the spoken word which already exists. The letter of the alphabet presented to the child may be compared with a watch-spring which gives off a sound and interests him much more than a surprise-box. Every now and then he remains absorbed in it (periods of concentration). The work of association described above is in vigorous action during a period of six or more months, from the age of about three and a half to four years—a period in which the word of the child is still uncertain and easy to break up (analyse) because it is still very near to and in sympathy with the preceding period in which is stabilized the articulate word in the language of the child.

It is only later (after four years and a few months) that the child masters the analytical mechanism and utilizes it fully in the interesting work of the composition of words. Then he displays his power over the mechanism as a peacock spreads out its feathers, and connects up the two analyses. He has become competent through the preceding exercises in perceiving words clearly sound by sound, and in recognizing with an ease which might be called the mechanism of them, the alphabetic sounds which correspond to them. Thus the word composed from the alphabet represents the external projection of the spoken word and the teacher is able to penetrate, if the expression may be permitted, into the inner labyrinths in which words are definitely elaborated. She can then intervene with help for the two languages, and lead the child on the one hand to the perfect spoken word and on the other to the perfect orthography of the written word.

The same mechanism exists fundamentally in the non-phonetic languages. The sounds represented by a letter of the alphabet or by a phonogram, when once they are associated with this, may be better determined in their analysis and finally projected into the composition of the word.

The exercise in composition lasts a still longer time than the other which is concerned in establishing the mechanism linking the two languages. It therefore suffices for the most part, for the acquisition of correct spelling, before writing suddenly comes into existence, which may reproduce a considerable number of words already found in the non-phonetic languages and almost all the words in the phonetic languages.

This association between the two languages, spoken and written, is of the highest importance and forms the key to the whole development of writing. Writing then becomes a second form of language associated with the mother tongue, and a way of communication is established between the two languages through these oft-repeated exercises.

On the other hand, with the usual methods, writing is a thing apart which is learnt independently of the spoken language and is studied objectively with supposed difficulties of sounds and syllables as if the whole language had to be built up *ex novo*, forgetting that the language already is formed and that the child already has been using it since the age of two, and that all the difficulties which the mother tongue presents are provided for by an act of nature.

Let us note the advantages of the method described.

The letters of the alphabet act on the spoken language, instigating almost mechanically the analysis of the spoken word.

It is the spoken word which is thrown into relief in the analysis of the sounds of which it is composed.

Once this association of signs with sounds is established, it is possible to reconstruct with the alphabet *all the words* which exist in the mind of the child and those which he hears pronounced.

Then, after merely having the trouble of associating signs with sounds, *all* spoken language can be composed with graphic signs, and suddenly ends in provoking the outburst of writing.

Alphabetic signs, as a matter of fact, are few in number; in the Italian language only 24 are distinguished. With the 24 letters all the words are formed; those which even a big dictionary is not enough to include.

Every word, whatever it may be, is always composed of one or more of these 24 sound-families.

If these are learnt by associating them with the 24 letters of the alphabet which represent them, then the whole language can be translated graphically, and the children, taking the letters relating to the sounds, are able to compose all possible words in a phonetic language like Italian.

A word demands the same effort, whether it be long or short. The supposed syllabic difficulties which are taught commonly, as in a systematic progression are always reduced to translating sounds into signs, to recognizing the signs relating to the sounds. To compose a simple word like " pipa," and to compose a difficult word like " stra-da " is really the same thing, because the two words already exist formed in the mother tongue. The key is that the child has succeeded in recognizing the sounds composing the words, so that he has made an analysis of the sounds which compose the words. If the child has succeeded in recognizing the sounds contained in the syllable " stra," and hears these sounds separately—" s-t-r-a," he will be able to compose the written word.

Hence there exists only one real difficulty, one single thing to do, one which is wholly internal—the mental analysis of sounds.

As for reproducing with the hand the design of the letters of the alphabet, even in this, our method cancels all those artificial difficulties which are taught in a supposed necessity for a progressive system. For example, *i, e, o,* are considered much easier than others, but the child who has exercised in a general manner his hand, which has been employed in all his sense exercises, and which has then specifically been exercised in tracing the letters and making so many geometrical drawing (of which, hereafter) has no difficulty either with the single letters or with combinations of them in the words which interest suggests to him and which he is keen to fix by means of graphic language. He breaks out into writing, writing at once whole sentences and not only words detached one from the other.

DEFECTS IN LANGUAGE DUE TO THE LACK OF EDUCATION

Defects and imperfections in speech are derived in part from organic causes consisting of malformations, or pathological alterations of the nervous system; but they are partly connected with functional defects acquired during the period when speech is developing, and they consist of a wrong pronunciation of the sounds composing the spoken word. Such errors are picked up by the child when he hears the word pronounced badly, or hears imperfect speech. Dialect defects come under this heading, but there also enter into it bad habits, which are responsible for the persistence in the child of defects natural to infantile speech. Again, the child imitates the faulty speech of the people who surround him in early childhood.

The normal defects of childish speech are to be traced to the fact that the complicated muscular apparatus of the organs of speech is not yet functioning properly, hence it is not able to reproduce the sound which was the sense-stimulus of this internal movement. The association of the movements necessary for the articulation of the spoken word is established gradually. This results in a speech in which sounds are imperfect and often left out (hence incomplete words). These defects are grouped together under the term *blaesitas*,[1] and are mainly due to the fact that the child cannot yet control the movements of the tongue. They comprise principally: sigmatism, or the imperfect pronunciation of the letter *S*; rhoticism, or excessive use of *R*; lambadism, or defective pronunciation of *L*; gammacism, wrong pronunciation of *G*; iotacism, imperfect pronunciation of the gutturals; mogilalia, imperfect pronunciation of the labials; according to some authors,

---

[1] Defective speech.

like Preyer, the suppression of the first sound of the word ought also to be included in mogilalia.

Some of the defects of pronunciation which concern the production of vowel sounds, like those of consonants, arise because the child reproduces perfectly sounds which have been heard in imperfect pronunciation.

In the first case we have functional inefficiency of the peripheral motor organ, and as a result, of the nerve tracts, when the cause is located in the individual. In the second case, the error is traced to the auditory stimulus, and the cause is located in the environment.

Such defects often persist, though in less marked degree, in the youth and the adult. They produce a definitely faulty language and also errors in spelling, like the wrong spelling of dialects.

When one thinks of the fascination of human speech, one realizes the inferiority of anyone who does not speak correctly, and one cannot picture an aesthetic conception of education which does not bestow special care on perfecting spoken language. Although the Greeks passed on to Rome the art of cultivating fine language, Humanism did not revive this practice, but devoted more attention to the aesthetics of the environment and the restoration of works of art than to the improvement of man.

Today there has been introduced the practice of correcting, by methods of teaching, the grave defects of speech like stammering, but there has not yet penetrated into our schools the idea of the gymnastics of language which tend to improve it, making them part of a universal method and treating them as a detail of the great work of the aesthetic improvement of man.

Some teachers of deaf-mutes and some intelligent seekers after correct speech are attempting today, with but slight practical success, to introduce into the elementary schools the correction of various forms of defective speech, influenced by statistical studies which show the wide prevalence of such defects among pupils. The exercises consist essentially in cures by silence, which will bring quiet and rest to the organs of speech. To these are added the patient repetition of single vowel sounds and consonants; breathing exercises form another part of the treatment. This is not the place to describe in detail the way in which these exercises are carried out; they are long and tedious and outside the range of school teaching. But in my methods all the exercises for the correction of speech have a place.

(a) The exercises in silence prepare the nerve tracts of speech to receive new stimuli in a perfect manner.

(b) The lesson stages secure first of all clear, detached pronunciation by the mistress of a few words (and specially of names which it is desired to connect with concrete objects or ideas); in this way there are set up clear and perfect auditory stimuli of language; these stimuli are repeated by the teacher when the child has added the idea of the object which the word represents (recognition of object) to the enunciation of the name. Further, there is involved the exciting of speech in the child, who must repeat that single word aloud and pronounce the separate sounds of which it is composed.

(c) The exercises in written language analyse the sounds of the word and get them repeated separately in many ways; this is done when the child is learning the separate letters of the alphabet, and when he is composing and writing words, repeating the sounds of them, which in each case leads to the composed or written word.

I believe that in the schools of the future there will disappear the idea which is coming into existence today of correcting faults of speech in the elementary schools, and that there will be substituted another more rational idea of avoiding them, by caring for the development of speech in the Children's Houses, at the age in which speech is establishing itself in children.

* * *

The process described above was confirmed so frequently in the innumerable schools which have arisen that the following conclusions may be stated:

The age which is most favourable for the development of written language is that of childhood, about the age of four, when there are in active operation the natural processes concerned in the development of spoken language, that is, during the sensitive period (v. *Secret of Childhood*) in which speech is developed and established naturally. It is the sensitiveness of the development from which arises the enthusiasm about the alphabet and which fixes spontaneously the phonetic analysis of the word into its component sounds. Later (six to seven years of age), his creative period being ended, there is no longer the same natural interest in these analyses, either of the spoken word or of the written (the alphabet). It is this which is responsible for the amazing fact that small children make better and more rapid progress than older children; instead of growing bored and tired like the latter, they display an inexhaustible activity which seems to strengthen them.

Besides the confirmation of this surprising fact which is related to the special psychology of childhood, other discoveries have led to interesting modifications in the application of the method which also must be referred to psychology.

The conclusion of this lengthy analysis is that *written* language in its mechanisms can be directly associated with spoken language, and almost derive from it as another form of expression. This is the case during the very period when, by nature, spoken language is established, i.e. during the sensitive period. Written language then becomes an exterior means to direct and perfect spoken language and to purify it from all its defects and errors. Written language thus becomes a means to educate spoken language.

Thus the *dictorium*, language that expresses thought, the work of intelligence, finds at its disposal two mechanisms which integrate each other; that of the spoken word and that of the written word.

The experience related above had its final result when the children read long sentences conveying an action to be fulfilled. Hence it was easy to pass on to the reading of books as soon as the children were capable of understanding them (5-6 years of age).

Afterwards, however, great progress was made. These later experiences almost confine those amazing miracles of children of 4 years of age who exploded into writing, to a surpassed epoch. The progress of the children has become even more precocious, the methods more quick and efficient in their success, the interest of the children is even intenser than before.

If one were to affirm all of a sudden that children under two years old are able to recognize more than twenty letters of the alphabet, and possess from 500 to 600 words, that at three years of age they begin to study grammar and to read, one would give an impression of utter unreality (it would seem a miracle). It would create the same stir and would draw the same attention as that which struck the learned world forty years ago when the children of San Lorenzo presented a new phenomenon.

A new book is certainly necessary to describe these subsequent achievements; here, however, we wish merely to mention them. Our attention was drawn to younger children, i.e. children from birth to three years of age. It is precisely in that epoch that the spoken language is naturally developed, it makes its first appearance at about two years of age. Spoken language follows certain rules in its development and the subsequent acquisitions are made in what could be called a ' grammatical ' order. This has been observed and recorded for the first time by Stern and subsequently by various other people interested in psychological observation.

The child begins to know nouns which refer to objects, and then words that refer to their qualities (adjectives), lastly prepositions (concerning the relative position of the objects) and conjunctions (which represent the conjunction of the objects). Briefly, there is in the first development a representation of things in the environment. It is a curious fact, however, that a few months before the age of two years words come out of the child as in an explosion of spoken language; and verbs, the exact forms of nouns and adjectives with their prefixes and suffixes; and finally the distinction (and conjugation) of verbal forms regarding the present, past and future tense, and pronouns are used.

After the age of two syntaxis is established, the construction of sentences and their mutual dependence.

In thus observing the development of language a real ' grammatical analysis ' is made. In fact, if one did not speak grammatically, it would not be possible to *express* thought in any language.

It is worthwhile mentioning that the *only language* anyone, educated or not, possesses perfectly as far as the sounds and the grammatical construction is concerned is the so-called ' mother tongue '. The child therefore not only acquires the spoken language, but he acquires it in a special way, because only thus that language becomes a ' personal characteristic,' hence a ' characteristic of the race '. It is *fixed* in the human individual.

When we studied and meditated upon this marvellous creative phenomenon, we recognized in the little child a mental form, different from ours, which we called: ' absorbent mind '.

The natural development of language in the child suggests the idea that in order to *help this development* in education we must proceed according to a grammatical scheme. And just as the mechanisms of written language had given help to and integrated spoken language in the first period of our experiment, so also written language in a grammatical form and succession, by means of objects, games and written words, can help a superior spoken language: the language of the dictorium, i.e. the expression of ideas.

The success of this second attempt surpassed by far the first. Although the methods used in the beginning have been retained fundamentally, there is this difference: the words of spoken language are no longer important only because they can be reproduced in written language, they are important too on account of their grammatical meaning. Thus also the union between words not only helps to ' translate into writing ' what one would say in speaking, it leads at once to the discovery of ' sentences full of meaning ' which are developed by and by on the lines of grammatical construction.

21

This second period of our experiments has a history much more important and surprising than that of the first period.

One of the practical sides of this new development lies in the facilitation, almost the complete revolution, of the problem of learning to write in a non-phonetic language. Here, in fact, the *intuition* of the child plays a part, being stimulated by his creative power. Thus, whilst in the first period we witnessed the phenomenon of children intuitively reading words written in printed or even gothic type, without any formal teaching, so here by means of intuition they read non-phonetic words (belonging to their own mother tongue) simply by using objects and attractive games. It is, after all, a spontaneous effort urged on by interest, something analogous to what urged modern scientists to interpret unknown inscriptions on prehistoric monuments.

The passionate interest of the children should be interpreted as the interest provoked by a ' discovery ' of those conquests, which they had made unconsciously during the first years of their life.

Let us give some practical illustration of grammatical grouping of words.

The substantives taken alone and read do not represent natural language, because one never says only, " Seat," or " Flower," but at least " the seat, the flower," etc.; that is, the article is always used along with the noun. In the same way there is often attached to the noun an adjective to indicate objects of the same kind; for example, we say, " the red flower, the yellow flower, the round table, the large table," and so on. And adjectives possess a very distinct significance for our children, who, in their sense-exercises, become acquainted through the senses with the sensations of qualities, learning in an exact manner the distinguishing terms—thick, thin, small, great, dark blue colour, light blue, etc. It is evident that at this period the child is doing the mental work of making himself conscious of the facts acquired by him unconsciously, and is extending and fixing them. This natural tendency was well illustrated by our successive attempts, and Signor Mario

M. Montessori was the builder of a magnificent construction, and in about twenty years of observations, has given us such a picture of the intellectual possibilities of the child that one might speak of it as a real educational monument.

There is no doubt that the child absorbs an enormous number of impressions from his environment, and external help given to this natural instinct rouses the greatest enthusiasm in him. With this, education gives real aid to natural mental development.

Although as already mentioned it is impossible to give here particulars of a colossal work which would need several volumes for its description in such a way as to make it of general use,[1] it is useful to state that written language leads not only to knowledge of grammar and of syntax at an apparently abnormally early age, but that there may also be made of this language, which delights the child so much, a vehicle of general education.

In the first period of our work, with which this volume is concerned, one sees how the mistress has to busy herself with finding more and more new names, in order to satisfy the insatiable requests of the children. This insatiability which education has revealed through the medium of written language, is certainly one which exists in nature, which spontaneously enlarges the vocabulary from 300 to 3,000 or more words in the period of three to five years of age, as has been ascertained by psychologists, who, however, have confined themselves to observing, counting and setting out the developments which have taken place, and not to point out the way in which to assist this natural development.

Still another fact has been demonstrated by our methods, which have shown themselves to be the means of gaining psychological information. It is that children are even interested in foreign words, and remember them in a surprising way during all the time

---

[1] Indeed, every subject requires a book to itself. There have already been printed in Spanish two volumes: *Psycho-Arithmetic* and *Psycho-Geometry*. Two others are in course of preparation: *Psycho-Grammar*, and a volume illustrating and explaining all the educational apparatus for the use of teachers who are preparing for practical work: *The Apparatus Book* by Maria M. Montessori.

employed in reproducing them with the movable alphabet. This reveals the fact that during the sensitive period (from three to five years) the child tends to accumulate words even when he does not understand them.

In fact, all words will be new until the child has understood them, and understanding them is just the conscious act which leads to clarifying, determining and conserving.

If there exist then these two natural facts—the tendency to accumulate words and the fact that the word may be acquired apart from its signification—it follows as a consequence that we may ask the question of why there should be given so many words confusedly mixed together by a mistress depending on her memory, and why, instead, there should not be utilized this period in the life of the child, first of all to introduce order among the words, and secondly to introduce some scientific terms.

This work, which has been full of surprises, has also been undertaken methodically by Mario M. Montessori. Instead of employing boxes of words of all kinds chosen by chance, we use sets of names referring to one special group of things, e.g. the five classes of vertebrates, animals placed in their groups, leaves, flowers, roots, etc. Illustrative figures then become interesting, because they give a meaning to new words. Not only pictures, but living things, the children's research into Nature, and so on, are utilized.

The success was so great that it has been possible to evolve a form of scientific instruction suited to the intellectual level of the children with unexpected success. It had to be considerably extended beyond the limits which were planned at the beginning of the exercise. The surprising result has been that the children like and remember the classifications, which confirms the idea that it is natural to collect words, and also the need for having a mental order based on the sense of the words. Thus there are two extremes in all these exercises; one is inward: grammar which prepares the order in which words ought to be arranged in order to express thought and therefore to construct language; the other

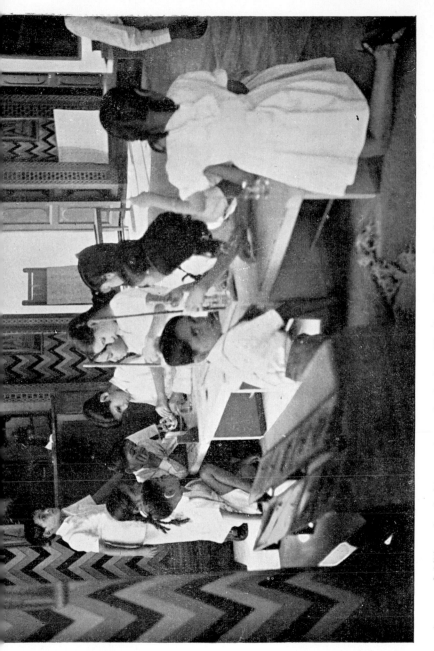

A group of children absorbed in experiments in physics. The " reading-slips " and " commands " of the language apparatus initiate them in simple experiments and technical terminology. Montessori School, Gwalior, India.

is the need for an order according to which external impressions may be classified.

This experiment has gone far beyond our estimations, and today children learn, having language as a guide, a great deal of precise knowledge about biology, geography and astronomy—knowledge which becomes elements sown in a fertile field like the mind of the child which develops of its own accord, through the promptings of nature and which urges the children onwards towards knowledge of the world.

Anyone who regards only from the psychological point of view these pure manifestations of natural development, as is usually done by those men of science who are called psychologists, will possibly discover that children five years old have a wide acquaintance with the outside world and recognize the new objects of civilization and their names, in a way which might almost seem mysterious. For example, they recognize the different makes of automobiles and know their names; their mothers cannot do that.

Astounded by similar facts, Stern concludes: " For thousands of years the child has been passing like an unknown being in the midst of humanity; and yet he possesses mental instincts which make us recognize him as a bond between successive generations in the development of civilization."

THE TEACHING OF NUMERATION AND THE APPROACH TO ARITHMETIC

THE first material which is used for numbers is the series of ten rods used for lengths, a ready part of the education of the senses; the rods are graduated in length from one to ten. The shortest rod is 10 cms long, the second 20 cms, and so on, up to the tenth which is 10 cms, or one metre. When they are to be used in teaching number, the rods are no longer all of the same colour, as when they are used as sense-material intended to make the eye estimate graduated lengths. Here, the various segments of 10 cms are coloured alternately in red and blue, and can therefore be distinguished and counted on every rod. If the first of them represents the quantity 1, the others represent successively the quantities 2, 3, 4, 5, 6, 7, 8, 9, 10. The advantage of this material is that it is possible to present united together, though distinct and countable, the units composing each of the numbers which they represent. The stick of 5, for instance, is a whole piece which corresponds to the number 5, but by means of the colours the five units are distinguished. By this means one overcomes a very great difficulty, that involved in the numbering which is done in adding separately one unit after the other. If they are used for counting any small objects, such as small equal cubes, why, in setting up the first, should we say one, and on adding another, two, and so on? The little child tends to say one about every new object which is added—" One, one, one, one, one," rather than " One, two, three, four, five."

The fact that with the addition of a new unit the group is enlarged, and that there must be considered this increasing whole which constitutes the real obstacle is met with in numeration, when it concerns children of three and a half to four years of age. The grouping together into one whole of units which are really separate from one another is a mental operation beyond the child's powers. Many small children can count, reciting from memory, the natural series of numbers, but they are confused when dealing with the quantities corresponding to them. Counting the fingers, the hands and the feet certainly forms something more concrete for the child, because he can always find the same objects, invariably joined together as a definite quantity. He will always know that he has two hands and two feet.

Rarely, however, will he be able to count with certainty the fingers of one hand and when he does succeed, the difficulty is to know why, if the hand has five fingers, he should have to say about the same object—" One, two, three, four, five." This confusion, which the rather more mature mind corrects, interferes with numeration in the earlier years. The extreme exactness and concreteness of the child's mind needs help which is precise and clear. When numerical rods are in use we find out that the very smallest children take the keenest interest in numbers.

The rods correspond to the numbers and increase in length gradually, unit by unit, hence they give not only the absolute but also the relative idea of number. The proportions have already been studied in the sense-exercise; here they are determined mathematically, constituting the first studies in arithmetic. These numbers, which can be handled and compared, lend themselves at once to combinations and comparisons. For example, by placing together the rod of one unit and that of two, there is produced a length equal to that of the rod of three. From the union of rods

THE DISCOVERY OF THE CHILD

of three and two, there results a length equal to the rod of five. The most interesting exercise consists in placing one alongside the other rods of successive lengths, as the whole series was arranged during the sense-exercises. The result is something resembling organ pipes in which the red and blue colours correspond, forming beautiful transverse stripes. By placing the rod of one on that of nine (that is, the rod farthest from the ten upon that nearest the ten), and repeating this with the two-rod on the eight, the three-rod on the seven, and the four on the six, there are built up lengths all equal to the ten-rod. What is this moving and combination of quantities if it is not the beginning of arithmetical operations? It is at the same time a delightful game to move objects about in this way, and the intelligence, instead of making a useless effort to conceive of the groups of separate units as total quantities representing one number, devotes its fresh energy to a higher exercise, which is that of estimating and adding together quantities. The obstacle having been removed, all the mental energy of the child is utilized, and the progress of learning advances to the extreme limits which age permits. When the child has begun to read and write it is quite easy for him to learn the figures which represent numbers. We give cards bearing the numbers in sandpaper at the same time as the alphabet, and the children trace the signs in order to learn how to write them and to learn their names. Every card when known is placed on the rod of the corresponding quantity. The union of the written figures with the quantities forms an exercise analogous to that of placing the card with the name on the corresponding objects. And when this is accomplished there is laid down a base for a long task which the child can continue alone. The sums of the rods can be written to agree with the figures placed beside the objects and children of five years of age sometimes fill whole copybooks with their little sums.

Although the rods constitute the principal aid to the child in beginning arithmetic, two other objects form part of the first material for the subject. One of these leads to the numbering of

First set of materials for number-work. The number-rods, spindle-boxes and counters give a clear understanding and knowledge of the first ten digits. The material of the decimal system (bottom) follows at once,

separate units, and initiates the child's mind into the idea of numerical groups, at the same time fixing before his eyes the succession of the signs 0, 1, 2, 3, 4, 5, 6, 7, 8, 9.   This material, called the tray of spindles, is divided into compartments each named with one of the ten figures, arranged in sequence.   Within these compartments, the child accumulates in group separate objects corresponding to the figures; that is, he groups the units.   In our case these objects are represented by long, spindle-shaped sticks.

The other material which has been mentioned consists of a group of cards in a box containing certain objects (coloured markers); the cards are separate (mixed) and on them are written the ten numbers from zero to nine.   The child must first of all arrange the cards in a row, by himself, showing by this that he has learned the numerical series, and recognizes the figures which represent the numbers.   Under each figure he then places an appropriate quantity of markers, arranging them two by two, that is one pair under the other; in this way there is made plain the difference between odd and even numbers.

This is all the material which we have considered necessary for laying the foundations of number-teaching and some arithmetical operations.

What follows here is a more detailed description which may be of practical assistance to the teacher.

The rods having been arranged together in juxtaposition according to length, the red and blue marks have to be counted, beginning with the smallest piece, that is: one; one and two; one, two and three, etc. always beginning again with the one for every piece, commencing from side A.   After that, the separate rods have to be named from the shortest to the longest, according to the number of sections which they contain, touching the extremities of them with the finger, starting from the side B where they go up in staircase style; there results from this the numbering of the longest piece: 1, 2, 3, 4, 5, 6, 7, 8, 9, 10.   This correspondence of the 10 on the three sides is verified by the child, who repeats the exercise many times of his own accord because it interests him.

Now to the sense exercises of recognizing the longer and shorter pieces, there are added those of numeration. The pieces having been placed on the ground or mixed up on a table, the teacher simply shows one of them to the child and counts its segments, e.g. five. Then she says to the child: " Give me a longer one." The child chooses by sight, and the teacher verifies if he has guessed rather than judged by comparing the lengths and counting the sections. Such exercises may be repeated many times. Every piece in the set is now given a name of its own by which it will be known henceforth: the piece of one, of two, of three, of four, etc.; finally, for shortness, they are spoken of as they are being handled as " the one, the two, the three, the four ", etc.

NUMBERS AND THE WRITTEN SYMBOLS WHICH REPRESENT THEM

At this point, if the child can write already, he is presented with the sandpaper numbers, which are used in the same way as all the other objects presented, that is, in the well-known stages: " This is one; " " This is two; " " Give me one; " " Give me two; " " Which number is this? " The numbers have to be traced in the same way as the letters.

EXERCISES ON NUMBERS; ASSOCIATION OF THE WRITTEN SIGN WITH THE QUANTITY

I have made two cases for counting. Each includes a horizontal tray, divided into five parts by small upright partitions, within each of which compartments small objects may be deposited; a second, a vertical board is attached to the first at right angles and is also divided into five parts by lines drawn vertically, a figure being placed within each space. In the first case are the figures 0, 1, 2, 3, 4; and in the second 5, 6, 7, 8, 9.

The exercise is obvious. It consists in placing within the enclosure of the horizontal plane a number of objects corresponding to the number drawn on the vertical plane. A variety of small objects are given to the child to make a change in the exercise. I use small spindles which I have made on purpose, Froebel's cubes, and the discs which are used in the game of draughts. A group of objects having been placed beside the child, he has to put them in position; for example, one disc corresponding to 1, two discs to 2, etc. When he thinks he has finished it correctly he asks the teacher to come and verify it.

LESSONS ON ZERO

Let us wait till the time comes when the child, pointing to the Zero compartments, asks: " What must I put in here? " and then answer, " Nothing, zero is nothing ".

But that is not enough; they must *feel* what nothing is. For this purpose we employ exercises which amuse the children immensely. I place myself in the midst of them as they sit around in their little chairs; I turn to one who has already performed the counting exercise and say to him: " Come, dear, come to me *zero* times." The child almost always runs to me and then returns to his place. " But, my child, you have come once, and I said zero times." He begins to wonder. " But what ought I to do then? " " Nothing, zero is nothing." " But how do I do nothing? " " Do nothing; you must stay where you are, you must not move, you must not come any times; zero means no times."

We repeat the exercise. " You, dear, throw me zero kisses with your finger-tips." " The baby gives himself little shake, laughs and stays where he is. " Have you understood," I repeat in an almost passionate tone of voice. " Send me zero kisses, zero kisses." A pause. General laughter. I make my voice harsh as if I were angry about their laughter, and I ask one very severely, " You come here zero times, come here zero times at once, do you understand? I am saying to you ' Come here zero times '." He does not move. The laughter grows more boisterous, excited all the more by my change of manner, first of begging, then of threatening. Then I groan in a pitiful, tearful voice: " But why do you not kiss me, why do you not come? " And every voice is raised in a shout, whilst the shining eyes are almost weeping with delight and laughter: " Zero is nothing, zero is nothing! " " Ah! yes," I say, smiling peacefully, " then all come here at once." They throw themselves on me.

EXERCISES ON THE MEMORY FOR NUMBERS

When the children know the written numbers and their numerical meaning, I make them do the following exercise.

I have various slips of paper on each of which is printed, or even written by hand, a number, from 0 to 9. (I often make use of the slips from block calendars, cutting off the upper and lower margins on which words are printed, and choosing, if possible, red numbers.) I fold the slips, put them into a box, and have a draw made. The child takes out a slip, carries it to his place, looks at it stealthily, folds it again to hide the *secret*. Then, one by one, or even in groups, the children possessing tickets (they are naturally the oldest, those who can read the figures), come up to the teacher's big table where objects are heaped together in piles— small cubes, Froebel's bricks, my tables for exercises in the baric sense; each one takes the quantity of objects which correspond to the number drawn. The number itself has remained at the child's place, the slip folded up as holding a mystery. The child, therefore, has to remember his number, not only during the time when he is moving among his companions to come to the table, but also whilst he is collecting his pieces, counting them one by one. The teacher has an opportunity for making interesting individual observations on the memory for numbers.

When the child has collected up his pieces, he places them in double file on the bench at his place. If the number is uneven he places at the bottom and half way between the last two, the uneven piece. The arrangement of the nine numbers is like this:

More advanced apparatus in arithmetic: number-frames, bead-frames and strip-boards for addition and substraction and the coloured bead-bars disposed for the snake-game

```
O      O       O       O      O      O       O      O      O
X    X X     X X     X X     X X    X X     X X    X X    X X
             X       X X     X X    X X     X X    X X    X X
                     X       X X    X X     X X    X X    X X
                                    X       X X    X X    X X
                                                   X       X
```

The numbers are represented by crosses; in the place indicated
by the small circle the child must place the folded ticket. That
done, he waits for his work to be inspected. The teacher comes,
opens the paper, reads and utters exclamations of pleasure and
praise when she declares that there are no mistakes.

At the beginning of the game it often happens that the children
take more objects than are required to match the number; that is
not really because they do not remember the figure, but owing to
their craving to possess more things. It is a little instinctive weakness which is common to primitive and untaught man. The
teacher tries to explain to the children that it is useless to have too
many things on the table, and that the only beauty of the game
lies in their guessing the exact number of the objects.

Little by little they grasp this idea, but not as easily as one
might imagine.

It is real exercise in self-control, one which keeps the child
within prescribed limits; it makes him take, for example, only two
of the things which are piled up at his disposal whilst he sees some
of his companions taking more.

I therefore consider this game to be more of an exercise in
will-power than an exercise in numbers.

The child who draws zero does not move from his place, while
he sees all those others who possess tickets getting up, moving
about, taking things freely from that far-away heap from which
he is debarred. Very often zero falls to a child who can count
readily, and who would also be delighted to put together a fine
group of objects and set them out in the required order on the
table, afterwards to wait with confident pride for the inspection.

It is very interesting to study the expressions on the faces of the possessors of the zero; the individual differences which appear form almost a revelation of the character of each individual. Some remain impassive, proudly trying to hide the inward pain of disillusion; others show by their momentary gestures that they are disappointed; others cannot hide the smile raised by the curious situation which will awaken the curiosity of their companions; some follow all the movements of their companions up till the end of the exercise with plainly shown feelings of longing, almost of envy; others show instant resignation.

Their attitude when they confess to zero is also interesting. When one asks, during the inspection: " And you, have you taken nothing?" " I have the zero," " It is zero," " I had zero." These are the common replies in spoken language, but the expressive gestures, the tone of the voice, express very diverse feelings. Rare are those who boldly seem to attribute the explanation to some extraordinary fact; most are irritated or resigned.

Some lessons on behaviour have to be given. " Take care, it is difficult to keep the secret of the zero; zero eludes you; be very watchful not to let it be known that you have nothing." After a while, pride and dignity prevail, and the little ones become accustomed to receiving the zero and the small numbers without disturbing themselves, satisfied if they no longer show the least trace of the feelings which at first overpowered them.

ADDITION AND SUBSTRACTION FROM ONE TO TWENTY
MULTIPLICATION AND DIVISION

The material which I use for teaching operations in arithmetic is the same as that already used for numeration, that is, rods graduated in length which already embody the first ideas of the decimal system.

The rods, as has been said, are called by the name of the number which they represent—one, two, three, etc. They are arranged according to length, that is to say in numerical order.

Three forms of early number-work: on top numerical rods, spindle-boxes and counters. The boy below penetrates the fascinating secrets of the decimal system enabling him to compose numbers up to 2,000. Top: Montessori School, Adyar, India, Photo by C. T. Nachiappan. Bottom: Montessori Centre, Laren, N. H., Holland.

The first exercise consists in trying to group together the piece shorter than ten, in such a manner as to make up ten. The simplest way of doing this is to take in succession the shortest rods, from one upwards, and place them at the top of the rods successively shorter from nine downwards. This work can be guided with orders; take one and add it to nine, take two and add it to eight, take three and add it to seven, take four and add it to six. Thus there are made up four sticks all equal to ten. There remains only the five, but when this is used twice lengthwise, it reaches from one extremity to the other of the ten; let us measure and we will see that 10 results from twice five.

Such an exercise is repeated many times, and little by little, a more technical language is taught to the child.

Nine plus one equals ten; eight plus two equals ten; seven plus three equals ten; six plus four equals ten; and finally five multiplied by two equals ten. The next step is to learn to write the signs which stand for 'plus,' 'equal to,' and 'multiplied by'. Here is the result, written in the nice little exercise-books of our little ones:

$$9+1=10$$
$$8+2=10$$
$$7+3=10$$
$$8+2=10$$
$$5\times2=10$$

When all this is thoroughly learnt and fixed on paper to the great satisfaction of the children, the attention is drawn to the work necessary to be done in putting back into their places all the pieces which have been grouped together to form tens. From the last piece of ten there is taken away the four and there remains alone the six; from another ten three is taken away, leaving the seven; from the other the two is removed, leaving the eight. We say more briefly: ten minus four equals six, ten minus three equals seven, ten minus two equals eight, ten minus one equals nine.

As for the remaining five, it is the half of ten, and if we had cut the long piece into two equal parts that would be dividing ten by two. In writing this would be:

$$10-4=6$$
$$10-3=7$$
$$10-2=8$$
$$10-1=9$$

$$10\div2=5$$

Once the children have mastered these exercises they are multiplied, also by the spontaneous work of the children. Can we make two pieces into a three? Let us put the one on the two, and then let us write in order to remember the completed exercise: $2+1=3$. Can a four be made from two pieces? $3+1=4$; $4-3=1$; and $4-1=3$.

The piece of two bears the same relationship to four as the five does to the ten; that is, when used twice over it goes from one end to the other, it enters into it exactly twice: $4\div2=2$; $2\times2=4$. Take this problem. Let us see with how many pieces we can do this game: the three does it with six, and the four with eight, thus—

$$2\times2=4; \quad 3\times2=6; \quad 4\times2=8; \quad 5\times2=10; \text{ and}$$
$$10\div2=5; \quad 8\div2=4; \quad 6\div2=3; \quad 4\div2=2.$$

At this point help may be got from the small cubes used in the game for memorizing numbers.

2	4	6	8	10
×	× ×	× ×	× ×	× ×
	×	× ×	× ×	× ×
		×	× ×	× ×
			×	× ×
				×

From the way in which they are arranged it is seen at a glance which numbers can be divided by two: all those which have no cube at the base. These are even numbers because they can be set out in pairs, that is, two by two; and the division into two is very easy because all that is needed is to separate the two lines of cubes which stand one under the other. Counting the cubes of each row, one gets the quotient. In order to reconstruct the original number it is enough to bring the two rows together again, e.g. $2 \times 3 = 6$.

None of this is difficult for children of five years old.

Here again repetition soon induces monotony; why should we not change the exercises? Let us take the series of the ten lengths, and instead of putting the one on the nine, let us put it on the ten; and the two on the nine instead of on the eight; and the three on the eight instead of on the seven. We can also place the two on the ten, the three on the nine, and the four on the eight. In every case the result is a length greater than ten, which has to be named—eleven, twelve, thirteen, etc. up to twenty. And why should the cubes be utilized for these games only up nine, that is, be so few?

The operations learnt on the ten are continued up to twenty without any difficulty; the only difficulty is that of the tens of units, for which several lessons are necessary.

LESSONS ON THE TENS OF UNITS
ARITHMETICAL CALCULATIONS BEYOND TEN

The material necessary consists of various rectangular cards on which is printed the 10 in figures five or six cms. high, and other rectangular cards equal in height and half in breadth of the first and bearing the separate numbers 1 to 9. The simple numbers are placed in a row—1, 2, 3, 4, 5, 6, 7, 8, 9. Then, as there are more numbers, it is necessary to start again and to take up the one again. This one resembles the piece which in the system of lengths extends beyond the nine in the ten stick. Counting along

22

the staircase up to the nine, there being no more figures, there still remains this last section which we again begin to mark with 1. But it is a 1 placed higher, and in order to distinguish it from the other we put near it a sign which has no value—the zero. Thus we have 10. Covering the zero with the separate rectangular numbers, in the order of their succession, there are formed: 11, 12, 13, 14, 15, 16, 17, 18, 19. These numbers are made up with the rods, putting in succession on the piece of ten that of one, and then again that of two; then three as a substitute until there is reached the piece of nine added to that of ten, in doing which we obtain a very long rod. Counting the alternate blue and red segments, nineteen is arrived at.

The teacher may then direct the movements of the system of length showing the cards of the ten and of the figure placed over the zero, e.g. 16; the child adds to the piece of ten that of six. The teacher takes from the ten card the 6, and places over the zero the rectangle which bears e.g. the number eight, giving 18; the child takes away the rod of the six and places that of the 8.

10		10
10		11
10		12
10		13
10	*A*	14
10		15
10		16
10		17
10		18
10		19

Every one of such exercises can then be written out, e.g. 10+6=16; 10+8=18, etc. The procedure would be the same for subtraction.

When the number itself begins to have a clear meaning for the child, the combinations are made with the cards alone, placing in various ways the rectangles which bear the nine figures on the two columns of numerals, which are drawn on long cards, as in the figures *A* and *B*.

In card *A* there is placed over the zero of the second 10 the rectangle with 1; and underneath, that with 2, etc.; whilst in the left column there remains

10
20
30
40
50
60
70
80
90
B

the 1 of the ten, in that of the right there follow all the figures from zero to nine.

In card *B* the operations are more complex. The cards bearing the figures are successively superposed and substituted in order of numerical progression on each 'ten'. After the nine, it is necessary to pass to the succeeding ten, and so one goes on to the end which is given at the 100.

Almost all our children count up to 100, a number which was given to them as a reward for the curiosity which they showed about it.

I do not think that such teaching requires further illustrations.

LATER DEVELOPMENTS IN ARITHMETIC

COUNTING up to 100 and the exercises connected therewith, which unite simple reckoning with a rational study of the first numbers, seemed to us an important matter, especially because the elements of reasoned arithmetic were given instead of numeration being entrusted to the memory and to a mnemonic repetition.

For more than twenty years these remained the limits of the development of the teaching.

I held, like everybody else, the prejudice that arithmetic presents great difficulty and that it was almost absurd to expect more than the result already obtained at so early an age.

Experience in fact demonstrated a lack of interest when compared with the enthusiasm and the surprising results obtained with written language. The superiority of interest in language apparently confirmed the prejudice about the difficulty and the dryness of arithmetic.

Meanwhile I had prepared for the older children in the elementary schools (where from the beginning the attempt was made to extend a method which had given such excellent results) material to represent the numbers under geometrical forms and with movable objects which would allow of combinations of the numbers being

made. It is the splendid material to which is given the name of
" material of the beads ". In it are represented the numbers in
their natural series from 1 to 10 with rods composed of beads
of coloured glass; every number has a different colour. The
number of these objects was so large that the numbers could be
combined into groups. The 10 was repeated ten times, uniting
ten rods in the form of a square, making the square of 10, composed of a hundred beds. Finally, ten squares superposed and
bound together form a cube (the cube of 10, that is 1,000). This
material is described in the book on advanced method for education
in the elementary schools. (*The Advanced Montessori Method, II.*)

Now it happened that some children of about four years old
were attracted to those things which were so brilliant, so easily
handled and moved about, and to our great surprise, they began
to use them as they had seen the older children doing.

The consequence was a development so enthusiastic about the
work with numbers and specially about the decimal system that
it is true to say that arithmetic became one of the favourite
exercises.

Children four years old composed numbers up to 1,000. And
later, from five to six years, the development became really
wonderful, so much so that today the six years old children can
perform the four operations on numbers with many thousands
of units.

Signor Mario M. Montessori has helped with this development, interpreting and materializing many calculations up to the
extraction of the square root of two, three and even four figures;
and the combination of the number-rods has made it possible to
introduce the first operations in algebra.

Urged by the evident pleasure which the children took in these
exercises, and by the skill which they possessed for manipulating
the small geometrical solids (as Froebel also understood when he
prepared his famous " gifts " of cubes and prisms collected in a
cubical box), I thought of preparing similar objects. Only, instead
of making all the cubes or all the bricks alike, I caused a large

wooden cube (about 10 cms. edge) to be divided according to the divisions of the face into two unequal parts, then another into three unequal parts; and by separating the parts according to these divisions there resulted small cubes and rectangular prisms of varied forms. This was the material representation of algebraic expressions, the cube of a binomial and a trinomial. The solids. which were equal in decimal value had the same colour, and groups of similar objects had different colours.

So on opening the box there was seen only one object, a cube painted in many colours, its individual components aligned and deposed separately in groups; for example, in the trinomial there were three cubes of different dimensions and of three diverse colours; similar prisms with a square face of one colour, e.g. green; three other prisms also having a square face, but of different shape, coloured perhaps yellow; and three other prisms with a square face, different from the other two groups, coloured perhaps blue; and finally six prisms all alike and with the faces rectangular, coloured black. The rectangular faces of the three groups of prisms mentioned are also black. These small coloured objects are fascinating, and it is a question first of all of grouping them together according to colour; then of disposing them of in various ways and inventing a kind of story, in which three cubes are three kings, each king having followers as high respectively as the other two kings, the guards being black. From the use of this material many results can be got; one is the order of the algebraic formula:

$$a^6 + 3a^2b + 3a^2c + b^3 + 3b^2a + 3b^2c + c^3 + 3c^2a + 3c^2b + 6abc.$$

Finally the cubes are placed in the box in a certain order and there is constructed the large cube of many colours: $(a+b+c)^3$.

Playing with this material, there is formed the visual image of the arrangement of the objects and therefore the memory of their quantity and their order.

This is a sense preparation of the mind. No object is more attractive to children of four years old. But later on, calling the

Two activities with the apparatus for arithmetics. The child on top composes the numbers between 10 and 100. Only genuine interest provokes such exact and graceful movements which, in their turn, assist the intelligence and make concentration possible. The boy below makes his own " tables of multiplication ". Top: Photo by Mrs. V. A. Baker in an English Montessori School. Bottom: Amsterdamsche Montessori School, Holland.

kings by the names *a*, *b*, *c* and writing the names of the separate pieces according to their dependence each on his own king, it happens that children, five years old and certainly those of six, store up in their minds the algebraic formula of the cube of a trinomial without looking at the material, because there is fixed the visual memory of the disposition of the various objects. This gives some idea of the possibilities that could be attained in practice.

All the teaching in arithmetic and in those principles of algebra in the form of reading and other memorizing cards and other material lead to results which might seem to be fabulous, and which show that the teaching of arithmetic ought to be completely transformed, starting from a sense preparation of the mind based on concrete knowledge.

It is clear that these children, six years old, on entering one of the ordinary schools, where they begin to count 1, 2, 3, are now out of place, and that a radical reform of the elementary schools is essential if there is to continue this wonderful development of education.

But, beyond the active method, in which there is always operating the movement of the hand which moves objects about, and in which the senses are so energetically employed, one must think of the special attitudes of the child mind towards mathematics. Because the children, leaving the material, very easily come to love writing out the operation, thus doing abstract mental work and acquiring a kind of natural and spontaneous leaning towards mental calculations.

For example, a child, when he left a London bus along with his mother, said: " If everybody had spat, £34 would have been collected." The child had noticed a card which said that spitting in the car carried a penalty of a certain number of shillings. Then the child had passed the time in calculating mentally the amount involved and in turning the shillings into pounds.

DRAWING AND REPRESENTATIVE ART

THE exercises which we have described as drawing were really an education of the hand intended to prepare it for writing. They were determined as an element in that complex preparation leading the small hand of the child, still uncertain in its motor co-ordinations, to execute that minute form of drawing known as writing. These elements, or factors, which are separated from one another (as we have seen from the movements leading up to writing) in order that they may move towards a synthesis which, in the case of writing, is one of the most characteristically " explosive," sometimes become an element which may be made to combine with other different syntheses. Thus this particular drawing which we have described becomes also an artistic element, a co-efficient of drawing proper. It is, therefore, neither drawing nor writing, but is a starting point for both.

Today one hears a good deal about ' free ' drawing, and for many people it is a matter of surprise that I have set up such rigid restrictions for drawing for the children, who are obliged to compose geometrical figures and then fill them in while holding their pencils in a special way, or who are limited to filling in with coloured pencils figures already drawn. I therefore feel obliged to

An exhibition of drawings made by children in the Amsterdamsche Montessori School, Holland

emphasize the point, in order that I may be clearly understood, that the proceedings which I describe form only one of the factors in the analysis of writing.

We have stated that our children do not produce of their own accord, which is left free, those dreadful drawings which are displayed and lauded in modern schools of advanced ideas. They, however, draw ornaments and figures which are much clearer and more harmonious than those strange daubs of the so-called " free drawing," where the child has to explain what he intends to represent by his incomprehensible attempts. We do not give lessons in drawing or in modelling, and yet many children are able to draw flowers, birds, scenes and even imaginary sketches in an admirable manner. Very frequently it is noticed that our children adorn with drawings even their pages of writing and arithmetic, sometimes adding to a page of numerical operations the figure of a child writing, or surrounding the page with fantastic ornamentation. Even the geometrical drawings sometimes become frames for figures, or the outline of the geometrical figure is garnished with ornamental drawings.

It must then be concluded that the preparation of the hand and of the senses gives natural aid not only to writing but also to expressive drawing.

We do not teach drawing by drawing, however, but by providing the opportunity to prepare the instruments of expression. This I consider to be a real aid to free drawing, which, not being dreadful and incomprehensible, encourages the child to continue.

Another form of assistance is that which we give to every kind of learning: the analysis of difficulties, or the analysis into components. In drawing itself there are various elements, such as outline and colour. Now for these two items, there is offered the tracing of the outlines of the insets and filling the drawings by means of lines, which prepare the hand for steady muscular exertion. For colour, we provide paint-brushes and water-colours, with which it is possible to represent drawings even without having an outline prepared. We give pastels also, and show how to use them.

Finally, it is possible to compose artistic representations by cutting out coloured paper, like those made for artistic purposes by Oswald, the famous Viennese physicist.

These papers, finely graded as to colour, prepared scientifically, lend themselves to the appreciation of harmony in the combination of colours.

These two separate facts, line and colour, are determined and perfected independently of each other. They are an acquisition of the individual, who becomes skilful in expressing himself artistically with the two things together.

Thus the individual is perfected by education without intervention in the work already carried out by him spontaneously. In fact, interfering in work done is always an obstacle which interrupts the inner trend of expression, as may happen when direct means are applied to the teaching of drawing.

Our way, for drawing as for writing, is called the " indirect method ". The result is that the children, growing more capable of expressing themselves, make hundreds and hundreds of drawings, sometimes producing ten in a single day, just as they are also unwearied in their writing.

Yet we do not find that progress continues indefinitely, as in written language, nor do the drawings indicate that all the children will become artists. At a certain moment there supervenes in almost all cases, a lack of interest in drawing, when other interests, such as writing, take precedence. This lessening of the artistic leaning towards drawing has been observed by many people, particularly by psychologists in art.

Cizek, for example, in his famous school of free art in Vienna, noticed that many children who seemed to have a passion for artistic work and to be artistically endowed by nature suddenly lost all interest in art and therefore ceased to make progress. And Dr. Revesz (a psychologist dedicated specially to art) says as a result of her experience: " There are children who, as their faculty of linguistic and cultural expression develop, gradually come to abandon drawing completely, either because it no longer interests them, or because they do not possess artistic talent, or because they concentrate on gifts of another character."

So, for example, it is often observed that children specially endowed for music and who are greatly attracted by abstract ideas (mathematics, logic) do not succeed at all in drawing, or abandon it.

Such a case has been very closely studied from the psychological point of view in a musical prodigy child. His drawings were evidence of what has just been stated, when we compare their inferiority and poor development with the pleasing musical compositions made at the same stage by the child. (Geza Revesz: *The Psychology of a Musical Prodigy.*)

Perhaps this is the reason why our children, when writing becomes a passion, leave off drawing for some time. And then it is only when writing is an accomplished fact that they betake themselves once more to decorating the borders of pages.

When, instead, the artistic spirit is present, it takes complete possession and creates an artist, as is told about Giotto, the shepherd boy whom the famous painter Cimabue, by teaching him, saved for the history of art as a never-to-be forgotten genius.

When there are found in the caves of primitive man those surprising coloured drawings of animals in movements, they tell us that artistic genius for drawing existed from the time of the origin of man; but these fine representations were not merely a way of finding expression or of communicating pleasing ideas, but are generally supposed to stand for religious ideas.

In a word, there exists an instinct for expression which seeks out its own ways; these ways are certainly two in number; one is writing, which is used for the expression of ideas, and the other is representative art. But in most cases this undeniable inclination of the child for drawing has no connection with an artistic gift pertaining to the child, nor to any ultimate leaning towards art. It is rather a kind of writing done with figures when the child is not able to express the ideas and sentiments which are taking shape within him about his surroundings, about the things which have impressed him.

This means that the hand takes part in speech, and just as the child speaks continually, so does he draw; he expresses himself with his phonetic organs, and he expresses himself with his hand, showing latent tendencies of which he is not yet conscious.

Indeed the history of writing shows that it was originally drawing, as it is in pictography. The many documents of the most primitive pictography of different pre-historic peoples very often resemble the free drawings of a child, especially in the representation of the human figure. These strange drawings have a very clear purpose, that of communicating with other men by means different from that of the human voice. Then from the primitive pictographs there came a transition in the course of the evolution of civilization to the symbolical representation of syllables which are not comprehensible (like many children's drawings), and therefore it is necessary to give them a conventional interpretation; for hieroglyphics like the spoken languages came to differ as the characters distinctive of a people, e.g. Egyptian and Hittite hieroglyphics.

Finally, in the alphabet, drawings are simplified, and no longer represent syllables or ideas, but the sounds themselves with which spoken language is composed and thus there is established an easy writing, which at the same time is the exact reproduction of spoken language, as if the mind inherited whole and intact the gift of expressing itself with the hand as well as with the spoken word.

To conclude, the best way to influence drawing is not to leave it free, but to prepare the natural means for producing it, which is to educate the hand. True talent will be manifested by itself, and there will be no harmful lessons in drawing intended to help it, those wicked lessons which might even stifle it. But the abandonment of the evident efforts of the child to express himself with the hand is an obstacle to the free development of drawing. To counteract this, we must enrich the environment with the means of expression, and indirectly prepare the hand for fulfiling its function to the utmost. The eye takes note of things with more accuracy, and opens the way to the inspirations which emanate from beautiful things, and the hand becomes more skilful and more flexible. The child will attain the object towards which nature urges him with more joy from having performed the preliminary exercises necessary to be able to draw.

Dr. Revesz, speaking of our method, and replying to the general criticisms made against it on the subject of " free drawing," says: " The Montessori School does not repress free drawing; rather does it make the children find the greatest pleasure in free drawing, along with the free development of their sense of colour and form, as with the constant exercise of the hand and the eye."

The education of the hand is specially important, because the hand is the expressive instrument of human intelligence; it is the organ of the mind.

Dr. Katz, who has made a special study of the functions of the hand in relation to psychology, says: " The Montessori Method, being dedicated to the development of the functions of the hand, makes very clear the surprising versatility of this organ. My studies, which have extended over a period of twelve years, have caused me to think how marvellous an instrument the hand is in respect of its tactile sensibility and its movement. The hand is the means which has made it possible for human intelligence to express itself and for civilization to move forward in its work. Without the hand the intrinsic value and the character of the functions of intelligent humanity would have been annihilated. The hand is the organ of expression, and it is the organ of creation; and in the world of the imagination also the hand has virtually held sway. The hand, in early infancy, aids the development of the intelligence and in the mature man, it is the instrument controlling his destiny on the earth."

THE BEGINNING OF MUSICAL ART

THE briefness of the reference to musical education which is made
in this book is not due to disparagement of the value of music in
education, but to the fact that with the child of tender age music
can only have a beginning; it has its development somewhat later.
Besides, success is bound up with the need for the production of
plenty of music around the child, so that there is set up an environment calculated to develop musical sense and intelligence. To
have available a good musical performer, or to possess simple
instruments adapted to children like those which Dolmetch makes
today for the equipment of his marvellous children's orchestras,
are things which we cannot lay down as being absolute essentials
in a school which has to be accessible to all. In the model
Montessori schools, however, musical education is cultivated in a
serious manner, trying to leave to the child free choice and free
expression, as in all branches of its development.

Already Signorina Maccheroni has made some beautiful ex-
periments, published in part in my book *L'Autoeducazione* (*The
Advanced Montessori Method*, II); and after some time, Lawrence
A. Benjamin, with the help of distinguished music teachers in
Vienna and London, has made important contributions to the

subject, especially with an accurate collection of musical pieces
chosen from classical music and the folk-music of every country,
agreed upon after being tried out for several years in the Model
Montessori School in Vienna.

Let us proceed now to a rapid review of the analysis and
development of the factors concerned in musical education.

RHYTHM AND RHYTHMICAL GYMNASTICS

The motor preparation for rhythmic gymnastics may be considered with reference to that exercise called 'walking on the line,'
through which little children acquire perfect assurance in equilibrium, and at the same time learn to control the movements of the
feet and hands.

It is during this slow, sustained walking that music may be
introduced as an aid to the effort which has to be sustained.
Having attained balance, however, education in rhythm must be
begun. Many lullabies are suitable for accompanying these slow,
uniform movements, which may be compared with the movement
of rocking. The addition of music to movement is in this case
a real accompaniment to the step which is already fixed, and it
penetrates it. In contrast with such music, there is a rhythm
which corresponds to running, and these two contrasting rhythms
are those to which small children are most responsive. As contrasts formed the first introduction to the education of the senses,
the same is true for rhythmic education. Besides, the steps,
slow and controlled by the difficulty of maintaining balance, and
the run are the two ways of moving preferred by children between
three and four years of age. On the contrary, the rhythmic jump
is not only a movement which follows the establishment of perfect
balance but it calls for a muscular effort to which the child is not
equal, owing to the special proportions of the child body. As for
the various steps corresponding to various rhythms, which would
correspond to the graduations in sense education, they can be
appreciated only at a later age (above five years of age).

The rhythmic marches on the line should be distinguished from the gymnastics done on the line which have as its aim to establish perfect balance and control of movements. These gymnastic exercises which consist of so many items (holding a banner in one hand, a glass of water, a burning candle or carrying a small basket on the head) require the line traced on the floor to guide the feet in a certain way. It is this definite direction that makes it rather difficult to keep balance and hence establishes and strengthens perfect equilibrium. In these exercises a uniform and delicate music accompanies the exercise in order to sustain the necessary effort to perform it exactly.

When, however, rhythmic exercises are started, the feet should be free and the line is merely a guide and helps to keep the children who walk, run, skip, etc. in line. It is then clear too, that passing on to the performance of dances the line has no reason of existence any longer, but perhaps to serve as an ornament useful to give a conscious order to movement.

The technique for the execution of music consists of grasping a single musical phrase of easy interpretation and repeating it many times. That is analogous to repeating an exercise. Besides the two initial contrasting steps specially suited to the little ones, there may be chosen and repeated rhythmic musical phrases in order to develop sensitiveness to music in the children, who have no other chance of receiving such impressions from the environment, as happens with colours and visual sensations in general. By repeating each phrase a very great number of times, some children between five and six become able to interpret rhythms which call for movements, slightly dissimilar, such as the slow step, the marching step, etc. (gradation).

Some teaching may usefully be given by the mistress in showing the step corresponding to a particular rhythm, as is done in the lessons when the teacher says, " This is big, this is small." However, after such a demonstration has been made, the child must be left to give his own interpretation of it, that is, to the recognizing of the same rhythms in different musical

THE BEGINNING OF MUSICAL ART   353

phrases.[1] Children feel the rhythm when it is played with musical expression, and often reproduce the rhythm not only with the foot but with the arms and with movements of the whole body. Sometimes even the smallest children show rhythmic expression. Beppino, about four years old, beats time with the index finger of his right hand extended; the music (a song) has two alternating parts, one *legato* and the other *staccato*. Beppino moves his hand with a smooth motion for the *legato*, and with a jerky one for the *staccato*.

Four-year old Nannina, when following sweetly melodious music, gracefully spreads out her wide skirt and throws her head back smiling happily; then, at the sound of a military march she stiffens up her body, assumes a grave expression and marches along with a firm step.

To intervene with an opportune lesson for teaching some step simply, or to improve some movement, gives the children pleasure.

In one class taken by Signorina Maccheroni, her small pupils Eriminia, Graziella, Peppinella, Sofia and Amelia embrace one another and their teacher enthusiastically after having learnt some movement in a rhythmic dance. Otello, Vincenzino and Teresa, having had their steps and gestures improved by a lesson, thank the mistress who has helped them.

Sometimes the children listen to music whilst they are seated round the room watching their companions walking on the line; they often beat time with their hands and reproduce it correctly. Occasionally a child specializes as what we call a conductor. Vincenzino, aged four and a half, used to stand with his two feet together in the middle of the ellipse drawn on the floor (the line) on which the children were walking, and beat time with his extended arm, bending his body at the correct angle at every beat. He lowered and raised his body in exact correspondence with the period between the beats, and assumed an expression perfectly in accord with that of the melody.

The exactitude with which the child succeeds in marking the tempo of the beat, without anyone having taught him the divisions

---

[1] L. A. Benjamin, *An Introduction to Music for Little Children.*

23

of three-beat, four-beat, etc. is a proof of the sense-education due to musical rhythm. At first the children follow the tempo without paying attention to the beat.

But there comes a moment in which, suddenly, they feel the beat, and then they mark it; that is, their movements correspond only to the first beat of the bar.

Marie Louise, little more than four, was walking to the sound of a march. Suddenly she cried out to the mistress: " Watch, see what I am doing." She was making a leaping step, and raising her arms gracefully at the first beat of each bar.

The study of the value of notes is made only by children of more advanced age. (For particulars of method see L. A. Benjamin, op. cit.). The interest in such a study will be associated with the fact that the children have already developed and analyzed in themselves the sense of rhythm.

MUSICAL REPRODUCTIONS

Music heard and accompanied by rhythmic movements forms only one element of musical education, dealing with the succession of sounds in time and the expressive tone of the phrase.

There follows the study of melody and harmony, which lends itself to individual performances only when the child has at his disposal instruments adapted to him not only in their dimensions but, especially, in their simplicity. He must be left free to use them, hampered by too rigid a technique. Then, with short initiations or lessons, similar to those which our mistresses give by our method to make useful the material in general, the child is rendered capable of carrying out his own performance, deriving from it, because of the simplicity of the musical instruments, a continually increasing interest. The musical performances of the children reach a surprising standard, when, united as a band, they give concerts, made possible by the fact that each one has made on his own instrument individual studies from which it is possible that true musical sentiment may be derived.

These results have been attained in England by Dolmetch, who, wishing to bring back into use the exquisite musical instruments of the past, now fallen into disuse owing to the predominance of the pianoforte, has had the brilliant idea of constructing simple instruments for children. The faith which Dolmetch has in the divine power of music, and also in the mind of the child, has led him to formulate a method which corresponds in principle with mine. (Properly adapted material; short introductions having the sole purpose of putting the child in touch with the material; and then the child left at liberty to play on his instrument.)

In the magnificent English institution of Bedales, where classes are held on the Montessori model, one may come across in the wood children playing the violin under a tree, or small groups trying to put together the tunes from some singular stringed instrument (between the simplified harp and the lyre). Again, we may hear delicate harmonies issuing from windows. Many of these children know nothing about theory or musical notes; they have never done rhythmic exercises. Musical development is fostered by the delightful performances into which the old, impassioned master breaks out wherever he may happen to be—in rooms, in the woods or in the fields. And the children sit all round about him, stretched out on the grass, listening with rapt attention. In addition to that, the training is represented by the opportunity which the children have of taking an instrument when the inspiration seizes them and trying to find some harmony which is rooted in their heart.

MUSICAL READING AND WRITING

It is also possible to make a start with the writing of musical notes in the Children's House.

It is based upon sense exercises consisting of the recognition of the musical sounds of the material of the bells, which, in the first exercises are paired and afterwards are placed in graduated order.

It is a great help to be able to ' handle ' the notes (that is, the objects which produce them), all alike in every respect (except in sound), separating them, mixing them up and putting them together again, because it represents the notes in material form, in the same way as for the other objects used in the education of the senses. The next thing to do is to attach its name to the note, as the children did in similar exercises. The names *do, re, mi, fa, sol, la, si*, are incised on separate wooden discs (representing the signs of the notes) and the children place one at the foot of each bell, according to its sound. In this way the child, by the repetition of the exercise, learns with certainty the names pertaining to the sounds. The discs which bear the names of the notes are thus not only signs to be arranged on the musical scale, but first of all are signs which signify a sound. When the children begin to study the notes on the scale, they will therefore do it as a written exercise based on musical facts already known.

In order that the child may be able to work alone, helped by his love of touching objects and moving them about, we have prepared for him a wooden board, on which are hollowed out circular spaces, corresponding to the places occupied by the notes *do, re, mi, fa, sol, la, si, do*. Into these spaces there can be inserted the discs corresponding to the notes which bear the names of them written on the upper face. To get the placing correct there is a corresponding number (1, 2, 3, 4, 5, 6, 7, 8) in every space and on the under face of every disc. In this way the child, by placing the objects according to the numbers, finds that he has set out on the scale all the notes of an octave.

For another exercise there exists another board of wood like the first but without the hollows and their numbers; accompanying this board there is a box of unnumbered discs, each of which has the name of a note inscribed on its upper face. The same name is repeated on several discs. The exercise tests the child's memory for the positions of the notes and proceeds thus. The discs are put into position as they chance to come to hand, each in its place on the stave, but as they are made to rest on the face which bears the written name, the black faces of the discs are thus exposed. Evidently many discs will find places on the same line or along the same space. When the notes are all placed they must be turned up without displacing them; the names can now be read and reveal to the child any mistake which he has made.

The third piece of material is a double board on which the notes are placed in a rhombus. By detaching the two boards, the notes are disposed as in the treble and bass staffs. Having learnt this the children are able to read little tunes and reproduce them on the bells. And, *vice versa*, they can write down little tunes after having played them from ear on the bells or on an instrument, and have thus found out the notes for them.

This part of musical writing has a noteworthy development at a slightly more advanced age, that is, in the elementary classes. In the Montessori school at Barcelona the children have music copybooks almost like those for writing.

It is seen that the three exercises dealt with—rhythmic movements, performances on musical instruments and the writing of music—may go on separately and independently. As an instance of this fact there may be cited not only the existence of independent exercises but also of complete methods which cover only one of these items. One example of the latter is the Dalcroze method which develops only rhythmic gymnastics and also that of Dolmetch which cultivates the art of drawing harmonies from an instrument. The old methods of teaching music began with knowledge of the notes on the musical scale, independently of music. But ours is an example of what we call analysis, that is, separating out the parts of a very difficult and complex whole into exercises which may by themselves constitute interesting work.

Rhythm, harmony, writing and reading are joined together in the end and form three interests, three stories of graded work and joyful experiences, which burst out into the full splendour of one single victory.

RELIGIOUS EDUCATION

RELIGIOUS education,[1] considered in accordance in the same general terms as the method as a whole, includes the preparation of an environment in which several divisions are distinguishable—those which might be referred to practical life, and those which, corresponding to what in the school refers to the development of the mind, deal with the development of religious sentiment, the education of the spirit, and the religious knowledge which constitutes the culture necessary to understand religion. It is, therefore, clear that it is impossible to go into the whole matter here and now. Such statements as are made will be directed towards opening up the necessary connections between the two branches of education, i.e. in a practical sense, the behaviour in the environment of daily life and the behaviour in the environment particular to religion (the Church).

It was at Barcelona, in the Model Montessori School, a civic school of the Province, but one in which the Catholic religion was established as a fundamental subject, that there were laid down the first bases of religious education planned according to my method.[2]

---

[1] Applied to Catholic education.

[2] cf. Maria Montessori: *The Child in the Church* (Sands & Co., London).

The first move made was to prepare an environment—the Children's Church in which this place reserved for the faithful was made to suit their small proportions. We furnished it with little chairs and kneeling stools, and we had the holy-water basins placed at the knee-height of an adult. Small pictures were hung low down, and changed often according to the season of the year; little statuettes and groups of statuettes represented the nativity, the flight into Egypt, etc. At the windows were hung light curtains, which the children could draw to shut out the light. They took turns to prepare the church—to put the seats in place, to fill the vases with flowers, to light some of the candles.

A priest instructed the children in religion and also officiated in the church. Directly the simple little church was prepared and opened for the use of the children there appeared, almost to our surprise, a fruit of our method which we had not anticipated. It was that the church is almost the end, up to which leads a great part of the education which the method sets out to give. Some exercises which, in the schools, seem to have no definite outside purpose, find their application here. The *silence*, which has prepared the child for withdrawing into himself, becomes the inner restraint to be observed in the House of God, in the half-dark surroundings, broken by the faint flickering of the candlelight. Walking in silence without making a noise, moving chairs without scraping the floor, rising up and sitting down quitely, passing amongst benches and people without creating any disturbance, carrying fragile objects in their hands and seeing that they are not damaged, as for example vases full of water to be filled with flowers and replaced on the altar, or lighted candles, the wax of which must not be spilt over hands or clothes—all of these were almost repetitions and at the same time applications of what the child had learnt to do within the classroom walls. They must appear to the tender intelligence as the purpose of the efforts so patiently persisted in; hence there would arise a sense of gratitude, joy and new dignity. At first the children carried out these exercises in obedience to an inward impulse, but without a purpose;

afterwards they get almost the revelation of a difference between the two occasions and the two different places—as between seed-time and harvest. The very act of differentiating between similar actions which have different applications and meanings constitutes in itself another source of intellectual development. The child of four does not miss the difference between the holy-water basin into which he dips the tip of his slender hand to make the sign of the Cross and the basin in the next room intended for the washing of his hands. These intuitions about differences between similar things is really an intelligent task which the small child, considered almost incapable of rising to conceptions beyond those of the senses, is initiating when he begins to feel that he is the son of God, lovingly entertained in the House of the great Heavenly Father.

Many who disbelieve in such impressions, I had already encountered. They said: " Do you know why my little nephew likes to come to school at the time for Mass? Because you make him put out the candles in a basin of water. That is all. Would you not be doing better by applying that pleasing exercise to arithmetic, taking for example ten lighted candles and then making him put them out whilst he counted one, two, three, etc.?" How little spiritual understanding and what slight insight into children did the critic, who talked to me in this way, possess. The arithmetic exercise with the candles would have lasted, at most, for a week, the average time necessary to learn to count from one to ten. But in the Church, those children, will continue for years to extinguish the candles which are consumed away as they burn before Jesus who has descended among them, and will also understand that this is not a childish game, but a religious act which is performed reverently because it is done in the holy place pertaining to the worship rendered there to the Lord.

The opinion expressed here is that the child who is interested in everything is all the more struck by what seems to him symbolical and clothed in majesty. At first the objects—the altar, the book, the holy vases, the priest's vestments—stand apart, and it is the acts in themselves which attract his attention—the various acts of the service, the sign of the Cross, the genuflection, the kiss. But, little by little, there is made clear also their relevance and the mystic meaning which is hidden within them.

When the priest began to explain the sacraments, using objects and reproducing, often with the active help of the children themselves, the scenes in the service, I thought that only the oldest children would concern themselves. But the youngest would not go away and followed everything with the deepest attention; even the little ones of three were enchanted as they followed the proceedings. The priest prepared, for example, the baptismal font and the ritual objects; he chose from the children themselves a god-father and a god-mother, and brought there an infant only a few days old, and set about performing one by one the sacred rites used in the administration of such a sacrament. On another occasion, it was a big boy who acted as a disciple and asked for baptism, and the children showed keen interest in learning that baptism, as in the early history of the church, was given always to adults when they were converted to Christianity. In this way the children acquired their first ideas about liturgical history.

When the children were able to read there was added another proceeding which gave them a chance of partly teaching themselves. It was to make, on a miniature scale, but with sufficient accuracy, the objects used in religious service, the priestly vestments, the altar and also some objects representing historical things and scenes from the Gospels. This was followed by attaching to the objects tickets on which were written names or simple descriptive sentences (as in the commands used in the first reading lessons). This gave the children the chance of repeating the exercise, as is the general way in the method. Another idea was to create groups of objects, as was described for the first reading lessons specially intended to teach phonetic languages, in which are grouped together words which present the same difficulty, the words then being placed along with the objects of which they are the names. Here, for a different purpose, the group of objects referred to the things necessary for making a sacrament valid. The separation between group and group seen in concrete form, and the breaking up and recomposing of each group repeated many times, all make it easier to understand the facts and to memorize every detail exactly, whilst reading and placing the cards ensures the learning of the exact terms. The exercise consists in setting out the objects of one group (e.g. the sacrament of extreme unction) and taking the whole of the cards which accompany it, placing above each object the word which stands for its name. The Sisters of Notre Dame in Glasgow (Scotland) have made complete models of such things; among others an altar in miniature, only 12 cms. broad, but showing the details which enter into it with great fidelity and with exquisite art. The children can observe it and place on every detail the card bearing the relative name.

Thus the children, from their tenderest infancy live, one might say, in the Church; and they acquire almost without being aware of it a knowledge of religious things—truly far from usual at their early age.

The habits which the children have already learnt at school of concentration in work, of silence, of calm in an environment where children in continual contact with one another have to make choice of their own actions and adapt their needs to those of others, predispose them to gain another moral victory of the greatest importance. It is in silence and when movements are ordered that the inner sensitivity that is called ' religious sense ' or ' spiritual sense ' can be developed.

In fact, it is only at the age of seven that the need is felt by the child to distinguish between good and evil. The young child does not have these problems: he accepts everything and believes everything. To him the only imaginable evil is ' naughtiness ' which attracts upon him the severity of the adult.

He is extremely ' receptive ' and an environment that touches his senses has a strong influence upon him. Therefore it is very necessary to realize that in the first age of growth the environment and the impressions it conveys are, so to say, sculptured in his soul in an indelible way. The mother who takes her little child with her to church, prepares a religious sense in him which could not be aroused by any teaching.

It is therefore a mistake to wish to teach the distinction between good and evil at a precocious age, in which interest for this problem has not awakened. That is why the development of moral conscience in this sense would be premature.

The sentiment for what is good can be cultivated at this age by affection and a sweet disposition in one's dealings with the child. What the children really need then is a feeling of security, through the protection given by their elders. Also education therefore must be in accordance with these natural conditions. The God who loves and protects the child and sends His angels to accompany him invisibly day and night is the foundation of their religion.

Only later on a social sense is awakened and a responsibility for one's actions felt; this is the time to accompany this new development with a guide—a guide in the world and especially a guide who directs one's own conscience.

To speak of evil to the small child is to teach him something which he is not capable of understanding, or at least which he cannot assimilate. Great prudence is therefore required in the teachers so that she may not hurt the soul of the child with arguments ill suited to his nature. For instance, on one occasion, one of the Franciscan Sisters Missionaries of Mary, in teaching sacred history and speaking of Cain, suggested that certainly when he was a very little boy he must have been unkind to Abel. Some hours after the lesson, a little one who was working (meditation!) burst into loud weeping, saying, " Oh, I shall become like Cain," and he confessed to the Sister, who was trying to console him, the little faults of which he had been guilty towards his companions.

Religious, and free in their intellectual operations and in the work which our method offers them, the little ones show that they are strong spirits, exceptionally robust as are the small bodies of

clean, well-nourished children. Growing up in this way, they have
no bashfulness, no timidity, no fear. They show pleasing self-
confidence, courage, a calm knowledge of things, above all, faith
in God, the author and preserver of life. The children are so
capable of distinguishing between natural and supernatural matters
that their insight has given us the idea that there exists a period
specially sensitive to religion. The age of childhood seems to be
bound closely to God, as the development of the body is strictly
dependent on the natural laws which are transforming it at that
time. I remember a baby girl of two, who, when put in front of
a statuette of the Child Jesus, said, " This is not a doll! "

FIELD LABOUR IN RELIGIOUS INSTRUCTION

We thought that it would be a proper and beautiful idea to
get the children to grow the grapes and the grain required for the
Sacrament of the Eucharist, and to infuse the religious activity of
the children into the work and the pleasure of the fields. We
therefore set apart a piece of a large meadow where the children
used to play in the afternoons, for the cultivation of grain and
grapes. Two rectangular spaces were marked off by the children
themselves—one on the extreme right and the other on the extreme
left of the field. A kind of grain which ripens quickly was chosen.
In the parallel furrows already prepared the children sowed the
seed, it being planned that each one of them shared in the sowing.
The movement in sowing, the care which had to be taken lest any
seed should fall outside the furrows, the solemn manner in which
this field ceremony was performed, showed clearly that it was an
act in keeping with the purpose which it was intended to serve.
A little later the vine plants were put in; they looked like dried
up roots, and their appearance gave small promise of the marvel
which the children had to wait for—the appearance one day of
bunches of real grapes. These young plants were placed in trenches,
in parallel rows, at equal distances apart. It seemed the best thing
to plant flowers all round them, as if offering perpetual homage

of perfume and beauty to the plants which were maturing to provide the fruit which would some day serve as material for the
Eucharistic Sacrament. The children continued to play in the
other part of the field; they made buildings with bricks, dug ditches,
made paved roads, ran about, played ball, whilst all around them
the flowers added gaiety to their games. Along with the joy of
play there was intermingled the deeper emotion of watching day
by day the marvels of growing life.

At last there began to appear in the grain-field long parallel
lines of little green plants; the green things grew and lengthened,
arousing great interest in the children. Then even the dry roots
began to send forth pale foliage. The children stood around in
groups and watched it all. Some of them were chosen to dis-
infect the vines, as protection against *Peronospora* (fungi). When
the grapes made their wonderful appearance, they were covered
up in little bags made of white gauze, to protect them from insects.

It was decided to organize for the opening and closing of the
scholastic year two outdoor festivals, one corresponding to the
grain-harvest, the other to the grape-harvest. It was thought that
the festivals might be made joyous with rustic music drawn from
primitive instruments and with folk-songs, some of which, very
old and full of harmony, have been used as sacred hymns in the
Church.

These notes about our experiment in religious education represent only one attempt, but already they show the practical
possibility of introducing religion into the life of the little child,
as a rich fount of joy and uplift.

The experiment in religious education was ultimately abolished
in our Children's Houses, because it referred solely to Catholic
religious education, in which it is possible to make the preparation
active by means of movements of the body and of objects, that is
' material '; whilst that cannot be done with other religions which
are quite abstract.

Nevertheless much was prepared and even written. I may
mention the books, *I Bambini viventi nella Chiesa* (The Child

in the Church), *La Tavola Apparecchiata* (The Mass explained to Children), *La Vita in Cristo* (Elementary Illustrations of the liturgic Year and of the Church Calendar) *Ill Libra Aperto*, (Advanced material for reading the Missal), and *Manuale per la Preparazions di un Messale per Bambini* (Manual for the Preparation of a Children's Missal).

But these practical attempts being beyond common use cannot be disseminated. Not possessing the diploma which today is rigorously required in order to have permission to teach the Catholic religion, I could not continue the work and its application.

DISCIPLINE IN THE CHILDREN'S HOUSE

THE experience gathered from the time when the first edition of the Italian book was printed up till today has confirmed over and over again this truth—that in our classes of small children reaching the size of forty or even fifty pupils, there prevails a discipline more nearly perfect than that existing in the ordinary schools. Anyone who visits well-managed schools is struck by the discipline of the children. Here you may find forty children from three to seven years of age, intent each on his own work; some are doing sense exercises, some arithmetic, some tracing letters, some drawing; some are busy with the clothes, some are dusting; some are seated at a table, some are stretched on mats on the ground. One hears a faint noise of objects being moved about lightly, of children going about on tip-toe. Every now and again there is a badly repressed cry of joy, a quick call of " Signorina, Signorina! ; " an exclamation of " See what I have done! "

But more frequently the peace is absolute.

The teacher moves about slowly and silently; she goes to any-one who calls her; she supervises in such a way that anyone who needs her is aware of her presence at once, whilst those who do not need her do not notice her existence.

Hours pass, and all is silent.

Some who have visited the Children's House call its inmates " little men," others, " senators in session ".

Whilst all this keen interest in work is in evidence it never happens that children get into disputes about objects. If anyone achieves something extraordinary, he will find some other who will admire and be delighted with it; no one is annoyed when another succeeds, but the triumph of one rouses wonder and pleasure in the others, often stimulates eager imitators. They all seem quite happy and satisfied with doing what they can, without the doings of others arousing envy and selfish emulation, without encouraging vanity and pride. The little one of three works peacefully alongside the boy of six, just as if he were contented with his lower stature and felt no envy for the tallness of the older boy. They all grow up in the most profound peace.

If the mistress wishes to engage the attention of the whole assembly, perhaps to get them to leave off all the work in which they are so much absorbed, she has only to say one word in a low voice, to make one gesture and everything is suspended; they turn their eyes to her full of interest, anxious to know how to carry out her wishes.

Many visitors have seen the teacher write some directions on the blackboard, and have watched how joyfully they have been carried out.

It is not only the mistress who is obeyed; but whoever asks anything from the children wonders at seeing how scrupulously they obey, how calmly and complacently. Often visitors would like to hear the singing of a child who is painting; the child leaves his painting to comply, but directly he has fulfilled the act of courtesy he returns to his interrupted work. Often, before obeying, the very little ones finish the work which they have begun.

One of the most wonderful examples of discipline happened during the teachers' examinations which we held after my first training courses. We then followed the practice of ordinary teachers' training colleges and part of the examination consisted in a practical lesson given to children. These pupils were there waiting for their turn and when they were called they came up to receive their lesson which the aspirant-teacher had drawn by lot. This was evidently no longer a lesson received after the child's own free choice, but the child was ready to lend himself to the task which the candidate asked him to do. The children were quite willing and seemed to understand the emotion of the pupil-teacher. While they were waiting, the little ones filled in their time in our presence just as they pleased; they worked continually and they returned to the interrupted work after their part in the examination was over. Every now and then some one of them came and offered us a painting finished whilst they were waiting.

We wondered at the patience, the perseverance, the inexhaustible satisfaction of the children, perhaps the impression might be given that the children are excessively dominated, if it were not for the absolute lack of timidity, the shining eyes, the gay, free bearing, the readiness with which they invite us to inspect their work or take us round to give explanations; or if they did not make us feel that we are among people who are masters in their own house. The fervour with which they clasp the teacher's knees, or with which they draw down her head and shoulders in order to kiss her face reveals a heart which is free to behave as it chooses.

Anyone who has seen them laying the table must have grown more and more apprehensive, been more and more filled with wonder: Little waitresses, four years old, carrying knives and placing them on the table with the things already there; bearing trays on which there may be as many as five glass tumblers; and later on moving from table to table bearing the great dish full of hot soup. No one cuts herself, breaks a glass, or spills a drop of soup, this would be a frightful accident! During the meal the waitresses are unintrusively and continually on the watch; no one finishes his soup without being asked at once to have a second helping, or if he has quite finished, the waitress makes haste to take away the empty plate. No child needs to ask for more soup or to give notice that he has finished.

24

Anyone who sees all this and who thinks of the usual behaviour of children four years old, who shout, break everything, and have to be waited on, is moved to surprise by a scene which evidently springs from the hidden fountains of energy, latent in the depths of the human soul. I have often seen tears flow down the cheeks of some who had been present at such little feasts.

Such discipline can never be attained by way of commands, by sermons, by any of the disciplinary methods universally known.

Such a discipline cannot be secured by reproofs, or by persuasive speeches. These may at first create the illusion of being effective, but very quickly, directly the true discipline appears, all that dissolves like something worthless, like an illusion before reality; night gives place to day.

The first glimmerings of discipline appear as the result of work. At some given moment it happens that the child becomes deeply interested in a piece of work; we see it in the expression of his face, his intense concentration, the devotion to his exercise. That child has entered upon the path of discipline. Whatever may be the application of it—to an exercise of the senses, to fastening up something, to washing plates—it is all the same. Our share in strengthening this experience is contributed through the repeated lessons in ' silence '. The perfect immobility, the attention on the alert to catch the sound of his name pronounced from a distance and in a toneless voice, and then the slight movements co-ordinated for the purpose of avoiding objects and of touching the floor very lightly with the feet—all these constitute a powerful preparation for controlling the individual personality, motor and mental.

The power to concentrate on work being established, we must superintend it with scrupulous exactitude, graduating the exercises as experience has taught us. Our duty as teachers in the creation of discipline is to apply the ' method ' rigorously.

Here is encountered the great difficulty of really disciplining man. It is not only by words that it will be done; neither is man disciplined by hearing another speak; there is required as preparation a series of complicated actions exemplified by those involved in the complete application of a method of eduation.

We find therefore that discipline comes by an indirect route, by developing activity in spontaneous work. Every individual must find out how to control himself by his own efforts and through calm, silent activity which is directed towards no external aim but is meant to keep alive that inner flame on which our life depends.

Work cannot be offered in an arbitrary manner; this is the principle embodied in the ' method '; it must be the work for which man craves in his inmost soul, the work which in some mysterious way is demanded by the latent requirements of life, and towards which the individual ascends step by step. It is work of this nature which determines the personality and which opens up the ill-defined road leading to expansion. Let us take as an example the undisciplined behaviour of the little child. The child is continually on the move, and in an irregular way; he throws himself on the ground, makes strange gestures, shouts, destroys things. Deep down in all this there lies hidden a tendency to try and co-ordinate the movements, which will be established later. The child is the man who is not yet quick in movement and in language, and who will have to become so; but he is passing through an experience full of mistakes and is struggling painfully towards the right goal which his instinct keeps hidden, which is not clear to his understanding. Whatever the movements which have to be established are those corresponding to the behaviour of man. The children must acquire the movements, the customs which they find in their environment. That is why he must have an opportunity to exercise them; it is not enough merely to see them done by others. His movements do not belong to an engine which only needs checking up; they belong to a mechanism with a definite task to be accomplished. Motor activity therefore must have a purpose and be connected with mental activity. There is a close link between movement and the intelligence eager to learn. The many children who are disorderly in their movements are not merely children who have not learned how to move, they are above all children whose mind is undernourished, who suffer from mental starvation.

Saying to the child " Stand still like me " does not enlighten him. It is not with a command that one can order the complex psycho-muscular system of an individual into the path of evolution. In doing so, we are confusing the case with that of the man who prefers to behave badly because of an innate bent, but who can (within the limits of possibility) obey a firm command which directs his will towards something different, towards an order which is well known and within the limits of his powers. But in the case of the small child it is a matter of helping forward the natural evolution of voluntary movement. All the co-ordinated movements must be taught by analyzing them as far as possible and developing them one by one. The child must be taught the various degrees of immobility leading up to the ' silence '. Included in these are the movements of getting up and sitting down, of walking naturally, of walking on the points of the toes, of walking on a line drawn on the ground whilst preserving erect balance; of removing objects, of setting them up more or less delicately; the complicated movements of dressing and undressing himself, which are analyzed in the fastening together of pieces of cloth, and for each one of these in the separate movements of the fingers; the movements required for keeping the body and the surroundings clean. Perfect immobility, and the perfecting of movements one after the other must be substituted for the customary " Stand still, keep quiet ".

All these exercises which promote the co-ordination of movements are done in order to reach a definite aim envisaged by the mind. These children did not only move their muscles, but ordered and enriched the mind. This activity developed the will which was built up in an environment of motives for their activity. Although, therefore, the movements were co-ordinated, the individual who actively co-ordinated them occupies the central place. By means of these motor exercises he expanded his intelligence and became ever more conscious of his environment and of himself.

Real co-ordination of movement is the result of a perfectionment
of the total personality.

These were therefore not children who had learned how to
move, they were disciplined because they had reached a superior
degree of development of their personality and which they had
done by means of a free choice of their occupations.

It is not wonderful, but really most natural, that the child
should have disciplined himself by these exercises, however great
may be the muscular unstability natural to his age. In fact, he is
responding to a natural urge when he is moving, but as his movements are infused with a purpose they no longer look like disorder
but like work. Here we have the discipline which represents an
aim which is attained through a multitude of victories; the child
disciplined in this way is not the child of other days who could
' be good,' but is an individual who has trained himself, who has
progressed beyond the usual limits of his age, who has made a
leap forward; in mastering the present he has mastered his own
future. He has grown up. He will not need anyone to be
constantly near him telling him repeatedly to keep still, to
be good—commands embodying two contradictory ideas. The
goodness which he has acquired can no longer make him keep
still in idleness; his goodness now is wholly expressed in
movement.

In truth, the ' good ' are those who move forward towards
the goodness which has been built up by their own efforts, and
by their orderly activity in external work.

The external work in our case constitutes the means for attain-
ing internal progress, and appears as the explanation of it; the
two factors are interwoven. Work leads to internal progress in
the child, but the child who has improved himself works better;
the improved work fascinates him; therefore he continues to develop
his inward powers.

Discipline, therefore, is not a fact, but a *way*, in the course
of which the child masters with a precision, which one might call
scientific, the idea of goodness.

But above all he tastes the supreme pleasures associated with the inward order which he has evolved through victories leading to the right goal.

In the course of the long preparation the child experiences joy, excitement and contentment, which form the intimate treasure of his mind, a treasure which is a fount of a special sweetness, a strength which will prove to be a source of goodness. The child has not only learnt to move about and to carry out useful operations, but he possesses a special grace of movement which makes his gestures more correct and beautiful and shows itself in beauty of the hand, the face and the calm shining eyes—the whole a revelation of the inward life which has been born in a man.

That the co-ordinated movements developing little by little spontaneously, that is, which are chosen and directed during the active and the resting periods by the child himself, are the equivalent of the inferior efforts belonging to the irregular movements which the child practices when left to himself, is easy to understand. Rest for the muscles, which are intended by nature to move, is found in orderly movement, just as rest for the lungs is represented by the normal rhythm of respiration in the open air. Just as the movements of the lungs aim at respiration, so the movements of the child are connected with the intelligence and the consciousness in course of development.

To deprive the muscles of all movement is to drive them in opposition to right motor impulses, and therefore not only tires them out but leads to their degeneration.

It is well to make clear to ourselves the idea that the *rest* of anything which moves resides in a definite form of motion acting in accord with the ruling of nature. To move in a proper manner, in obedience to the hidden decrees of life—that is rest. And in this special case, since man is intelligent, the movements are the more restful, the more intelligent they are. The effort made by the child who is jumping about aimlessly and without restraint is wearing out nerves and heart, whereas the intelligent movement which gives the child inward satisfaction, almost inward pride in having conquered himself, in finding himself in a world from which he was supposed to be debarred, enveloped by the silent consideration of one who guides him without showing it—such effort increases his strength.

This 'multiplication of strength' is a way of saying that it may be analyzed physiologically into the development of organs by reasonable use, the improvement of the blood supply, the renewal of the substance of the tissues—all these are factors which favour the development of the body and ensure physical health.

The spirit assists in the growth of the body; the heart, the nerves, the muscles, will all develop better in their several ways, because there is only one way.

One might say the same about the intellectual development of the child: child mentality, characteristically unregulated, yet pursues its own purposes, suffering sometimes from neglect and too often from general persecution.

Once in the public gardens of the Pincio in Rome I saw a child of about a year and a half, very beautiful, brimming over with laughter; he had an empty bucket and a small spade and he was busy collecting pebbles from the path to fill the bucket. Near him sat a superior-looking nurse, one who might be expected to bestow affectionate and intelligent care on the child. It was time to go away, and the maid patiently begged the child to leave his work and let himself be put into his carriage. All her exhortations having had no effect on the eager little worker, she herself filled the pail with gravel, then placed baby and bucket in the carriage, quite convinced that she had pleased him. The child's loud cries, the expression of protest against violence and injustice which his little face bore struck me forcibly. What a weight of resentment filled that young heart! The little one did not want to have his pail full of gravel; he wanted the exercise involved in filling it, in which he would be responding to the call made by his vigorous organism. The end pursued by the child was his internal growth, not the external matter of getting a pailful of stones. His apparently very close connection with the outside world was illusory; that need of his a reality. If he had filled the bucket he would perhaps have emptied it, to refill it many times until his *ego* was completely satisfied. In pursuit of this satisfaction, I had, a short time before, seen him with a rosy, smiling countenance: inward happiness, exercise and the sun constituted the three beams of light which were helping to build up that splendid life.

This simple episode forms an illustration of what happens to children all over the world, to the best and the most dearly loved of them. They are not understood because the adult judges them by his own standard; he believes that the child is bent upon external projects, and in a friendly way helps him to attain them, whereas the child is dominated unconsciously by the need to develop himself. For that reason he disparages what is done and loves what there is to be done. For instance, he prefers the act of dressing himself to the time when he sees himself dressed, even grandly; he likes the act of washing himself better than the comfort of feeling clean; he likes to build a house rather than to possess one. This is because what he has to do is to form life for himself, not just to enjoy it. In this formation exists his true and almost only enjoyment. That very beautiful baby of the Pincio is the symbol of it. He wanted to co-ordinate his voluntary movements, to exert his muscular energy in lifting things, to use his eyes in measuring distances, to use his intelligence in the reasoning needed for the work of filling his bucket, to develop his own will in deciding what should be done. Instead of that, some one who loved him, imagining that his desire was to possess stones, made him unhappy.

Similar to this error, and of very common occurrence is the assumption that the object to be aimed at for the pupil is intellectual knowledge, and the teacher teaches children just as the mother or the nurse washes them and dresses them. Children, however, must acquire knowledge by their own activity according to the dictates of nature.

But by leaving our children at liberty we have been able to follow them with great certainty along the paths in which their powers develop spontaneously.

To have learnt something is for the child a starting point; when he has learnt, then he begins to get enjoyment from the repetition of the exercise; he repeats what he has learnt an indefinite number of times, with evident satisfaction; he enjoys doing things, because in this he is developing his mental power. Having regard to this fact, criticism may be directed towards what is done today in many schools: when, for example, in the course of questioning pupils, it happens that the master says to some one who has offered to answer " No, you may not answer because you know," and he questions the scholar who, he thinks, does not know.

Those who do not know must answer, those who do know must keep silent. That is because it is considered useless to go outside knowledge. Yet how often it happens to us in the common course of life to repeat what we know best, that which enthrals us, which corresponds to a life within us!

That is why we love to sing musical themes which are well known, and therefore savoured, lived. We love to repeat the story of things which have delighted us, which we know well, even if we are quite well aware that we have nothing new to say, that we have recited this story many times. The prayers which we have learnt are always repeated with a renewal of interest.

But in order to repeat in this way, it is necessary that there should first exist the thing to be repeated; knowledge corresponds to this existence, to this *sine qua non*, to what is indispensable for beginning the repetition of actions; and it is the repetition, not the learning, which affords the exercise which develops life.

Now when the child has reached the stage of repeating an exercise, he is on the way set for the development of his life, and this shows itself externally in his being a disciplined child.

The phenomenon does not always occur. The same exercises are not repeated at all ages. The repetition must answer a need. In this is to be found the experimental method of education; the exercises offered must respond to the necessity for development of the organism, and if the definite necessity has disappeared as the result of age, the child will no longer have a chance of reaching the fullness of development which was missed at the opportune time. Thus it is that children often grow up fatally, permanently imperfect.

Another interesting observation is that which relates to the length of time required for carrying out actions. Children who are making their first attempts by themselves are very slow in doing things. Their life is governed by special laws quite different from ours.

Little children perform slowly and deliberately many complicated actions which they love—dressing and undressing themselves, setting the table, eating, etc. In doing all these things they show extreme patience, and they carry on to a conclusion their laborious tasks, overcoming every difficulty which arises from an organism being still in the process of development. Seeing them ' toiling ' and ' wasting time ' in doing something which we could manage in a moment without any trouble, we substitute ourselves for the child and do it ourselves.

Always animated by the same prejudice that the object to strive for is the completion of an external act, we clothe and wash the child, take out of his hands the things which he loves to handle, pour the soup into his basin for him, feed him, set the table for him. And after rendering such services, we most unjustly judge him to be incapable, inept, as always happens when someone suppresses another whilst apparently benefiting him. We often consider the child impatient just because we cannot find the patience to wait for the conclusion of these doings of his which are obeying time-laws different from ours; or, being powerful, we use our power over him. This blot, this brand, this calumny is like a dogma which presses hard on the patient and gentle nature of the child.

He, as does every strong character who defends the rights of life within him, rebels against anyone who opposes this something which he feels within him, which is a voice of nature which he must obey; then he shows in violent actions, in screams and weeping that he has been thwarted in his mission. In the eyes of those who do not understand him and who, whilst thinking they are helping him, are pushing him backward along the ways of life, he appears as a rebel, a revolutionary, a destroyer. Thus the adult who loves him fastens on his bent neck still another slander, confusing the defence of obstructed life with a form of original sin natural in children of tender age.

How would we feel if we were plunged into the midst of *Fregoli* people, who are extravagantly rapid in their movements, like those who astound us and make us laugh in our theatre by their rapid transformations? And if, continuing to move in our usual way, we found ourselves assaulted by these *Fregoli*, dressed and undressed badly by them, made to put our food so fast into our mouths that we had no time to swallow it, had our work taken out of our hands to be done by them much more rapidly, found ourselves reduced to impotency and an idleness indescribably humiliating—we, not knowing how to express ourselves better, would defend ourselves from these madmen with our fists and with shouts, and they, solely animated with the desire to serve us, would say that we were bad, rebels, unfit for anything. We, who knew our own country, would say to such: " Come to our country, and you will see a splendid civilization built up there by us, you will see our marvellous works." These *Fregoli* would admire us delightedly, not able to believe their own eyes, when they saw how our world went on—so beautiful, busy, orderly, peaceful and kindly, but much slower than their world.

Something similar happens between us and the children.

The education of the senses is completely provided for by the repetition of the exercises. Its object is not that the child should acquire knowledge of the colours, shapes and qualities of the various objects but that his senses should be sharpened by exercises in observation, comparison, judgement—which constitute true intellectual gymnastics. Such gymnastics, thoughtfully carried out with various stimuli, aid in intellectual development, just as physical gymnastics improve the health and regulate the growth of the body.

The child who is exercising himself in receiving stimuli from the different senses taken separately concentrates his attention and develops his mental powers one by one, just as, by means of movements prepared for separately, he regulates his muscular activity. He is not limited to psycho-sensorial gymnastics, but prepares a special activity of spontaneous association among ideas, an order of reasoning basing itself on positive knowledge, a harmonious balance of the intellect. Out of such unseen gymnastic work are born and developed the roots of those psychic outbursts—which bring so much joy to the child when he makes discoveries in the world around him, when he meditates and at the same time admires the new things which reveal themselves outside himself, and the exquisite inward emotions of his growing consciousness, when, finally, there is born in him almost for spontaneous maturing, like phenomena of interior development, the products of knowledge—writing and reading.

I once happened to see a child two years of age, the son of a doctor-colleague of mine, who almost dragged himself out of the arms of the mother who had brought him to me and flung himself on things heaped up on his father's desk—the rectangular block of papers, the round cover of the inkstand. I was touched to see this intelligent little one who was trying to do the very things which our little ones, with so much devotion, repeat again with the plane insets. The father and the mother drew him away, scolding him and explaining that they found it impossible to prevent him from meddling with his father's papers and other things—the child was restless and naughty. How often do we see all the children of the world when they are reproved for touching everything, rebelling against every correction.

Yet it is by guiding and developing this natural instinct for ' touching everything ' and for recognizing the harmony of geometrical figures, that our little men of four and a half have found the sources of so many joys and emotions in the acquirement of self-taught writing.

The child who flung himself on the pile of papers, on the ink-well and such things, trying in vain to reach his object, always opposed and overborne by persons stronger than himself, always agitated and weeping over the frustration of his desperate efforts—that child is wasting his nervous energy, and his parents are suffering from an illusion when they believe that such a child should rest; just as it is an ignorant calumny to consider to be wicked that little man who is striving already to lay the foundation for his intellectual edifice. On the contrary, children are really resting ardently and happily when they are left at liberty to displace and replace the geometrical plaques of the plane insets offered to their better developed powers. They enjoy themselves in the most perfect mental peace, quite unaware that eye and hand are being initiated into the mysteries of a new language.

Most of our children grow calm over their exercises; the nervous system rests. Then we say that these little ones are good and quiet; the external discipline so much sought after in ordinary schools is already far surpassed.

But as a calm man and a disciplined man are not the same, so here the fact which reveals itself to the world in the calmness of the children is too physical a symptom, too partial and superficial, compared with the true discipline which is being established within them.

Often, and in this there exists another prejudice, we believe that in order to obtain a willing act from the child it is necessary to give him an order. We pretend that this is so, and we call such a pretence the ' obedience of the child '. We find very small children particularly disobedient; also, their resistance when they are three or four years old is enough to drive us to despair and into giving up the attempt to obtain obedience. We extol to the children the value of obedience which, according to us, ought to be peculiar to childhood, an infantile virtue, just because we do not find it in children except with great difficulty.

It is a very common illusion that one should seek with prayer or command, or with agitation, anything which is difficult or impossible to obtain. We ask for obedience from children; children ask for the moon.

Obedience can be secured only through a complex formation of the mental personality; in order to obey there is necessary not only the desire to obey but also the ability to obey. Since, when we order anything, we expect an active or an inhibitory result, obedience must include an act of the will and an intellectual act. To prepare for this active growth in detail, by means of separate exercises, is to urge the child, although indirectly, towards obedience.

The method which we advocate contains in every part of it a voluntary exercise; when the child carries out movements co-ordinated for a definite purpose he reaches a goal which he had set up, repeats an exercise patiently, exercises his will.

Similarly, in fairly complicated series of exercises he brings into action inhibitory powers. For instance, the silence lessons demand prolonged control forbidding all movement: when the child is waiting for the call, and also strict control of the acts which follow when the child would like to shout for joy and rush out at the call; instead of that he is silent and moves lightly, taking care to avoid obstacles so as to make no noise. Other inhibitory exercises are those of arithmetic: when the child, having taken out a number, has to take from the great heap which is all apparently at his disposal, only the number of objects corresponding to his numeral, whereas (as experiment has shown) he would like to take the greatest possible quantity, and if fate deals out to him the *zero*, he waits patiently with empty hands. Another exercise which forbids action is found in the *zero* lesson: when the child, having been invited in so many ways to come *zero* times, and give us *zero* kisses, remains motionless, mastering the impulse which would carry him at once to obey this call. The child who is carrying the great pan full of hot soup must shut out every outside attraction, must resist the temptation to jump about, must put up with the itch from the fly on his face, and be completely absorbed in the great responsibility of preventing the pan from tipping up or falling.

One baby girl of four and a half, every time she was resting the pan on the table till the little guests should be served, made two or three little jumps; then she took up the dish and carried it to another table, always repeating her jumping. But never did she interrupt her long round of work in serving twenty tables with her soup-dish, and never did she relax the vigilance required for controlling her movements.

The will, like every other function, is strengthened and developed by methodical exercise. In our method exercises of the will are incorporated with all intellectual exercises and in the everyday life of the child. Outwardly the child is learning accuracy and grace of movement, refines his sensations, learns to count and to write, but, as a more deep-seated result, he becomes master of himself, the forerunner of the man of strong, ready will.

One often hears it said that the child's will should be subordinated in obedience, and that in this way that will is being trained, because the child ought to submit and obey. But this theory is irrational, because the child cannot give up what he does not possess. It is in this way that we prevent him from cultivating his own will-power, and commit the greatest sins against the child. He is never allowed either the time or the means to test himself, to evaluate his own strength or his limitations, because he is always being interrupted and overborne by our superior power; he loses heart over the injustice of his treatment when he hears himself reproved sharply because he does not possess what is continually being destroyed within him.

In this way there originates in the child timidity, which is a kind of malady acquired by a will which cannot develop, and which, in the usual slanderous fashion in which the tyrant, deliberately or not, covers up his own errors, is considered among us to be a characteristic of childhood.

Our children are never timid. One of the most fascinating of their qualities is the fearlessness with which they approach those with whom they are working in the presence of others, and show what they are doing freely and with a desire to get them to participate in their doings.

That moral monster, the precise, timid child who breaks out when he is alone with companions and becomes a ' little rascal ' because he had not been allowed to exercise his will except stealthily, disappears in our Children's Houses.

Besides the action of will-power there is another factor in obedience which consists of knowledge of the act which has to be performed.

One of the most interesting observations made by my pupil Anna Maccheroni, first in the Children's House in Milan, and then in that in the Via Giusti in Rome, referred to the way in which the development of obedience is dependent on the extent of the child's knowledge.

Obedience springs up in the child as a latent instinct, directly his personality has begun, as we say, to control itself. For example, a child begins to try to do a certain exercise, and once, all of a sudden, he does it perfectly. He is surprised about it, he looks at it, then he tries to do it again, but not for some time does he get the same results. In the end he almost always manages to succeed, but if anyone asks him to do it, he does not always succeed, indeed he almost always makes a mistake. The external command does not yet elicit the voluntary act. When, however, he has reached the stage when his efforts always succeed with absolute accuracy, then the external invitation calls forth orderly actions adequate for the task; the child can always fulfil the order received.

That these facts, individual variations being disregarded, are laws of mental growth is seen as a matter of common experience repeatedly in schools and in life. One may often hear a child say: " I have done that, but I can no longer do it." Or a master, on giving a command, is misled by the inability of the child and says: " Yet the child used to do it well, now he cannot do it." Finally, there is the period of finished development, consisting in this: that when he can do a thing there remains as a permanency the capacity to reproduce it.

There exist three periods of development. The first is a sub-conscious condition in which in the intelligence of the child order is being produced by some mysterious inward impulse out of disorder, showing itself in a perfect external act which, however, as it lies outside the field of consciousness, the individual cannot reproduce at will. In a second period, of a conscious character now, there appears the influence of the will which can assist in the process of the growth and of the fixation of actions. In the third period the will is able to direct and instigate the acts themselves, responding also to external commands.

Now obedience follows a parallel course. In the first period, that of internal disorder, the child does not obey, as if he were mentally deaf, impervious to commands. In the second period, he would like to obey, seems to understand an order and be willing to comply with it, but he cannot, or at least he does not, always succeed in obeying because he is not ready, does not show any pleasure in obeying. In the third period, he responds at once and joyfully; and, as he perfects himself in the exercise, there is born in the child the delight of being able to obey.

This last is the period in which he hastens with eager pleasure to leave whatever he is doing at the slightest command.

From the order thus established in the conscience, where before there had been chaos, there emanates the whole picture of the events associated with discipline and intellectual development, which expands from within outwards like a creation. In such orderly minds, in which light has been separated from darkness, there are born unexpected sentiments and intellectual victories. Already there are perceived the first flowers of kindliness, of love, of the sincere desire for goodness, which send forth their perfume from the hearts of these children, and which give promise of St. Paul's 'fruits of spiritual life'—"Love, joy, peace, longsuffering, gentleness, goodness, faith, meekness."

25

CONCLUSIONS AND IMPRESSIONS

I THINK that the part of the method which is described here will be clear enough to enable teachers to apply it practically. Anyone who has grasped as a whole the idea embodied in this method will understand why the part referring to the material application of it is excessively simple and easy.

The figure of the common mistress who maintains, so painfully, the discipline of immobility and who expends her lung power in loud and continuous talking, has disappeared.

For verbal teaching there has been substituted a " material for development," which includes in itself the control of error, and which permits individual children to teach themselves by their own efforts. Thus the teacher becomes a director of the spontaneous work of the children; she is a " patient one," a " silent one ".

Each child is occupied with different work, and the teacher can, whilst supervising them, make mental observations; these, collected and arranged in orderly, scientific form, may serve as a base for formulating a reconstruction of child psychology and preparing for experimental pedagogy. I think I have, in my method, created the conditions of study necessary for building up a scheme of scientific teaching, and anyone who adopts this method will open by the use of this alone, in every school and every class, a laboratory of experimental pedagogy.

Henceforth we must wait for the real, positive solution of all the teaching problems of which we talk, as there have already been reached solutions for others, such as the liberty of the pupils, self-education and the harmonizing of household work with scholastic work for the common purpose of educating the children.

Turning to the practical side of the school, we have, according to our methods, the advantage of drawing together children in very different stages of advancement. In our first Children's Houses, there associated together in their work little ones of two and a half, still unable to carry out the simplest of the sense exercises, and children over five, who, judged by their acquirements, might in a few months pass into the third class of the elementary school. Each one of them is training himself, and carries on according to his own individual ability. What an immense advantage belongs to this method, one which would make very easy the instruction in rural schools and in schools in small villages in the provinces, in which there are a few children and in which many different classes could not be formed and which would have a few teachers. The result of our experiment is that a single mistress can handle children who are at such varying levels as those between three years of age in the infant school and the third class in the elementary school. In addition to this practical advantage there appears another, the extreme facility with which written language is learned, which means that illiteracy can be fought, and the national language cultivated.

As for the mistress, she is able, without danger of exhausting her strength, to remain all day with children who belong to such diverse grades of development, just as in a home the mother is in company with her children of all ages, from morning till night, and does not grow weary.

The children work by themselves, thus becoming endowed with active discipline—independence in practical daily life, and the progressive development of intelligence. Directed by an intelligent teacher, in their physical development as much as in the intellectual and moral, the children may, through our methods, acquire not only a remarkably fine physical organism, but also the magnificence possible to the human mind.

There are still some who believe erroneously that the natural education of little children ought to be wholly physical; but the spirit also has its nature, and it is spiritual life which dominates existence throughout all its stages.

Our methods take into consideration the spontaneous mental development of children, and assist it with means derived from observation and experience.

If physical care gives the children the chance of enjoying a healthy body, intellectual and moral care brings them to the lofty joys of the spirit and urges them forward to continual surprises, to discoveries both in the environment and in the intimate world of their soul.

These are the joys which prepare for the life of man and which alone are capable of giving true education to the childhood of humanity.

Our children are markedly different from all others met with up till now in the subdued flock in the schools; they display the serene aspect of those who are happy, and the fearlessness of those who feel that they are masters of their doings. When they run to meet visitors, they speak to them frankly, gravely holding out their tiny little hands for a cordial handshake; they offer thanks for the visit, received more with their shining eyes than with their shrill voices; they make one fancy that they are extraordinary little men. When they display their accomplishments in so simple and confidential a manner they seem to be asking for a mother's opinion from all those who are observing them; when, in the neighbourhood of two visitors who are talking together, they squat on the ground close to their feet, and silently write their names with a polite word of thanks, it is almost as if they wanted to express affectionate, gratitude to those who had come to call on them.

When they give proof of their respect by the most profound silence, then we feel their behaviour as being touching enough to stir our hearts.

The Children's House seems to have a spiritual influence on everybody. I have seen business men, men of high position, men overburdened with heavy work, or full of a sense of their own social importance, become serene, shake off some of the stiff formality of their rank, become lost in pleasant forgetfulness of themselves. It is the effect of the spectacle of the human mind expanding in accordance with its true nature; it is this which makes us call our little ones wonderful children, happy children, the infancy of a humanity developed further than our own.

I understand the great English poet Wordsworth, who, in love with Nature, began to hear the mysterious voices of her colours and of her silences and asked from her the secret of all life. At last, as in a vision, the revelation came to him: the secret of all Nature dwells in the heart of a little child.

He discloses for us the true meaning of the life which is found in the soul of humanity. But that spirit which envelops us in childhood is afterwards obscured because the "shades of the prison-house begin to close upon the growing boy," and the man sees the vision " die away and fade into the light of common day ". Truly our social life is very often the gradual darkening and the death of the natural life which is within us.

THE TRIUMPHAL CHARIOT

THE results of instruction reached in the Children's Houses represent the limit of the education which separates such schools from the elementary classes which follow them. It is well to fix this boundary line, though it is in part artificial. The Children's House is not a preparation for the elementary classes but forms a beginning of education which goes on uninterruptedly. With our method we can no longer distinguish the ' pre-scholastic ' from the ' scholastic ' period. Indeed we have not in this case a programme governing the instruction of the child, but a case in which the child himself, whilst living and developing himself with the help of physical and intellectual work, indicates stages of culture corresponding, generally speaking, to successive ages.

The need for observing, reflecting, learning and also the need for concentration, for isolating himself, and for suspending his activities in silence from time to time has been demonstrated so clearly in the child that we can confidently declare to be wrong the idea that the small child, when outside a place intended to educate him, *rests.* It is rather our duty to direct childish activity, spare the baby from those useless efforts which dissipate his energy, thwart his instinctive search after knowledge, and so often give

Classified reading material imparting fundamental information in geography and botany.　　Photo by C. T. Nachiappan

rise in him to nervous disturbances and check his development.
The duty of employing oneself in the education of the very youngest
children does not have for its external aim the facilitation of their
entry into the obligatory period of instruction, but is a duty towards
the life, and therefore the health, of the child. What now interests
us to ascertain is the level of attainment which can be fixed as a
separation between the two kinds of school—the Children's House
and the Elementary School.

The children of the Children's Houses have begun four
branches of learning—drawing, writing, reading and arithmetic—
all of which will be continued by degrees in the elementary schools.
Our recent experiences may add to these: Geometry, Biology,
Geography, Grammar and others.

These branches of learning depend upon the education of the
senses, in which exist the preparations and the initial impulses of
the four branches, which germinate from them in a kind of sudden
outburst. Arithmetic is derived from a sense-exercise in estimating
dimensions, that is, the quantitative relations between things.
Drawing originates from educating the eye in the valuation of
forms and in distinguishing colours, together with the preparation
of the hand in following the outlines of specially chosen objects.
Writing begins with the more complicated group of touch exercises
in which the light hand is trained to move in specified directions,
the eye is taught to analyse outlines and abstract forms, the hearing
to perceive the sound of the voice which speaks framing the words
according to their component sounds. Reading arises from
writing, and extends the individual conquest into the wealth of
language revealed in the writing of others.

Such conquests are powerful manifestations of internal energy,
and occur like sudden irruptions; the outbreak of the higher
activities is accompanied by the enthusiasm and joy of the child.
It was not then a mere matter of dry learning, but a triumphant
manifestation of personality, which found the means for linking
up with the profound needs of life. And like an ancient Roman
conqueror who drove through the streets in his superb quadriga,

the spirit of the child, erect and balanced, is guiding by itself the four intellectual victories—the four horses of the triumphal chariot which races onward, instinct with strength, towards the far distant goals of culture.

The real centre of this great experience is, however, a *discovery* in the field of child psychology. Every further development follows that first revelation by the children of San Lorenzo, that strange, inexplicable capacity to reproduce such long words, the meaning of which was not even always known to them, by means of the movable alphabet, that surprising phenomenon of the explosion into writing, but also the almost miraculous fact of the establishment of spontaneous discipline in such young children. All this happened in the most inexplicable way, because they were not taught directly, neither were they submitted to any compulsion. Yet these phenomena did not happen only once in a special environment, they were repeated in every part of the world where our procedure was followed with sincerity and exactitude.

These extraordinary phenomena revealed a hidden part of the soul of the child. This is the real pivot of all our work, because it was developed round these phenomena and guided by them. That is also why these experiments and the method that was built upon them cannot be understood lest recognition is given to the fact that it is connected with a special mental form found only in the creative period of early infancy.

Above all else there emerges from this great experiment the demonstration of the fact that in the child under six years of age there exists a " mental form " different from that which is developed after six or seven years of age, and which is therefore different from that of the adult. The difference is accentuated in the smallest children, back to the time of birth. We call this the " absorbent mind " of the child, and a first account has already appeared in the book, " *Nuova Educazione per un Nuovo Mondo* " (*Education for a New World*); but there is in preparation a book, " *La Mente Assordente* " (*The Absorbent Mind*), dealing with child psychology, which will soon be published.

It is certain that mysterious facts, referrable to the unconscious mind at first and then to the subconscious at the same time as conscious ideas are appearing, reveal in the child a power to absorb images from the environment even when these are deposited in the mental labyrinths—as it reveals itself in the truly miraculous fact that the child can absorb what is erroneously called " the mother tongue " with all its phonetic and grammatical peculiarities, when it does not yet possess the mental faculties which are necessary in order to *learn*: the voluntary attention, the memory, the reasoning power. It is also true that things absorbed at the unconscious age, by force of nature, are those which persist in such a profound manner that they become identified with the person, so that the mother tongue actually becomes a character of the race, the property of the human individual.

On the other hand adults, who learn a foreign language when the mind is mature, do it with difficulty and do not succeed in imitating to perfection the spoken sounds, never losing their foreign accent and always making some grammatical mistake.

The child, in the first two years of its life, is preparing with its absorbent mind all the characters of the individual, although he is unaware of it. At three years of age there is shown the motor activity through which experiences are establishing the definite " conscious mind ". The motor organ employed in the transformation is essentially the hand which has to make use of objects. It is well known that the child wants to touch everything and concentrates on games which are carried out by the intelligence and the hand in partnership.

The importance of the hand as an organ which co-operates in the age of childhood in the building up of the conscious mind is not yet utilized in education.

The powers of the absorbent mind are obscured by degrees as the organization of the conscious mind advances; they are, however, still in existence during childhood, and permit, as is shown in our universal experience (that is, among almost all the human races), the " absorption " of culture to a vastly surprising extent.

Whilst the child in its earliest years (two years and a little more) is capable of miraculous achievements simply by his unconscious absorbing power, whilst he is immobile, after the age of three he becomes capable of obtaining a great deal of knowledge by his own efforts in exploring his surroundings. It is in this period that he seizes things by his own activity, and lays hold of his mental world as if he were gathering it with his two hands.

He has not yet, however, acquired that maturity which enables him later to learn through the speech of an adult. This is the reason why the small child has been considered incapable of profiting by the teaching of the ordinary school.

But it is certain that things gained during the absorbing period are those which are fixed, not in the memory, but in the living organism, when they become the guide for the formation of the mind, for the character of the individual. Hence if educational help can be given at that age it must be through the environment, and not through oral teaching. What is taken in by the child in the form of culture is like a permanent victory which kindles a blaze of enthusiasm, as if he were launched into a sudden conflagration. From this childhood-culture sparks of intelligence are given off which lead to expansion, to more victories in the future.

That is the age during which man works without growing weary and takes in knowledge like a life-giving food. Without the possibility of functioning in accordance with the mental characters which nature has furnished as a key to the secret of the creation of a human intelligence, the child suffers and deviates from normality.

Today psychologists are beginning to recognize a form of " mental starvation " in difficult children, who seem to be arrested in their development and to have wandered from the straight way which human development ought to follow.

The surprising results obtained in our schools and described in these pages are therefore not caused by a more perfect method of education, they are the exponents of a special mental form, of psychological sensibilities found only in the creative period of growth.

Credit therefore should not be given to our scientific work, neither to the method we used with defective children as applied to the education of normal children. The point of departure for any true understanding of our work is not to consider a " method of education " rather the reverse: the method is the consequence of having assisted the development of psychological phenomena which had remained unobserved and hence unknown for thousands of years.

The problem, therefore, is not pedagogic; 'but psychologic'; and the education which aids life is a problem which concerns humanity.

SEQUENCE AND GRADES IN THE PRESENTATION OF THE MATERIAL

In the practical application of the method it is necessary to know the serial arrangement of the exercises, which must be presented in succession to the child. In the course of this book there has been indicated a progressive course for every exercise. But in the Children's Houses, the most varied exercises are begun at the same time, and it happens that there exist grades in the presentation of the material in its entirety. That is indicated as follows:

FIRST GRADE

Practical life: moving chairs silently, carrying objects, walking on the points of the feet.

Fastening up.

The solid insets (sense exercises).

Within the group of the insets is found the following gradation from easy to difficult—

(a) Insets of the same height and decreasing diameter.

(b) Insets decreasing in all dimensions.

(c) Insets decreasing only in height.

The globe is a source of profound interest and a starting point for great spontaneous activity
in geography. Montessori School, Gwalior, India.

SECOND GRADE

Practical life: Dressing and undressing themselves, washing themselves, etc.
Various cleaning operations in the surroundings.
Eating properly, using table-ware.
Exercises in movement.

THIRD GRADE

Practical life: dressing and undressing themselves, washing themselves, etc.
Various cleaning operations in the surroundings.
Eating properly, using the table-ware.
Exercises in movement.
Various exercises in the control of movements, whilst walking on the line.
All the sense-exercises according to gradation.
Drawing.
Exercises in silence.

FOURTH GRADE

Practical life: laying the table, washing the dishes, keeping the room in order, etc.
Exercises in movement: rhythmic marches.
Analyses of movement.
The alphabet.
Drawing.
Arithmetic: various exercises with the material.
Entry of the children into the Church.

FIFTH GRADE

Practical life: all the exercises in practical life as set out above, besides applications to personal details of the toilet such as cleaning the teeth and the nails.
Learning external social manners, such as greeting people.

Water-colours and drawing.

Writing and reading words.   Commands.

First operations in written arithmetic.

Reading scientific words—geographical, historical, biological, geometrical, etc.

Development of reading through grammatical details accompanied by games.

In the same class there ought to be mixed together children of three ages; the youngest, who of their own accord interest themselves in the work of the oldest and learn from them, ought to be helped.   A child who shows a desire to work and to learn must be left free to do so, even if the work lies outside the regular programme, which is indicated only for the mistress who is beginning a class.